ABOUT THIS PUBLICATION

FOR SERVICE ASSISTANCE

Customer Service
1.704.898.0770

North Carolina General Statues is published by The Muliti-Media Group of Greater Charlotte in Charlotte, North Carolina. Copyright 2015 by the Multi-Media Group of Greater Charlotte. This book or parts thereof may not be reproduced in any form, stored in a retrieval system, or transmitted in any form by any means—electronic, mechanical, photocopy, recording or otherwise—without prior written permission of the publisher, except as provided by United States of America copyright law.

The records required by U.S. Code 2257(a) through (c) and the pertinent regulations 28 C.F.R. Cli. 1, Part 75 with respect to this publication and all materials associated with such records are maintained by The Multi-Media Group of Greater Charlotte, Publisher and available for review by Attorney General.

www.visionbooks.org

Copyright © 2015 by MMGGC
All rights reserved!

TID: 5061721
ISBN (10) digit: 1502915308
ISBN (13) digit: 978-1502915306

123-4-56789-01239-Paperback
123-4-56789-01239-Hardback

First Edition

090520140547

Printed in the United States of America

2015 EDITION

North Carolina Criminal Law And Procedure-Pamphlet # 48

Printed In conjunction with the Administration of the Courts

North Carolina Criminal Law and Procedure
Pamphlet Reference Guide

Chapters	Pamphlet
Chapter 1 Civil Procedure	1
Chapter 1 Civil Procedure (Continue)	2
Chapter 1A Rules of Civil Procedure	2
Chapter 1B Contribution.	2
Chapter 1C Enforcement of Judgments.	2
Chapter 1D Punitive Damages.	2
Chapter 1E Eastern Band of Cherokee Indians.	2
Chapter 1F North Carolina Uniform Interstate Depositions and Discovery Act.	2
Chapter 2 - Clerk of Superior Court [Repealed and Transferred.]	3
Chapter 3 - Commissioners of Affidavits and Deeds [Repealed.]	3
Chapter 4 - Common Law	3
Chapter 5 - Contempt [Repealed.]	3
Chapter 5A - Contempt	3
Chapter 6 - Liability for Court Costs	3
Chapter 7 - Courts [Repealed and Transferred.]	3
Chapter 7A – Judicial Department	3
Chapter 7A – Continuation (Judicial Department)	4
Chapter 7A – Continuation (Judicial Department)	5
Chapter 7B - Juvenile Code	5
Chapter 8 - Evidence	6
Chapter 8A - Interpreters for Deaf Persons [Recodified.]	6
Chapter 8B - Interpreters for Deaf Persons	6
Chapter 8C - Evidence Code	6
Chapter 9 - Jurors	6
Chapter 10 - Notaries [Repealed.]	6
Chapter 10A - Notaries [Recodified.]	6
Chapter 10B - Notaries	6
Chapter 11 - Oaths	6
Chapter 12 - Statutory Construction	6
Chapter 13 - Citizenship Restored	6
Chapter 14 - Criminal Law	7
Chapter 14 –Criminal Law (Continuation)	8
Chapter 15 - Criminal Procedure	9
Chapter 15A - Criminal Procedure Act (Continuation)	10
Chapter 15A - Criminal Procedure Act (Continuation)	11
Chapter 15B - Victims Compensation	11
Chapter 15C - Address Confidentiality Program	11
Chapter 16 - Gaming Contracts and Futures	11
Chapter 17 - Habeas Corpus	11

Chapter 17A - Law-Enforcement Officers [Recodified.]	11
Chapter 17B - North Carolina Criminal Justice Education and Training System [Recodified.] Chapter 17C - North Carolina Criminal Justice Education and Training Standards Commission	11
	11
Chapter 17D - North Carolina Justice Academy	11
Chapter 17E - North Carolina Sheriffs' Education and Training Standards Commission	11
Chapter 18 - Regulation of Intoxicating Liquors [Repealed.]	12
Chapter 18A - Regulation of Intoxicating Liquors [Repealed.]	12
Chapter 18B - Regulation of Alcoholic Beverages	12
Chapter 18C - North Carolina State Lottery	12
Chapter 19 - Offenses against Public Morals	12
Chapter 19A - Protection of Animals	12
Chapter 20 - Motor Vehicles	13
Chapter 20 - Motor Vehicles (Continuation)	14
Chapter 20 - Motor Vehicles (Continuation)	15
Chapter 20 - Motor Vehicles (Continuation)	16
Chapter 21 - Bills of Lading	17
Chapter 22 - Contracts Requiring Writing	17
Chapter 22A - Signatures	17
Chapter 22B - Contracts Against Public Policy	17
Chapter 22C - Payments to Subcontractors	17
Chapter 23 - Debtor and Creditor	17
Chapter 24 – Interest	17
Chapter 25 – Uniform Commercial Code	18
Chapter 25 – Uniform Commercial Code (Continuation)	19
Chapter 25A – Retail Installment Sales Act	20
Chapter 25B - Credit	20
Chapter 25C - Sales of Artwork	20
Chapter 26 - Suretyship	20
Chapter 27 - Warehouse Receipts [Repealed.]	20
Chapter 28 - Administration [Repealed.]	20
Chapter 28A - Administration of Decedents' Estates	20
Chapter 28B - Estates of Absentees in Military Service	20
Chapter 28C - Estates of Missing Persons	20
Chapter 29 - Intestate Succession	21
Chapter 30 - Surviving Spouses	21
Chapter 31 - Wills	21
Chapter 31A - Acts Barring Property Rights	21
Chapter 31B - Renunciation of Property and Renunciation of Fiduciary Powers Act	21
Chapter 31C - Uniform Disposition of Community Property Rights at Death Act	21
Chapter 32 - Fiduciaries	21
Chapter 32A - Powers of Attorney	21
Chapter 33 - Guardian and Ward [Repealed and Recodified.]	21

Chapter 33A - North Carolina Uniform Transfers to Minors Act	21
Chapter 33B - North Carolina Uniform Custodial Trust Act	21
Chapter 34 - Veterans' Guardianship Act	22
Chapter 35 - Sterilization Procedures	22
Chapter 35A - Incompetency and Guardianship	22
Chapter 36 - Trusts and Trustees [Repealed.]	22
Chapter 36A - Trusts and Trustees	22
Chapter 36B - Uniform Management of Institutional Funds Act [Repealed.]	22
Chapter 36C - North Carolina Uniform Trust Code	22
Chapter 36D - North Carolina Community Third Party Trusts, Pooled Trusts	23
Chapter 36E - Uniform Prudent Management of Institutional Funds Act	23
Chapter 37 - Allocation of Principal and Income [Repealed.]	23
Chapter 37A - Uniform Principal and Income Act	23
Chapter 38 - Boundaries	23
Chapter 38A - Landowner Liability	23
Chapter 39 - Conveyances	23
Chapter 39A - Transfer Fee Covenants Prohibited	23
Chapter 40 - Eminent Domain [Repealed.]	23
Chapter 40A - Eminent Domain	23
Chapter 41 - Estates	23
Chapter 41A - State Fair Housing Act	23
Chapter 42 - Landlord and Tenant	23
Chapter 42A - Vacation Rental Act	23
Chapter 43 - Land Registration	23
Chapter 44 - Liens	24
Chapter 44A - Statutory Liens and Charges	24
Chapter 45 - Mortgages and Deeds of Trust	24
Chapter 45A - Good Funds Settlement Act	24
Chapter 46 - Partition	24
Chapter 47 - Probate and Registration	25
Chapter 47A - Unit Ownership	25
Chapter 47B - Real Property Marketable Title Act	25
Chapter 47C - North Carolina Condominium Act	25
Chapter 47D - Notice of Settlement Act [Expired.]	25
Chapter 47E - Residential Property Disclosure Act	25
Chapter 47F - North Carolina Planned Community Act	25
Chapter 47G - Option to Purchase Contracts	25
Chapter 47H - Contracts for Deed	25
Chapter 48 - Adoptions +	26
Chapter 48A - Minors	26
Chapter 49 - Bastardy	26
Chapter 49A - Rights of Children	26
Chapter 50 - Divorce and Alimony	26
Chapter 50A - Uniform Child-Custody Jurisdiction and	

Enforcement Act	26
Chapter 50B - Domestic Violence	26
Chapter 50C - Civil No-Contact Orders	26
Chapter 51 - Marriage	26
Chapter 52 - Powers and Liabilities of Married Persons	27
Chapter 52A - Uniform Reciprocal Enforcement of Support Act [Repealed.]	27
Chapter 52B - Uniform Premarital Agreement Act	27
Chapter 52C - Uniform Interstate Family Support Act	27
Chapter 53 - Banks	27
Chapter 53A - Business Development Corporations and North Carolina Capital Resource Corporations	28
Chapter 53B - Financial Privacy Act	28
Chapter 54 - Cooperative Organizations	28
Chapter 54A - Capital Stock Savings and Loan Associations [Repealed.]	28
Chapter 54B - Savings and Loan Associations	29
Chapter 54C - Savings Banks	29
Chapter 55 - North Carolina Business Corporation Act	30
Chapter 55A - North Carolina Nonprofit Corporation Act	31
Chapter 55B - Professional Corporation Act	31
Chapter 55C - Foreign Trade Zones	31
Chapter 55D - Filings, Names, and Registered Agents for Corporations, Nonprofit Corporations, and Partnerships	31
Chapter 56 - Electric, Telegraph and Power Companies [Repealed.]	31
Chapter 57 - Hospital, Medical and Dental Service Corporations [Recodified.]	31
Chapter 57A - Health Maintenance Organization Act [Recodified.]	31
Chapter 57B - Health Maintenance Organization Act [Recodified.]	31
Chapter 57C - North Carolina Limited Liability Company Act.	31
Chapter 58 - Insurance.	32
Chapter 58A - North Carolina Health Insurance Trust Commission [Recodified.]	32
Chapter 58A - North Carolina Health Insurance Trust Commission [Recodified.] (Continuation)	33
Chapter 58A - North Carolina Health Insurance Trust Commission [Recodified.] (Continuation)	34
Chapter 58A - North Carolina Health Insurance Trust Commission [Recodified.] (Continuation)	35
Chapter 58A - North Carolina Health Insurance Trust Commission [Recodified.] (Continuation)	36
Chapter 58A - North Carolina Health Insurance Trust Commission [Recodified.] (Continuation)	37
Chapter 58A - North Carolina Health Insurance Trust	

Commission [Recodified.] (Continuation)	38
Chapter 59 - Partnership.	39
Chapter 59B - Uniform Unincorporated Nonprofit Association Act.	39
Chapter 60 - Railroads and Other Carriers [Repealed and Transferred.]	39
Chapter 61 - Religious Societies	39
Chapter 62 - Public Utilities	39
Chapter 62 - Public Utilities (Continuation)	40
Chapter 62A - Public Safety Telephone Service And Wireless Telephone Service	40
Chapter 63 - Aeronautics	40
Chapter 63A - North Carolina Global TransPark Authority	40
Chapter 64 - Aliens	40
Chapter 65 – Cemeteries	40
Chapter 66 - Commerce and Business	41
Chapter 67 - Dogs	41
Chapter 68 - Fences and Stock Law	41
Chapter 69 - Fire Protection	41
Chapter 70 - Indian Antiquities, Archaeological Resources and Unmarked Human Skeletal Remains Protection	42
Chapter 71 - Indians [Repealed.]	42
Chapter 71A - Indians	42
Chapter 72 - Inns, Hotels and Restaurants	42
Chapter 73 - Mills	42
Chapter 74 - Mines and Quarries	42
Chapter 74A - Company Police [Repealed.]	42
Chapter 74B - Private Protective Services Act [Repealed.]	42
Chapter 74C - Private Protective Services	42
Chapter 74D - Alarm Systems	42
Chapter 74E - Company Police Act	42
Chapter 74F - Locksmith Licensing Act	42
Chapter 74G - Campus Police Act	42
Chapter 75 - Monopolies, Trusts and Consumer Protection	42
Chapter 75A - Boating and Water Safety	43
Chapter 75B - Discrimination in Business	43
Chapter 75C - Motion Picture Fair Competition Act	43
Chapter 75D - Racketeer Influenced and Corrupt Organizations	43
Chapter 75E - Unlawful Activities in Connection With Certain Corporate Transactions	43
Chapter 76 - Navigation	43
Chapter 76A - Navigation and Pilotage Commissions	43
Chapter 77 - Rivers, Creeks, and Coastal Waters	43
Chapter 78 - Securities Law [Repealed.]	43
Chapter 78A - North Carolina Securities Act	43
Chapter 78B - Tender Offer Disclosure Act [Repealed.]	43
Chapter 78C - Investment Advisers	43
Chapter 78D - Commodities Act	43

Chapter 79 - Strays [Repealed.]	43
Chapter 80 - Trademarks, Brands, etc.	44
Chapter 81 - Weights and Measures [Recodified.]	44
Chapter 81A - Weights and Measures Act of 1975.	44
Chapter 82 - Wrecks [Repealed.]	44
Chapter 83 - Architects [Recodified.]	44
Chapter 83A - Architects	44
Chapter 84 - Attorneys-at-Law	44
Chapter 84A - Foreign Legal Consultants	44
Chapter 85 - Auctions and Auctioneers [Repealed.]	44
Chapter 85A - Bail Bondsmen and Runners [Recodified.]	44
Chapter 85B - Auctions and Auctioneers	44
Chapter 85C - Bail Bondsmen and Runners [Recodified.]	44
Chapter 86 - Barbers [Recodified.]	44
Chapter 86A - Barbers	44
Chapter 87 - Contractors	44
Chapter 88 - Cosmetic Art [Repealed.]	44
Chapter 88A - Electrolysis Practice Act	44
Chapter 88B - Cosmetic Art	45
Chapter 89 - Engineering and Land Surveying [Recodified.]	45
Chapter 89A - Landscape Architects	45
Chapter 89B - Foresters	45
Chapter 89C - Engineering and Land Surveying	45
Chapter 89D - Landscape Contractors	45
Chapter 89E - Geologists Licensing Act	45
Chapter 89F - North Carolina Soil Scientist Licensing Act	45
Chapter 89G - Irrigation Contractors	45
Chapter 90 - Medicine and Allied Occupations	45
Chapter 90 - Medicine and Allied Occupations (Continuation)	46
Chapter 90 - Medicine and Allied Occupations (Continuation)	47
Chapter 90 - Medicine and Allied Occupations (Continuation)	48
Chapter 90A - Sanitarians and Water and Wastewater Treatment Facility Operators	48
Chapter 90B - Social Worker Certification and Licensure Act	48
Chapter 90C - North Carolina Recreational Therapy Licensure Act	48
Chapter 90D - Interpreters and Transliterators	48
Chapter 91 - Pawnbrokers [Repealed.]	48
Chapter 91A - Pawnbrokers Modernization Act of 1989	48
Chapter 92 - Photographers [Deleted.]	48
Chapter 93 - Certified Public Accountants	48
Chapter 93A - Real Estate License Law	49
Chapter 93B - Occupational Licensing Boards	49
Chapter 93C - Watchmakers [Repealed.]	49
Chapter 93D - North Carolina State Hearing Aid Dealers and Fitters Board.	49
Chapter 93E - North Carolina Appraisers Act	49

Chapter 94 - Apprenticeship	49
Chapter 95 - Department of Labor and Labor Regulations	49
Chapter 95 - Department of Labor and Labor Regulations (Continuation)	50
Chapter 96 - Employment Security	50
Chapter 97 - Workers' Compensation Act	50
Chapter 97 - Workers' Compensation Act (Continuation)	51
Chapter 98 - Burnt and Lost Records	51
Chapter 99 - Libel and Slander	51
Chapter 99A - Civil Remedies for Criminal Actions	51
Chapter 99B - Products Liability	51
Chapter 99C - Actions Relating to Winter Sports Safety and Accidents	51
Chapter 99D - Civil Rights	51
Chapter 99E - Special Liability Provisions	51
Chapter 100 - Monuments, Memorials and Parks	51
Chapter 101 - Names of Persons	51
Chapter 102 - Official Survey Base	51
Chapter 103 - Sundays, Holidays and Special Days	51
Chapter 104 - United States Lands	51
Chapter 104A - Degrees of Kinship	51
Chapter 104B - Hurricanes or Other Acts of Nature	51
Chapter 104C - Atomic Energy, Radioactivity and Ionizing Radiation [Repealed and Recodified.]	51
Chapter 104D - Southern States Energy Compact	51
Chapter 104E - North Carolina Radiation Protection Act	51
Chapter 104F - Southeast Interstate Low-Level Radioactive Waste Management Compact [Repealed]	51
Chapter 104G - North Carolina Low-Level Radioactive Waste Management Authority Act of 1987 [Repealed]	51
Chapter 105 - Taxation	51
Chapter 105 - Taxation (Continuation)	52
Chapter 105 - Taxation (Continuation)	53
Chapter 105 - Taxation (Continuation)	54
Chapter 105A - Setoff Debt Collection Act	55
Chapter 105B - Defaulted Student Loan Recovery Act	55
Chapter 106 - Agriculture	55
Chapter 106 - Agriculture (Continue)	56
Chapter 106 - Agriculture (Continue)	57
Chapter 107 - Agricultural Development Districts [Repealed.]	57
Chapter 108 - Social Services [Repealed and Recodified.]	57
Chapter 108A - Social Services	57
Chapter 108B - Community Action Programs	58
Chapter 108C Medicaid and Health Choice Provider Requirements.	58
Chapter 108D Medicaid Managed Care for Behavioral Health Services.	58
Chapter 109 - Bonds [Recodified.]	58

Chapter 110 - Child Welfare	58
Chapter 111 - Aid to the Blind	58
Chapter 112 - Confederate Homes and Pensions [Repealed.]	58
Chapter 113 - Conservation and Development	58
Chapter 113 - Conservation and Development (Continuation)	59
Chapter 113A - Pollution Control and Environment	59
Chapter 113A - Pollution Control and Environment (Continuation)	60
Chapter 113B - North Carolina Energy Policy Act of 1975	60
Chapter 114 - Department of Justice	60
Chapter 115 - Elementary and Secondary Education [Repealed.]	60
Chapter 115A - Community Colleges, Technical Institutes, and Industrial Education Centers [Repealed.]	60
Chapter 115B - Tuition and Fee Waivers	60
Chapter 115C - Elementary and Secondary Education	60
Chapter 115C - Elementary and Secondary Education (Continuation)	61
Chapter 115C - Elementary and Secondary Education (Continuation)	62
Chapter 115C - Elementary and Secondary Education (Continuation)	63
Chapter 115D - Community Colleges	63
Chapter 115E - Private Educational Facilities Finance Act [Recodified]	63
Chapter 116 - Higher Education	63
Chapter 116 - Higher Education (Continuation)	63
Chapter 116A - Escheats and Abandoned Property [Repealed.]	64
Chapter 116B - Escheats and Abandoned Property	64
Chapter 116C - Continuum of Education Programs	64
Chapter 116D - Higher Education Bonds	64
Chapter 117 - Electrification	64
Chapter 118 - Firemen's and Rescue Squad Workers' Relief and Pension Funds [Recodified.]	64
Chapter 118A - Firemen's Death Benefit Act [Repealed.]	64
Chapter 118B - Members of a Rescue Squad Death Benefit Act [Repealed.]	64
Chapter 119 - Gasoline and Oil Inspection and Regulation	64
Chapter 120 - General Assembly	65
Chapter 120 - General Assembly (Continuation)	66
Chapter 120 - General Assembly (Continuation)	67
Chapter 120C - Lobbying	67
Chapter 121 - Archives and History	67
Chapter 122 - Hospitals for the Mentally Disordered [Repealed.]	67
Chapter 122A - North Carolina Housing Finance Agency	67
Chapter 122B - North Carolina Agricultural Facilities	

Finance Act [Repealed.]	67
Chapter 122C - Mental Health, Developmental Disabilities, and Substance Abuse Act of 1985	67
Chapter 122C - Mental Health, Developmental Disabilities, and Substance Abuse Act of 1985 (Continuation)	68
Chapter 122D - North Carolina Agricultural Finance Act	68
Chapter 122E - North Carolina Housing Trust and Oil Overcharge Act	68
Chapter 123 - Impeachment	69
Chapter 123A - Industrial Development [Repealed.]	69
Chapter 124 - Internal Improvements	69
Chapter 125 - Libraries	69
Chapter 126 - State Personnel System	69
Chapter 127 - Militia [Repealed.]	69
Chapter 127A - Militia	69
Chapter 127B - Military Affairs	69
Chapter 127C - Advisory Commission on Military Affairs	69
Chapter 128 - Offices and Public Officers	69
Chapter 128 - Offices and Public Officers (Continuation)	70
Chapter 129 - Public Buildings and Grounds	70
Chapter 130 - Public Health [Repealed.]	70
Chapter 130A - Public Health	70
Chapter 130A - Public Health (Continuation)	71
Chapter 130A - Public Health (Continuation)	72
Chapter 130B - Hazardous Waste Management Commission [Repealed.]	72
Chapter 131 - Public Hospitals [Repealed.]	72
Chapter 131A - Health Care Facilities Finance Act	72
Chapter 131B - Licensing of Ambulatory Surgical Facilities [Repealed.]	72
Chapter 131C - Charitable Solicitation Licensure Act [Repealed.]	72
Chapter 131D - Inspection and Licensing of Facilities	72
Chapter 131E - Health Care Facilities and Services	72
Chapter 131E - Health Care Facilities and Services (Continuation)	73
Chapter 131F - Solicitation of Contributions	73
Chapter 132 - Public Records	73
Chapter 133 - Public Works	74
Chapter 134 - Youth Development [Recodified.]	74
Chapter 134A - Youth Services [Repealed.]	74
Chapter 135 - Retirement System for Teachers and State Employees; Social Security; Health Insurance Program for Children	74
Chapter 135 - Retirement System for Teachers and State Employees; Social Security; Health Insurance Program for Children	75

Chapter 136 - Transportation	75
Chapter 136 - Transportation (Continuation)	76
Chapter 137 - Rural Rehabilitation [Repealed.]	76
Chapter 138 - Salaries, Fees and Allowances	76
Chapter 138A - State Government Ethics Act	76
Chapter 139 - Soil and Water Conservation Districts	76
Chapter 140 - State Art Museum; Symphony and Art Societies	76
Chapter 140A - State Awards System	76
Chapter 141 - State Boundaries	76
Chapter 142 - State Debt	76
Chapter 143 - State Departments, Institutions, and Commissions	77
Chapter 143 - State Departments, Institutions, and Commissions (Continuation)	78
Chapter 143 - State Departments, Institutions, and Commissions (Continuation)	79
Chapter 143 - State Departments, Institutions, and Commissions (Continuation)	80
Chapter 143A - State Government Reorganization	80
Chapter 143B - Executive Organization Act of 1973	80
Chapter 143B - Executive Organization Act of 1973 (Continuation)	81
Chapter 143B - Executive Organization Act of 1973 (Continuation)	82
Chapter 143C - State Budget Act	83
Chapter 143D - The State Governmental Accountability and Internal Control Act	83
Chapter 144 - State Flag, Official Governmental Flags, Motto, and Colors	83
Chapter 145 - State Symbols and Other Official Adoptions.	83
Chapter 146 - State Lands	83
Chapter 147 - State Officers	83
Chapter 148 - State Prison System	84
Chapter 149 - State Song and Toast	84
Chapter 150 - Uniform Revocation of Licenses [Repealed.]	84
Chapter 150A - Administrative Procedure Act [Recodified.]	84
Chapter 150B - Administrative Procedure Act	84
Chapter 151 - Constables [Repealed.]	84
Chapter 152 - Coroners	84
Chapter 152A - County Medical Examiner [Repealed.]	84
Chapter 152A - County Medical Examiner [Repealed.] (Continuation)	85
Chapter 153 - Counties and County Commissioners [Repealed.]	85
Chapter 153A - Counties	85

Chapter 153B - Mountain Resources Planning Act	85
Chapter 153C - Uwharrie Regional Resources Act	85
Chapter 154 - County Surveyor [Repealed.]	85
Chapter 155 - County Treasurer [Repealed.]	85
Chapter 156 - Drainage	85
Chapter 156 – Drainage (Continuation)	86
Chapter 157 - Housing Authorities and Projects	86
Chapter 157A - Historic Properties Commissions [Transferred.]	86
Chapter 158 - Local Development	86
Chapter 159 - Local Government Finance	86
Chapter 159 - Local Government Finance (Continuation)	87
Chapter 159A - Pollution Abatement and Industrial Facilities Financing Act [Unconstitutional.]	87
Chapter 159B - Joint Municipal Electric Power and Energy Act	87
Chapter 159C - Industrial and Pollution Control Facilities Financing Act	87
Chapter 159D - The North Carolina Capital Facilities Financing Act	87
Chapter 159E - Registered Public Obligations Act	87
Chapter 159F - North Carolina Energy Development Authority [Repealed.]	87
Chapter 159G - Water Infrastructure	87
Chapter 159H - [Reserved.]	87
Chapter 159I - Solid Waste Management Loan Program and Local Government Special Obligation Bonds	87
Chapter 160 - Municipal Corporations [Repealed And Transferred.]	87
Chapter 160A - Cities and Towns	88
Chapter 160A - Cities and Towns (Continuation)	89
Chapter 160B - Consolidated City-County Act	89
Chapter 160C - Baseball Park Districts [Repealed.]	90
Chapter 161 - Register of Deeds	90
Chapter 162 - Sheriff	90
Chapter 162A - Water and Sewer Systems	90
Chapter 162B Continuity of Local Government in Emergency.	90
Chapter 163 Elections and Election Laws.	90
Chapter 163 Elections and Election Laws. (Continuation)	91
Chapter 164 Concerning the General Statutes of North Carolina.	92
Chapter 165 Veterans.	92
Chapter 166 Civil Preparedness Agencies [Repealed.]	92
Chapter 166A North Carolina Emergency Management Act.	92
Chapter 167 State Civil Air Patrol [Repealed.]	92
Chapter 168 Persons with Disabilities.	92
Chapter 168A Persons With Disabilities Protection Act.	92

§ 90-288.17. Posting certificates.

Every person issued a certificate under this Article shall display the certificate prominently in the assisted living residence where the person works. (1999-443, s. 1.)

§ 90-288.18. Adverse action on a certificate.

(a)   Subject to subsection (b) of this section, the Department shall have the authority to deny a new or renewal application for a certificate, and to amend, recall, suspend, or revoke an existing certificate upon a determination that there has been a substantial failure to comply with the provisions of this Article or any rules promulgated under this Article.

(b)   The provisions of Chapter 150B of the General Statutes shall govern all administrative action and judicial review in cases where the Department has taken action as described in subsection (a) of this section. A petition for a contested case shall be filed within 30 days after the Department mails the certificate holder a notice of its decision to deny a renewal application, or to recall, suspend, or revoke an existing certificate. (1999-443, s. 1.)

§ 90-288.19. Reporting requirement.

The holder of a facility license issued under G.S. 131D-2.4 shall report any incidents of suspected abuse, neglect, or exploitation of persons residing in an assisted living residence by a person certified under this Article to the Health Care Personnel Registry. (1999-443, s. 1; 2009-462, s. 4(d).)

§ 90-288.20. Penalties.

A person who serves as an assisted living administrator without first obtaining a certificate from the Department is guilty of a Class 1 misdemeanor. Each act of unlawful practice constitutes a distinct and separate offense. (1999-443, s. 1.)

Article 21.

Determination of Need for Medical Care Facilities.

§§ 90-289 through 90-291: Repealed by Session Laws 1973, c. 113.

Article 22.

Licensure Act for Speech and Language Pathologists and Audiologists.

§ 90-292. Declaration of policy.

It is declared to be a policy of the State of North Carolina that, in order to safeguard the public health, safety, and welfare; to protect the public from being misled by incompetent, unscrupulous, and unauthorized persons and from unprofessional conduct on the part of qualified speech and language pathologists and audiologists and to help assure the availability of the highest possible quality speech and language pathology and audiology services to the communicatively handicapped people of this State, it is necessary to provide regulatory authority over persons offering speech and language pathology and audiology services to the public. (1975, c. 773, s. 1.)

§ 90-293. Definitions.

As used in this Article, unless the context otherwise requires:

(1)   "Audiologist" means any person who engages in the practice of audiology. A person is deemed to be an audiologist if he offers services to the public under any title incorporating the terms of "audiology," "audiologist," "audiological," "hearing clinic," "hearing clinician," "hearing therapist," or any similar title or description of service.

(2)   "Board" means the Board of Examiners for Speech and Language Pathologists and Audiologists.

(3)   "License" means a license issued by the Board under the provisions of this Article, including a temporary license.

(4) "Person" means an individual, organization, or corporate body, except that only individuals can be licensed under this Article.

(5) "Speech and language pathologist" means any person who represents himself or herself to the public by title or by description of services, methods, or procedures as one who evaluates, examines, instructs, counsels, or treats persons suffering from conditions or disorders affecting speech and language or swallowing. A person is deemed to be a speech and language pathologist if the person offers such services under any title incorporating the words "speech pathology," "speech pathologist," "speech correction," "speech correctionist," "speech therapy," "speech therapist," "speech clinic," "speech clinician," "language pathologist," "language therapist," "logopedist," "communication disorders," "communicologist," "voice therapist," "voice pathologist," or any similar title or description of service.

(6) "The practice of audiology" means the application of principles, methods, and procedures of measurement, testing, evaluation, prediction, consultation, counseling, instruction, habilitation, or rehabilitation related to hearing and vestibular disorders for the purpose of identifying, preventing, ameliorating, or modifying such disorders and conditions in individuals or groups of individuals. For the purpose of this subdivision, the words "habilitation" and "rehabilitation" shall include auditory training, speech reading, aural rehabilitation, hearing aid use evaluation and recommendations, and fabrication of earmolds and similar accessories for clinical testing purposes.

(7) "The practice of speech and language pathology" means the application of principles, methods, and procedures for the measurement, testing, evaluation, prediction, counseling, treating, instruction, habilitation, or rehabilitation related to the development and disorders of speech, voice, language, and swallowing for the purpose of identifying, preventing, ameliorating, or modifying such disorders.

(8) Repealed by Session Laws 1987, c. 665, s. 1.

(9) "Accredited college or university" means an institution of higher learning accredited by the Southern Association of Colleges and Universities, or accredited by a similarly recognized association of another locale. (1975, c. 773, s. 1; 1987, c. 665, s. 1; 2007-436, s. 1.)

§ 90-294. License required; Article not applicable to certain activities.

(a) Licensure shall be granted in either speech and language pathology or audiology independently. A person may be licensed in both areas if qualified in both areas.

(b) No person may practice or hold himself or herself out as being able to practice speech and language pathology or audiology in this State unless the person holds a current, unsuspended, unrevoked license issued by the Board or is registered with the Board as an assistant. The license required by this section shall be kept conspicuously posted in the person's office or place of business at all times. Nothing in this Article, however, shall be construed to prevent a qualified person licensed in this State under any other law from engaging in the profession or occupation for which such person is licensed.

(c) Repealed by Session Laws 2013-410, s. 47.7(a), effective August 23, 2013.

(c1) The provisions of this Article do not apply to:

(1) The activities, services, and use of an official title by a person employed by an agency of the federal government and solely in connection with such employment.

(2) The activities and services of a student or trainee in speech and language pathology or audiology pursuing a course of study in an accredited college or university, or working in a training center program approved by the Board, if these activities and services constitute a part of the person's course of study.

(3) Individuals licensed under Chapter 93D of the General Statutes.

(d) Nothing in this Article shall apply to a physician licensed to practice medicine, or to any person employed by a physician licensed to practice medicine in the course of the physician's practice of medicine.

(e) This Article shall not be construed to prevent any person licensed in this State under Chapter 93D of the General Statutes of North Carolina from the practice of fitting and selling hearing aids.

(f)   The provisions of this Article do not apply to registered nurses and licensed practical nurses or other certified technicians trained to perform audiometric screening tests and whose work is under the supervision of a physician, consulting physician, or licensed audiologist.

(g)   The provisions of this Article do not apply to persons who are now or may become engaged in counseling or instructing laryngectomees in the methods, techniques or problems of learning to speak again.

(h)   No license under this Article is required for persons originally employed by any agency of State government between October 1, 1975, and July 1, 1977, for the practice of speech and language pathology or audiology within and during the course and scope of employment with such agency.

(i)   Nothing in this Article shall apply to a licensed physical therapy or occupational therapy practitioner providing evaluation and treatment of swallowing disorders, cognitive/communication deficits, and balance functions within the context of his or her licensed practice. (1975, c. 773, s. 1; 1977, c. 692, s. 3; 1981, c. 572, ss. 1, 2; 1987, c. 665, s. 2; 1989, c. 770, s. 17; 1993 (Reg. Sess., 1994), c. 688, s. 1; 1997-443, s. 11A.118(a); 2007-436, ss. 2, 3(a), 3(b); 2013-410, s. 47.7(a), (b).)

§ 90-295. Qualifications of applicants for permanent licensure.

(a)   To be eligible for permanent licensure by the Board as a speech and language pathologist, the applicant must:

(1)   Possess at least a master's degree in speech and language pathology or qualifications deemed equivalent by the Board under rules duly adopted by the Board under this Article. The degree or equivalent qualifications shall be from an accredited institution.

(2)   Submit transcripts from one or more accredited colleges or universities presenting evidence of the completion of 75 semester hours constituting a well-integrated program of course study dealing with the normal aspects of human communication, development thereof, disorders thereof, and clinical techniques for evaluation and management of such disorders.

a. Fifteen of these 75 semester hours must be obtained in courses that provide information that pertains to normal development and use of speech, language and hearing.

b. Thirty-six of these 75 semester hours must be in courses that provide information relative to communication disorders and information about and training in evaluation and management of speech, language, and hearing disorders. At least 24 of these 30 semester hours must be in courses in speech and language pathology.

c. Credit for study of information pertaining to related fields that augment the work of the clinical practitioner of speech and language pathology or audiology may also apply toward the total 75 semester hours.

d. Thirty-six of the total 75 semester hours that are required for a license must be in courses that are acceptable toward a graduate degree by the college or university at which they are taken. Moreover, 21 of those semester hours must be in graduate level courses in speech and language pathology.

(3) Submit evidence of the completion of a minimum of 400 clock hours of supervised, direct clinical experience with individuals who present a variety of communication disorders. This experience must have been obtained within the training institution or in one of its cooperating programs in the following areas: (i) Speech - Adult (20 diagnostic and 20 therapeutic); Children (20 diagnostic and 20 therapeutic); and (ii) Language - Adult (20 diagnostic and 20 therapeutic); Children (20 diagnostic and 20 therapeutic). Each new applicant must submit a verified clinical clock hour summary sheet signed by the clinic or program director, in addition to completion of the license application.

(4) Present written evidence of nine months of full-time professional experience in which bona fide clinical work has been accomplished in speech and language pathology. The professional work must have been supervised by a speech and language pathologist who is State-licensed or certified by the American Speech-Language-Hearing Association. This experience must follow the completion of the requirements listed in subdivisions (1), (2) and (3). Full time is defined as at least nine months in a calendar year and a minimum of 30 hours per week. Half time is defined as at least 18 months in two calendar years and a minimum of 20 hours per week. The supervision must be performed by a person who holds a valid license under this Article, or certificate of clinical competence from the American Speech-Language-Hearing Association, in speech and language pathology.

(5) Pass an examination established or approved by the Board.

(6) Exercise good moral conduct as defined in rules adopted by the Board or in a code of moral conduct adopted by the Board.

(b) To be eligible for permanent licensure by the Board as an audiologist, the applicant must:

(1) Possess a doctoral degree in audiology or qualifications deemed equivalent by the Board under rules duly adopted by the Board under this Article. The degree or equivalent qualifications shall be from an accredited institution.

(2) Persons who were engaged in the practice of audiology and do not possess a doctoral degree in audiology before October 1, 2007, shall be exempt from the degree requirement in subdivision (1) of this subsection provided those persons remain continuously licensed in the field.

(3) Submit transcripts from one or more accredited colleges or universities presenting evidence of the completion of 90 semester hours constituting a well-integrated program of course study dealing with the normal aspects of human communication, the development of human communication, the disorders associated with human communication, and the clinical techniques for evaluation and management of such disorders.

(4) Present written evidence documenting 1,800 clock hours of professional experience directly supervised by an audiologist who is State-licensed or certified by the American Speech-Language-Hearing Association or other Board-approved agency. The clock hours of professional experience must be with individuals who present a variety of communication and auditory disorders and must have been obtained within the training program at an accredited college or university or in one of its cooperating programs.

(5) Pass an examination established or approved by the Board.

(6) Exercise good moral conduct as defined in rules adopted by the Board or in a code of moral conduct adopted by the Board. (1975, c. 773, s. 1; 1987, c. 665, s. 3; 2007-436, s. 4; 2009-138, s. 1; 2013-410, s. 47.7(c).)

§ 90-296. Examinations.

(a)   An applicant for licensure who has satisfied the academic requirements of G.S. 90-295, shall pass a written examination approved or established by the Board.

(b)   The Board shall administer or approve at least two examinations of the type described in subsection (a) of this section each year, and additional examinations as the volume of applications makes appropriate.

(c)   An examination shall not be required as a prerequisite for a license for:

(1)   A person who holds a certificate of clinical competence issued by the American Speech-Hearing-Language Association in the specialized area for which such person seeks licensure; or

(2)   A person who has met the educational, practical experience, and examination requirements of another state or jurisdiction which has requirements equivalent to or higher than those in effect pursuant to this Article for the practice of audiology or speech pathology. (1975, c. 773, s. 1; 1981, c. 572, s. 3; 1987, c. 665, s. 4; 2013-410, s. 47.7(d).)

§ 90-297. Repealed by Session Laws 1987, c. 665, s. 5.

§ 90-298. Qualifications for applicants for temporary licensure.

(a)   To be eligible for temporary licensure an applicant must:

(1)   Meet the academic and clinical practicum requirements of G.S. 90-295(1), (2), and (3); and

(2)   Submit a plan of supervised experience complying with the provisions of G.S. 90-295(4); and

(3)   Pay the temporary license fee required by G.S. 90-305(5).

(b) A temporary license is required when an applicant has not completed the required supervised experience and passed the required examination.

(c) A temporary license issued under this section shall be valid only during the period of supervised experience required by G.S. 90-295(4), and shall not be renewed. (1975, c. 773, s. 1; 1987, c. 665, s. 6; 2013-410, s. 47.7(e).)

§ 90-298.1. Registered assistant.

A licensed speech and language pathologist or a licensed audiologist may register with the Board an assistant who works under the licensee's supervision if all of the following requirements are met:

(1) The assistant meets the qualifications for registered assistants adopted by the Board.

(2) The licensee who supervises the assistant pays the registration fee set by the Board.

A registration of an assistant must be renewed annually. To renew the registration of an assistant, the licensee who supervises the assistant must submit an application for renewal and pay the renewal fee. An initial or renewal fee for registering an assistant may not exceed the renewal license fee set under G.S. 90-305. (1993 (Reg. Sess., 1994), c. 688, s. 2.)

§ 90-299. Licensee to notify Board of place of practice.

(a) A person who holds a license shall notify the Board in writing of the address of the place or places where he engages or intends to engage in the practice of speech and language pathology or audiology.

(b) The Board shall keep a record of the places of practice of licensees.

(c) Any notice required to be given by the Board to a licensee may be given by mailing it to him at the address of the last place of practice of which he has notified the Board. (1975, c. 773, s. 1.)

§ 90-300. Renewal of licenses.

A licensee shall annually pay to the Board a fee in an amount established by the General Assembly for a renewal of his license. A 30-day grace period shall be allowed after expiration of a license during which the license may be renewed on payment of a fee in an amount established by the General Assembly. The Board may suspend the license of any person who fails to renew his license before the expiration of the 30-day grace period. After expiration of the grace period, the Board may renew such a license upon the payment of a fee in an amount established by the General Assembly. No person who applies for renewal whose license was suspended for failure to renew shall be required to submit to any examination as a condition of renewal. (1975, c. 773, s. 1.)

§ 90-301. Grounds for suspension or revocation of license.

Any person licensed under this Article may have his license revoked or suspended for a fixed period by the Board under the provisions of North Carolina General Statutes, Chapter 150B, for any of the following causes:

(1)   His license has been secured by fraud or deceit practiced upon the Board.

(2)   Fraud or deceit in connection with his services rendered as an audiologist or speech and language pathologist.

(3)   Unethical or immoral conduct as defined in this Article or in a code of ethics adopted by the Board.

(4)   Violation of any lawful order, rule or regulation rendered or adopted by the Board.

(5)   Failure to exercise a reasonable degree of professional skill and care in the delivery of professional services.

(6)   Any violation of the provisions of this Article.

(7)   Failure to exercise good moral conduct as defined in rules adopted by the Board or in a code of moral conduct adopted by the Board. (1975, c. 773, s. 1; 1981, c. 572, s. 4; 1987, c. 665, s. 7; c. 827, s. 1; 2013-410, s. 47.7(f).)

§ 90-301A. Unethical acts and practices.

Unethical acts and practices shall be defined as including:

(1)   Obtaining or attempting to obtain any fee by fraud or misrepresentation.

(2)   Employing directly or indirectly any suspended or unlicensed person to perform any work covered by this Article.

(3)   Using, or causing or promoting the use of any advertising matter, promotional literature, testimonial, guarantee, warranty, label, brand, insignia, or any other representation, however disseminated or published, which is misleading, deceiving, improbable, or untruthful.

(4)   Aiding, abetting, or assisting any other person or entity in violating the provisions of this Article.

(5)   Willfully harming any person in the course of the delivery of professional services licensed by this Article.

(6)   Treating a person who cannot reasonably be expected to benefit from treatment.

(7)   Charging a fee for treatment or services not rendered.

(8)   Providing or attempting to provide services or supervision of services by persons not properly prepared or legally qualified to perform or permitting services to be provided by a person under such person's supervision who is not properly prepared or legally qualified to perform such services.

(9)   Guaranteeing the result of any therapeutic or evaluation procedure. (1987, c. 665, s. 8.)

§ 90-302. Prohibited acts and practices.

No person, partnership, corporation, or other entity may:

(1)   Sell, barter, transfer or offer to sell or barter a license.

(2) Purchase or procure by barter a license with intent to use it as evidence of the holder's qualification to practice audiology or speech and language pathology.

(3) Alter a license.

(4) Use or attempt to use a valid license which has been purchased, fraudulently obtained, counterfeited or materially altered.

(5) Make a false, material statement in an application for a North Carolina license.

(6) Aid, assist, abet, or direct any person licensed under this Article in violation of the provisions of this Article. (1975, c. 773, s. 1; 1987, c. 665, s. 9; 2013-410, s. 47.7(g).)

§ 90-303. Board of Examiners for speech and language pathology and audiology; qualifications, appointment and terms of members; vacancies; meetings, etc.

(a) There shall be a Board of Examiners for Speech and Language Pathologists and Audiologists, which shall be composed of seven members, who shall all be residents of this State. Two members shall have a paid work experience in audiology for at least five years and hold a North Carolina license as an audiologist. Two members shall have paid work experience in speech pathology for at least five years and hold a North Carolina license as a speech and language pathologist. One member shall be a physician who is licensed to practice medicine in the State of North Carolina. Two members shall be appointed by the Governor to represent the interest of the public at large. These two members shall be neither licensed speech and language pathologists nor audiologists. These members shall be appointed not later than July 1, 1981; one shall be initially appointed for a term of two years; the other shall be appointed for a term of three years. Thereafter all public members shall serve three-year terms.

(b) The members of the Board shall be appointed by the Governor.

(c) The initial Board shall have members appointed for terms of one year, two years, three years, four years, and five years. All board members serving on

June 30, 1981, shall be eligible to complete their respective terms. No member appointed to a term on or after July 1, 1981, shall serve more than two complete consecutive three-year terms.

(d) Members of the Board shall receive no compensation for their service, but shall receive the same per diem, subsistence and travel allowance as provided in G.S. 138-5. (1975, c. 773, s. 1; 1981, c. 572, ss. 5, 6; 2007-436, s. 5.)

§ 90-304. Powers and duties of Board.

(a) The powers and duties of the Board are as follows:

(1) To administer, coordinate, and enforce the provisions of this Article, establish fees, evaluate the qualifications of applicants, supervise the examination of applicants, and issue subpoenas, examine witnesses, and administer oaths, and investigate persons engaging in practices which violate the provisions of this Article.

(2) To conduct hearings and keep records and minutes as necessary to an orderly dispatch of business.

(3) To adopt responsible rules including rules that establish ethical standards of practice and require continuing professional education and to amend or repeal the same.

(4) To issue annually a list stating the names of persons currently licensed under the provisions of this Article.

(5) To employ such personnel as determined by its needs and budget.

(6) To adopt seals by which it shall authenticate their proceedings, copies of the proceedings, records and the acts of the Board, and licenses.

(7) To bring an action to restrain or enjoin violations of this Article in addition to and not in lieu of criminal prosecution or proceedings to revoke or suspend licenses issued under this Article.

(b) The Board shall not adopt or enforce any rule or regulation which prohibits advertising except for false or misleading advertising. (1975, c. 773, s. 1; 1981, c. 572, s. 7; 1987, c. 665, s. 10; 2007-436, s. 6.)

§ 90-305. Fees.

Persons subject to licensure under this Article shall pay fees to the Board not to exceed the following:

(1) Application fee $30.00

(2) Examination fee 30.00

(3) Initial license fee 100.00

(4) Renewal license fee 100.00

(5) Temporary license 40.00

(6) Delinquency fee .... 25.00.

(1975, c. 773, s. 1; 1987, c. 665, s. 11; 2003-222, s. 1.)

§ 90-306. Penalty for violation.

Any person, partnership, or corporation who or which willfully violates the provisions of this Article shall be guilty of a Class 2 misdemeanor. (1975, c. 773, s. 1; 1987, c. 665, s. 12; 1993, c. 539, s. 650; 1994, Ex. Sess., c. 24, s. 14(c).)

§ 90-307. Severability.

If any part of this Article is for any reason held unconstitutional, inoperative, or void, such holding of invalidity shall not affect the remaining portions of the Article; and it shall be construed to have been the legislative intent to pass this Article without such unconstitutional, invalid, or inoperative part therein; and the remainder of this Article, after the exclusion of such part or parts, shall be valid as if such parts were not contained therein. (1975, c. 773, s. 1.)

§§ 90-308 through 90-319. Reserved for future codification purposes.

Article 23.

Right to Natural Death; Brain Death.

§ 90-320. General purpose of Article.

(a) The General Assembly recognizes as a matter of public policy that an individual's rights include the right to a peaceful and natural death and that a patient or the patient's representative has the fundamental right to control the decisions relating to the rendering of the patient's own medical care, including the decision to have life-prolonging measures withheld or withdrawn in instances of a terminal condition. This Article is to establish an optional and nonexclusive procedure by which a patient or the patient's representative may exercise these rights. A military advanced medical directive executed in accordance with 10 U.S.C. § 1044 or other applicable law is valid in this State.

(b) Nothing in this Article shall be construed to authorize any affirmative or deliberate act or omission to end life other than to permit the natural process of dying. Nothing in this Article shall impair or supersede any legal right or legal responsibility which any person may have to effect the withholding or withdrawal of life-prolonging measures in any lawful manner. In such respect the provisions of this Article are cumulative. (1977, c. 815; 1979, c. 715, s. 1; 1983, c. 313, s. 1; 2007-502, s. 10.)

§ 90-321. Right to a natural death.

(a) The following definitions apply in this Article:

(1) Declarant. - A person who has signed a declaration in accordance with subsection (c) of this section.

(1a) Declaration. - Any signed, witnessed, dated, and proved document meeting the requirements of subsection (c) of this section.

(2) Repealed by Session Laws 2007-502, s. 11(a), effective October 1, 2007.

(2a) Life-prolonging measures. - As defined in G.S. 32A-16(4).

(3) Physician. - Any person licensed to practice medicine under Article 1 of Chapter 90 of the laws of the State of North Carolina.

(4) Repealed by Session Laws 2007-502, s. 11(a), effective October 1, 2007.

(b) If a person has expressed through a declaration, in accordance with subsection (c) of this section, a desire that the person's life not be prolonged by life-prolonging measures, and the declaration has not been revoked in accordance with subsection (e) of this section; and

(1) It is determined by the attending physician that the declarant's present condition is a condition described in subsection (c) of this section and specified in the declaration for applying the declarant's directives, and

(2) There is confirmation of the declarant's present condition as set out in subdivision (b)(1) of this section by a physician other than the attending physician;

then the life-prolonging measures identified by the declarant shall or may, as specified by the declarant, be withheld or discontinued upon the direction and under the supervision of the attending physician.

(c) The attending physician shall follow, subject to subsections (b), (e), and (k) of this section, a declaration:

(1) That expresses a desire of the declarant that life-prolonging measures not be used to prolong the declarant's life if, as specified in the declaration as to any or all of the following:

a. The declarant has an incurable or irreversible condition that will result in the declarant's death within a relatively short period of time; or

b. The declarant becomes unconscious and, to a high degree of medical certainty, will never regain consciousness; or

c. The declarant suffers from advanced dementia or any other condition resulting in the substantial loss of cognitive ability and that loss, to a high degree of medical certainty, is not reversible.

(2) That states that the declarant is aware that the declaration authorizes a physician to withhold or discontinue the life-prolonging measures; and

(3) That has been signed by the declarant in the presence of two witnesses who believe the declarant to be of sound mind and who state that they (i) are not related within the third degree to the declarant or to the declarant's spouse, (ii) do not know or have a reasonable expectation that they would be entitled to any portion of the estate of the declarant upon the declarant's death under any will of the declarant or codicil thereto then existing or under the Intestate Succession Act as it then provides, (iii) are not the attending physician, licensed health care providers who are paid employees of the attending physician, paid employees of a health facility in which the declarant is a patient, or paid employees of a nursing home or any adult care home in which the declarant resides, and (iv) do not have a claim against any portion of the estate of the declarant at the time of the declaration; and

(4) That has been proved before a clerk or assistant clerk of superior court, or a notary public who certifies substantially as set out in subsection (d1) of this section. A notary who takes the acknowledgement may but is not required to be a paid employee of the attending physician, a paid employee of a health facility in which the declarant is a patient, or a paid employee of a nursing home or any adult care home in which the declarant resides.

(d) Repealed by Session Laws 2007-502, s. 11(b), effective October 1, 2007.

(d1) The following form is specifically determined to meet the requirements of subsection (c) of this section:

ADVANCE DIRECTIVE FOR A NATURAL DEATH ("LIVING WILL")

NOTE: YOU SHOULD USE THIS DOCUMENT TO GIVE YOUR HEALTH CARE PROVIDERS INSTRUCTIONS TO WITHHOLD OR WITHDRAW LIFE-PROLONGING MEASURES IN CERTAIN SITUATIONS. THERE IS NO LEGAL REQUIREMENT THAT ANYONE EXECUTE A LIVING WILL.

GENERAL INSTRUCTIONS: You can use this Advance Directive ("Living Will") form to give instructions for the future if you want your health care providers to withhold or withdraw life-prolonging measures in certain situations. You should talk to your doctor about what these terms mean. The Living Will states what choices you would have made for yourself if you were able to communicate. Talk to your family members, friends, and others you trust about your choices. Also, it is a good idea to talk with professionals such as your doctors, clergypersons, and lawyers before you complete and sign this Living Will.

You do not have to use this form to give those instructions, but if you create your own Advance Directive you need to be very careful to ensure that it is consistent with North Carolina law.

This Living Will form is intended to be valid in any jurisdiction in which it is presented, but places outside North Carolina may impose requirements that this form does not meet.

If you want to use this form, you must complete it, sign it, and have your signature witnessed by two qualified witnesses and proved by a notary public. Follow the instructions about which choices you can initial very carefully. Do not sign this form until two witnesses and a notary public are present to watch you sign it. You then should consider giving a copy to your primary physician and/or a trusted relative, and should consider filing it with the Advanced Health Care

Directive Registry maintained by the North Carolina Secretary of State: http://www.nclifelinks.org/ahcdr/

My Desire for a Natural Death

I, _____, being of sound mind, desire that, as specified below, my life not be prolonged by life-prolonging measures:

1. When My Directives Apply

My directions about prolonging my life shall apply IF my attending physician determines that I lack capacity to make or communicate health care decisions and:

NOTE: YOU MAY INITIAL ANY AND ALL OF THESE CHOICES.

_____ I have an incurable or irreversible condition that will result
(Initial) in my death within a relatively short period of time.

_____ I become unconscious and my health care providers
(Initial) determine that, to a high degree of medical certainty, I will
           never regain my consciousness.

_____ I suffer from advanced dementia or any other condition
(Initial)   which results in the substantial loss of my cognitive
ability

and my health care providers determine that, to a high
degree of medical certainty, this loss is not reversible.

2. These are My Directives about Prolonging My Life:

In those situations I have initialed in Section 1, I direct that my health care providers:

NOTE: INITIAL ONLY IN ONE PLACE.

_____   may withhold or withdraw life-prolonging measures.

(Initial)

_____   shall withhold or withdraw life-prolonging measures.

(Initial)

3. Exceptions - "Artificial Nutrition or Hydration"

NOTE: INITIAL ONLY IF YOU WANT TO MAKE EXCEPTIONS TO YOUR INSTRUCTIONS IN PARAGRAPH 2.

EVEN THOUGH I do not want my life prolonged in those situations I have initialed in Section 1:

_____
(Initial)

I DO want to receive BOTH artificial hydration AND artificial nutrition (for example, through tubes) in those situations.

NOTE: DO NOT INITIAL THIS BLOCK IF ONE OF THE BLOCKS BELOW IS INITIALED.

_____
(Initial)

I DO want to receive ONLY artificial hydration (for example, through tubes) in those situations.

NOTE: DO NOT INITIAL THE BLOCK ABOVE OR BELOW IF THIS BLOCK IS INITIALED.

_____
(Initial)

I DO want to receive ONLY artificial nutrition (for example, through tubes) in those situations.

NOTE: DO NOT INITIAL EITHER OF THE TWO BLOCKS ABOVE IF THIS BLOCK IS INITIALED.

4. I Wish to be Made as Comfortable as Possible

I direct that my health care providers take reasonable steps to keep me as clean, comfortable, and free of pain as possible so that my dignity is maintained, even though this care may hasten my death.

5. I Understand my Advance Directive

I am aware and understand that this document directs certain life-prolonging measures to be withheld or discontinued in accordance with my advance instructions.

6. If I have an Available Health Care Agent

If I have appointed a health care agent by executing a health care power of attorney or similar instrument, and that health care agent is acting and available and gives instructions that differ from this Advance Directive, then I direct that:

_____
(Initial)
Follow Advance Directive: This Advance Directive will override instructions my health care agent gives about prolonging my life.

_____
(Initial)
Follow Health Care Agent: My health care agent has authority to override this Advance Directive.

NOTE: DO NOT INITIAL BOTH BLOCKS. IF YOU DO NOT INITIAL EITHER BOX, THEN YOUR HEALTH CARE PROVIDERS WILL FOLLOW THIS ADVANCE DIRECTIVE AND IGNORE THE INSTRUCTIONS OF YOUR HEALTH CARE AGENT ABOUT PROLONGING YOUR LIFE.

7. My Health Care Providers May Rely on this Directive

My health care providers shall not be liable to me or to my family, my estate, my heirs, or my personal representative for following the instructions I give in this instrument. Following my directions shall not be considered suicide, or the cause of my death, or malpractice or unprofessional conduct. If I have revoked this instrument but my health care providers do not know that I have done so, and they follow the instructions in this instrument in good faith, they shall be entitled to the same protections to which they would have been entitled if the instrument had not been revoked.

8. I Want this Directive to be Effective Anywhere

I intend that this Advance Directive be followed by any health care provider in any place.

9. I have the Right to Revoke this Advance Directive

I understand that at any time I may revoke this Advance Directive in a writing I sign or by communicating in any clear and consistent manner my intent to revoke it to my attending physician. I understand that if I revoke this instrument I should try to destroy all copies of it.

This the _____ day of _____, _____.

_____

Print Name

_____

I hereby state that the declarant, _____, being of sound mind, signed (or directed another to sign on declarant's behalf) the foregoing Advance Directive for a Natural Death in my presence, and that I am not related to the declarant by blood or marriage, and I would not be entitled to any portion of the estate of the declarant under any existing will or codicil of the declarant or as an heir under the Intestate Succession Act, if the declarant died on this date without a will. I also state that I am not the declarant's attending physician, nor a licensed health care provider who is (1) an employee of the declarant's attending physician, (2) nor an employee of the health facility in which the declarant is a patient, or (3) an employee of a nursing home or any adult care home where the declarant resides. I further state that I do not have any claim against the declarant or the estate of the declarant.

Date: _____   Witness:
_____

Date: _____   Witness:
_____

_____COUNTY, _____STATE

Sworn to (or affirmed) and subscribed before me this day by
_____

of declarant)   (type/print name

_____

(type/print name of witness)

_____

type/print name of witness)

Date _____
       _____

(Official Seal)   Signature of Notary Public

                                         _____,
Notary Public

                                         Printed or typed name

                                         My commission expires:

_____

(e)   A declaration may be revoked by the declarant, in writing or in any manner by which the declarant is able to communicate the declarant's intent to revoke in a clear and consistent manner, without regard to the declarant's mental or physical condition. A health care provider shall have no liability for acting in accordance with a revoked declaration unless the provider has actual notice of the revocation. A health care agent may not revoke a declaration unless the health care power of attorney explicitly authorizes that revocation; however, a health care agent may exercise any authority explicitly given to the health care agent in a declaration. A guardian of the person of the declarant or general guardian may not revoke a declaration.

(f)   The execution and consummation of declarations made in accordance with subsection (c) shall not constitute suicide for any purpose.

(g) No person shall be required to sign a declaration in accordance with subsection (c) as a condition for becoming insured under any insurance contract or for receiving any medical treatment.

(h) The withholding or discontinuance of life prolonging measures in accordance with this section shall not be considered the cause of death for any civil or criminal purposes nor shall it be considered unprofessional conduct or a lack of professional competence. Any person, institution or facility against whom criminal or civil liability is asserted because of conduct in compliance with this section may interpose this section as a defense. The protections of this section extend to any valid declaration, including a document valid under subsection (l) of this section; these protections are not limited to declarations prepared in accordance with the statutory form provided in subsection (d1) of this section, or to declarations filed with the Advance Health Care Directive Registry maintained by the Secretary of State. A health care provider may rely in good faith on an oral or written statement by legal counsel that a document appears to meet the statutory requirements for a declaration.

(i) Use of the statutory form prescribed in subsection (d1) of this section is an optional and nonexclusive method for creating a declaration and does not affect the use of other forms of a declaration, including previous statutory forms.

(j) The form provided by this section may be combined with or incorporated into a health care power of attorney form meeting the requirements of Article 3 of Chapter 32A of the General Statutes; provided, however, that the resulting form shall be signed, witnessed, and proved in accordance with the provisions of this section.

(k) Notwithstanding subsection (c) of this section:

(1) An attending physician may decline to honor a declaration that expresses a desire of the declarant that life-prolonging measures not be used if doing so would violate that physician's conscience or the conscience-based policy of the facility at which the declarant is being treated; provided, an attending physician who declines to honor a declaration on these grounds must not interfere, and must cooperate reasonably, with efforts to substitute an attending physician whose conscience would not be violated by honoring the declaration, or transfer the declarant to a facility that does not have policies in force that prohibit honoring the declaration.

(2) An attending physician may decline to honor a declaration if after reasonable inquiry there are reasonable grounds to question the genuineness or validity of a declaration. The subsection imposes no duty on the attending physician to verify a declaration's genuineness or validity.

(l) Notwithstanding subsection (c) of this section, a declaration or similar document executed in a jurisdiction other than North Carolina shall be valid in this State if it appears to have been executed in accordance with the applicable requirements of that jurisdiction or this State. (1977, c. 815; 1979, c. 112, ss. 1-6; 1981, c. 848, ss. 1-3; 1991, c. 639, s. 3; 1993, c. 553, s. 28; 2001-455, s. 4; 2001-513, s. 30(b); 2007-502, ss. 11(a)-(e).)

§ 90-322. Procedures for natural death in the absence of a declaration.

(a) If the attending physician determines, to a high degree of medical certainty, that a person lacks capacity to make or communicate health care decisions and the person will never regain that capacity, and:

(1) Repealed by Session Laws 2007-502, s. 12, effective October 1, 2007.

(1a) That the person:

a. Has an incurable or irreversible condition that will result in the person's death within a relatively short period of time; or

b. Is unconscious and, to a high degree of medical certainty, will never regain consciousness; and

(2) There is confirmation of the person's present condition as set out above in this subsection, in writing by a physician other than the attending physician; and

(3) A vital bodily function of the person could be restored or is being sustained by life-prolonging measures;

(4) Repealed by Session Laws 2007-502, s. 12, effective October 1, 2007.

then, life-prolonging measures may be withheld or discontinued in accordance with subsection (b) of this section.

(b) If a person's condition has been determined to meet the conditions set forth in subsection (a) of this section and no instrument has been executed as provided in G.S. 90-321, then life-prolonging measures may be withheld or discontinued upon the direction and under the supervision of the attending physician with the concurrence of the following persons, in the order indicated:

(1) A guardian of the patient's person, or a general guardian with powers over the patient's person, appointed by a court of competent jurisdiction pursuant to Article 5 of Chapter 35A of the General Statutes; provided that, if the patient has a health care agent appointed pursuant to a valid health care power of attorney, the health care agent shall have the right to exercise the authority to the extent granted in the health care power of attorney and to the extent provided in G.S. 32A-19(b) unless the Clerk has suspended the authority of that health care agent in accordance with G.S. 35A-1208(a);

(2) A health care agent appointed pursuant to a valid health care power of attorney, to the extent of the authority granted;

(3) An attorney-in-fact, with powers to make health care decisions for the patient, appointed by the patient pursuant to Article 1 or Article 2 of Chapter 32A of the General Statutes, to the extent of the authority granted;

(4) The patient's spouse;

(5) A majority of the patient's reasonably available parents and children who are at least 18 years of age;

(6) A majority of the patient's reasonably available siblings who are at least 18 years of age; or

(7) An individual who has an established relationship with the patient, who is acting in good faith on behalf of the patient, and who can reliably convey the patient's wishes.

If none of the above is reasonably available then at the discretion of the attending physician the life-prolonging measures may be withheld or discontinued upon the direction and under the supervision of the attending physician.

(c) Repealed by Session Laws 1979, c. 715, s. 2.

(d) The withholding or discontinuance of such life-prolonging measures shall not be considered the cause of death for any civil or criminal purpose nor shall it be considered unprofessional conduct. Any person, institution or facility against whom criminal or civil liability is asserted because of conduct in compliance with this section may interpose this section as a defense. (1977, c. 815; 1979, c. 715, s. 2; 1981, c. 848, s. 5; 1983, c. 313, ss. 2-4; c. 768, s. 5.1; 1991, c. 639, s. 4; 1993, c. 553, s. 29; 2007-502, s. 12.)

§ 90-323. Death; determination by physician.

The determination that a person is dead shall be made by a physician licensed to practice medicine applying ordinary and accepted standards of medical practice. Brain death, defined as irreversible cessation of total brain function, may be used as a sole basis for the determination that a person has died, particularly when brain death occurs in the presence of artificially maintained respiratory and circulatory functions. This specific recognition of brain death as a criterion of death of the person shall not preclude the use of other medically recognized criteria for determining whether and when a person has died. (1979, c. 715, s. 3.)

§§ 90-324 through 90-328. Reserved for future codification purposes.

Article 24.

Licensed Professional Counselors Act.

§ 90-329. Declaration of policy.

It is declared to be the public policy of this State that the activities of persons who render counseling services to the public be regulated to insure the protection of the public health, safety, and welfare. (1983, c. 755, s. 1; 1993, c. 514, s. 1.)

§ 90-330. Definitions; practice of counseling.

(a) Definitions. - As used in this Article certain terms are defined as follows:

(1) Repealed by Session Laws 1993, c. 514, s. 1.

(1a) The "Board" means the Board of Licensed Professional Counselors.

(2) A "licensed professional counselor" is a person engaged in the practice of counseling who holds a license as a licensed professional counselor issued under the provisions of this Article.

(2a) A "licensed professional counselor associate" is a person engaged in the supervised practice of counseling who holds a license as a licensed professional counselor associate issued under the provisions of this Article.

(2b) A "licensed professional counselor supervisor" is a person engaged in the practice of counseling who holds a license as a licensed professional counselor and is approved by the Board to provide clinical supervision under the provisions of this Article.

(3) The "practice of counseling" means holding oneself out to the public as a professional counselor offering counseling services that include, but are not limited to, the following:

a. Counseling. - Assisting individuals, groups, and families through the counseling relationship by evaluating and treating mental disorders and other conditions through the use of a combination of clinical mental health and human development principles, methods, diagnostic procedures, treatment plans, and other psychotherapeutic techniques, to develop an understanding of personal problems, to define goals, and to plan action reflecting the client's interests, abilities, aptitudes, and mental health needs as these are related to personal-social-emotional concerns, educational progress, and occupations and careers.

b. Appraisal Activities. - Administering and interpreting tests for assessment of personal characteristics.

c. Consulting. - Interpreting scientific data and providing guidance and personnel services to individuals, groups, or organizations.

d.   Referral Activities. - Identifying problems requiring referral to other specialists.

e.   Research Activities. - Designing, conducting, and interpreting research with human subjects.

The "practice of counseling" does not include the facilitation of communication, understanding, reconciliation, and settlement of conflicts by mediators at community mediation centers authorized by G.S. 7A-38.5.

(4)   A "supervisor" means any licensed professional counselor supervisor or, when one is inaccessible, a licensed professional counselor or an equivalently and actively licensed mental health professional, as determined by the Board, who meets the qualifications established by the Board.

(b)   Repealed by Session Laws 1993, c. 514, s. 1.

(c)   Practice of Marriage and Family Therapy, Psychology, or Social Work. - No person licensed as a licensed professional counselor or licensed professional counselor associate under the provisions of this Article shall be allowed to hold himself or herself out to the public as a licensed marriage and family therapist, licensed practicing psychologist, psychological associate, or licensed clinical social worker unless specifically authorized by other provisions of law. (1983, c. 755, s. 1; 1993, c. 514, s. 1; 1995, c. 157, s. 4; 1999-354, s. 3; 2001-487, s. 40(j); 2009-367, s. 1.)

§ 90-331.   Prohibitions.

It shall be unlawful for any person who is not licensed under this Article to engage in the practice of counseling, use the title "Licensed Professional Counselor Associate," "Licensed Professional Counselor," or "Licensed Professional Counselor Supervisor," use the letters "LPCA," "LPC," or "LPCS," use any facsimile or combination of these words or letters, abbreviations, or insignia, or indicate or imply orally, in writing, or in any other way that the person is a licensed professional counselor. (1983, c. 755, s. 1; 1993, c. 514, s. 1; 2001-487, s. 40(k); 2009-367, s. 2.)

§ 90-332. Use of title by firm.

It shall be unlawful for any firm, partnership, corporation, association, or other business or professional entity to assume or use the title of licensed professional counselor unless each of the members of the firm, partnership, or association is licensed by the Board. (1983, c. 755, s. 1; 1993, c. 514, s. 1.)

§ 90-332.1. Exemptions from licensure.

(a) It is not the intent of this Article to regulate members of other regulated professions who do counseling in the normal course of the practice of their profession. Accordingly, this Article does not apply to:

(1) Lawyers licensed under Chapter 84, doctors licensed under Chapter 90, and any other person registered, certified, or licensed by the State to practice any other occupation or profession while rendering counseling services in the performance of the occupation or profession for which the person is registered, certified, or licensed.

(2) Any school counselor certified by the State Board of Education while counseling within the scope of employment by a board of education or private school.

(3) Any student intern or trainee in counseling pursuing a course of study in counseling in a regionally accredited institution of higher learning or training institution, if the intern or trainee is a designated "counselor intern" and the activities and services constitute a part of the supervised course of study.

(4) Repealed by Session Laws 2009-367, s. 3, effective October 1, 2009.

(4a) Any person counseling within the scope of employment at: (i) a local community college as defined in G.S. 115D-2(2); (ii) a public higher education institution as defined in G.S. 116-2(4); or (iii) a nonprofit postsecondary educational institution as described in G.S. 116-280.

(4b) Repealed by Session Laws 2009-367, s. 3, effective October 1, 2009.

(5) Any ordained minister or other member of the clergy while acting in a ministerial capacity who does not charge a fee for the service, or any person

invited by a religious organization to conduct, lead, or provide counseling to its members when the service is not performed for more than 30 days a year.

(6)   Any nonresident temporarily employed in this State to render counseling services for not more than 30 days in a year, if the person holds a license or certificate required for counselors in another state.

(7)   Any person employed by State, federal, county, or municipal government while counseling within the scope of employment.

(8)   through (10) Repealed by Session Laws 2009-367, s. 3, effective October 1, 2009.

(b)   Persons who claim to be exempt under subsection (a) of this section are prohibited from advertising or offering themselves as "licensed professional counselors".

(c)   Persons licensed under this Article are exempt from rules pertaining to counseling adopted by other occupational licensing boards.

(d)   Nothing in this Article shall prevent a person from performing substance abuse counseling or substance abuse prevention consulting as defined in Article 5C of this Chapter. (1993, c. 514, s. 1; 1993 (Reg. Sess., 1994), c. 591, ss. 12, 16(a), 16(b); c. 685, s. 2; 1997-456, s. 27; 2001-487, s. 40(l); 2009-367, s. 3; 2011-145, s. 9.18(e).)

§ 90-333. North Carolina Board of Licensed Professional Counselors; appointments; terms; composition.

(a)   For the purpose of carrying out the provisions of this Article, there is hereby created the North Carolina Board of Licensed Professional Counselors which shall consist of seven members appointed by the Governor in the manner hereinafter prescribed. Any State or nationally recognized professional association representing professional counselors may submit recommendations to the Governor for Board membership. The Governor may remove any member of the Board for neglect of duty or malfeasance or conviction of a felony or other crime of moral turpitude, but for no other reason.

(b) At least five members of the Board shall be licensed professional counselors except that initial appointees shall be persons who meet the educational and experience requirements for licensure as licensed professional counselors under the provisions of this Article; and two members shall be public-at-large members appointed from the general public. Composition of the Board as to the race and sex of its members shall reflect the population of the State and each member shall reside in a different congressional district.

(c) At all times the Board shall include at least one counselor primarily engaged in counselor education, at least one counselor primarily engaged in the public sector, at least one counselor primarily engaged in the private sector, and two licensed professional counselors at large.

(d) All members of the Board shall be residents of the State of North Carolina, and, with the exception of the public-at-large members, shall be licensed by the Board under the provisions of this Article. Professional members of the Board must be actively engaged in the practice of counseling or in the education and training of students in counseling, and have been for at least three years prior to their appointment to the Board. The engagement in this activity during the two years preceding the appointment shall have occurred primarily in this State.

(e) The term of office of each member of the Board shall be three years; provided, however, that of the members first appointed, three shall be appointed for terms of one year, two for terms of two years, and two for terms of three years. No member shall serve more than two consecutive three-year terms.

(f) Each term of service on the Board shall expire on the 30th day of June of the year in which the term expires. As the term of a member expires, the Governor shall make the appointment for a full term, or, if a vacancy occurs for any other reason, for the remainder of the unexpired term. Appointees to the Board shall continue to serve until a successor is appointed and qualified.

(g) Members of the Board shall receive compensation for their services and reimbursement for expenses incurred in the performance of duties required by this Article, at the rates prescribed in G.S. 93B-5.

(h) The Board may employ, subject to the provisions of Chapter 126 of the General Statutes, the necessary personnel for the performance of its functions, and fix their compensation within the limits of funds available to the Board. (1983, c. 755, s. 1; 1993, c. 514, s. 1; 2009-367, s. 4.)

§ 90-334. Functions and duties of the Board.

(a) The Board shall administer and enforce the provisions of this Article.

(b) The Board shall elect from its membership, a chairperson, a vice-chairperson, and secretary-treasurer, and adopt rules to govern its proceedings. A majority of the membership shall constitute a quorum for all Board meetings.

(c) The Board shall examine and pass on the qualifications of all applicants for licenses under this Article, and shall issue a license or renewal of license to each successful applicant therefor.

(d) The Board may adopt a seal which may be affixed to all licenses issued by the Board.

(e) The Board may authorize expenditures deemed necessary to carry out the provisions of this Article from fees paid to the Board pursuant to this section. No State appropriations shall be subject to the administration of the Board.

(f) The Board shall establish and receive fees not to exceed two hundred dollars ($200.00) for initial or renewal application and not to exceed seventy-five dollars ($75.00) for late renewal, maintain Board accounts of all receipts, and make expenditures from Board receipts for any purpose which is reasonable and necessary for the proper performance of its duties under this Article.

(g) The Board shall have the power to establish or approve study or training courses and to establish reasonable standards for licensure and license renewal, including but not limited to the power to adopt or use examination materials and accreditation standards of any recognized counselor accrediting agency and the power to establish reasonable standards for continuing counselor education.

(h) Subject to the provisions of Chapter 150B of the General Statutes, the Board shall have the power to adopt, amend, or repeal rules to carry out the purposes of this Article, including but not limited to the power to adopt ethical and disciplinary standards.

(i) The Board shall establish the criteria for determining the qualifications constituting "supervised professional practice".

(j)   The Board may examine, approve, issue, deny, revoke, suspend, and renew the licenses of counselor applicants and licensees under this Article, and conduct hearings in connection with these actions.

(k)   The Board shall investigate, subpoena individuals and records, and take necessary appropriate action to properly discipline persons licensed under this Article and to enforce this Article. (1983, c. 755, s. 1; 1987, c. 827, s. 1; 1993, c. 514, s. 1; 2009-367, s. 5.)

§ 90-335. Board general provisions.

The Board shall be subject to the provisions of Chapter 93B of the General Statutes. (1983, c. 755, s. 1.)

§ 90-336. Title and qualifications for licensure.

(a)   Each person desiring to be a licensed professional counselor associate, licensed professional counselor, or licensed professional counselor supervisor shall make application to the Board upon such forms and in such manner as the Board shall prescribe, together with the required application fee.

(b)   The Board shall issue a license as a "licensed professional counselor associate" to an applicant who meets all of the following criteria:

(1)   Has earned a minimum of 48 semester hours or 72 quarter credit hours of graduate training as defined by the Board, including a master's degree in counseling or a related field from a regionally accredited institution of higher education if the applicant enrolled in the master's program before July 1, 2009; a minimum of 54 semester hours or 81 quarter credit hours of graduate training as defined by the Board, including a master's degree in counseling or a related field from a regionally accredited institution of higher education if the applicant enrolled in the master's program before July 1, 2013, but after June 30, 2009; or a minimum of 60 semester hours or 90 quarter credit hours of graduate training as defined by the Board, including a master's degree in counseling or a related field from a regionally accredited institution of higher education if the applicant enrolled in the master's program after June 30, 2013.

(2) Repealed by Session Laws 2009-367, s. 6, effective October 1, 2009.

(3) Has passed an examination in accordance with rules adopted by the Board.

(c) The Board shall issue a license as a "licensed professional counselor" to an applicant who meets all of the following criteria:

(1) Has met all of the requirements under subsection (b) of this section.

(2) Has completed a minimum of 3,000 hours of supervised professional practice as determined by the Board.

(d) (See Editor's note) A licensed professional counselor may apply to the Board for recognition as a "licensed professional counselor supervisor" and receive the credential "licensed professional counselor supervisor" upon meeting all of the following criteria:

(1) Has met all of the requirements under subsection (c) of this section.

(2) Has one of the following:

a. At least five years of full-time licensed professional counseling experience, including a minimum of 2,500 hours of direct client contact;

b. At least eight years of part-time licensed professional counseling experience, including a minimum of 2,500 hours of direct client contact; or

c. A combination of full-time and part-time professional counseling experience, including a minimum of 2,500 hours of direct client contact as determined by the Board.

(3) Has completed minimum education requirements in clinical supervision as approved by the Board.

(4) Has an active license in good standing as a licensed professional counselor approved by the Board. (1983, c. 755, s. 1; 1993, c. 514, s. 1; 2009-367, s. 6.)

§ 90-337. Persons credentialed in other states.

The Board may license any person who is currently licensed, certified, or registered by another state if the individual has met requirements determined by the Board to be substantially similar to or exceeding those established under this Article. (1983, c. 755, s. 1; 1993, c. 514, s. 1.)

§ 90-338. Exemptions.

Applicants holding certificates of registration as Registered Practicing Counselors and in good standing with the Board shall be issued licenses as licensed professional counselors without meeting the requirements of G.S. 90-336(c). The following applicants shall be exempt from the academic qualifications required by this Article for licensed professional counselor associates or licensed professional counselors and shall be licensed upon passing the Board examination and meeting the experience requirements:

(1)   An applicant who was engaged in the practice of counseling before July 1, 1993, and who applied to the Board prior to January 1, 1996.

(2)   An applicant who holds a masters degree from a college or university accredited by one of the regional accrediting associations or from a college or university determined by the Board to have standards substantially equivalent to a regionally accredited institution, provided the applicant was enrolled in the masters program prior to July 1, 1994. (1983, c. 755, s. 1; 1993, c. 514, s. 1; 1993 (Reg. Sess., 1994), c. 685, s. 3; c. 769, s. 25.19; 1995, c. 157, s. 3; 2009-367, s. 7.)

§ 90-339. Renewal of licenses.

(a)   All licenses shall be effective upon the date of issuance by the Board, and shall expire on the second June 30 thereafter.

(b)   All licenses issued hereunder shall be renewed at the times and in the manner provided by this section. At least 45 days prior to expiration of each license, the Board shall mail a notice for license renewal to the person licensed for the current licensure period. At least 10 days before the current license expires, the applicant must return the notice properly completed, together with a renewal fee established by the Board and evidence of continuing counselor education as approved by the Board, upon receipt of which the Board shall issue to the person to be licensed the renewed license for the period stated on the license.

(c)   Any person licensed who allows the license to lapse for failure to apply for renewal within 45 days after notice shall be subject to the late renewal fee. Failure to apply for renewal of a license within one year after the license's expiration date will require that a license be reissued only upon application as for an original license. (1983, c. 755, s. 1; 1993, c. 514, s. 1.)

§ 90-340. Protection of the public.

(a)   The Board may, in accordance with the provisions of Chapter 150B of the General Statutes, deny, suspend, or revoke licensure, discipline, place on probation, limit practice, or require examination, remediation, or rehabilitation of any person licensed under this Article on one or more of the following grounds:

(1)   Has been convicted of a felony or entered a plea of guilty or nolo contendere to any felony charge under the laws of the United States or of any state of the United States.

(2)   Has been convicted of or entered a plea of guilty or nolo contendere to any misdemeanor involving moral turpitude, misrepresentation, or fraud in dealing with the public, or conduct otherwise relevant to fitness to practice professional counseling, or a misdemeanor charge reflecting the inability to practice professional counseling with due regard to the health and safety of clients or patients.

(3)   Has engaged in fraud or deceit in securing or attempting to secure or renew a license under this Article or has willfully concealed from the Board material information in connection with application for a license or renewal of a license under this Article.

(4)   Has practiced any fraud, deceit, or misrepresentation upon the public, the Board, or any individual in connection with the practice of professional counseling, the offer of professional counseling services, the filing of Medicare,

Medicaid, or other claims to any third-party payor, or in any manner otherwise relevant to fitness for the practice of professional counseling.

(5) Has made fraudulent, misleading, or intentionally or materially false statements pertaining to education, licensure, license renewal, certification as a health services provider, supervision, continuing education, any disciplinary actions or sanctions pending or occurring in any other jurisdiction, professional credentials, or qualifications or fitness for the practice of professional counseling to the public, any individual, the Board, or any other organization.

(6) Has had a license or certification for the practice of professional counseling in any other jurisdiction suspended or revoked, or has been disciplined by the licensing or certification board in any other jurisdiction for conduct which would subject him or her to discipline under this Article.

(7) Has violated any provision of this Article or any rules adopted by the Board.

(8) Has aided or abetted the unlawful practice of professional counseling by any person not licensed by the Board.

(9) Has been guilty of immoral, dishonorable, unprofessional, or unethical conduct as defined in this subsection or in the current code of ethics of the American Counseling Association. However, if any provision of the code of ethics is inconsistent and in conflict with the provisions of this Article, the provisions of this Article shall control.

(10) Has practiced professional counseling in such a manner as to endanger the welfare of clients.

(11) Has demonstrated an inability to practice professional counseling with reasonable skill and safety by reason of illness, inebriation, misuse of drugs, narcotics, alcohol, chemicals, or any other substance affecting mental or physical functioning, or as a result of any mental or physical condition.

(12) Has practiced professional counseling outside the boundaries of demonstrated competence or the limitations of education, training, or supervised experience.

(13) Has exercised undue influence in such a manner as to exploit the client, patient, student, supervisee, or trainee for the financial or other personal

advantage or gratification of the licensed professional counselor associate, licensed professional counselor, or a third party.

(14) Has harassed or abused, sexually or otherwise, a client, patient, student, supervisee, or trainee.

(15) Has failed to cooperate with or to respond promptly, completely, and honestly to the Board, to credentials committees, or to ethics committees of professional associations, hospitals, or other health care organizations or educational institutions, when those organizations or entities have jurisdiction.

(16) Has refused to appear before the Board after having been ordered to do so in writing by the chair.

(17) Has a finding listed on the Division of Health Service Regulation of the Department of Health and Human Services Health Care Personnel Registry.

(b) The Board may, in lieu of denial, suspension, or revocation, take any of the following disciplinary actions:

(1) Issue a formal reprimand or formally censure the applicant or licensee.

(2) Place the applicant or licensee on probation with the appropriate conditions on the continued practice of professional counseling deemed advisable by the Board.

(3) Require examination, remediation, or rehabilitation for the applicant or licensee, including care, counseling, or treatment by a professional or professionals designated or approved by the Board, the expense to be borne by the applicant or licensee.

(4) Require supervision of the professional counseling services provided by the applicant or licensee by a licensee designated or approved by the Board, the expense to be borne by the applicant or licensee.

(5) Limit or circumscribe the practice of professional counseling provided by the applicant or licensee with respect to the extent, nature, or location of the professional counseling services provided, as deemed advisable by the Board.

(6) Discipline and impose any appropriate combination of the types of disciplinary action listed in this section.

In addition, the Board may impose conditions of probation or restrictions on continued practice of professional counseling at the conclusion of a period of suspension or as a requirement for the restoration of a revoked or suspended license. In lieu of or in connection with any disciplinary proceedings or investigation, the Board may enter into a consent order relative to discipline, supervision, probation, remediation, rehabilitation, or practice limitation of a licensee or applicant for a license.

(c)   The Board may assess costs of disciplinary action against an applicant or licensee found to be in violation of this Article.

(d)   When considering the issue of whether an applicant or licensee is physically or mentally capable of practicing professional counseling with reasonable skill and safety with patients or clients, upon a showing of probable cause to the Board that the applicant or licensee is not capable of practicing professional counseling with reasonable skill and safety with patients or clients, the Board may petition a court of competent jurisdiction to order the applicant or licensee in question to submit to a psychological evaluation by a psychologist to determine psychological status or a physical evaluation by a physician to determine physical condition, or both. The psychologist or physician shall be designated by the court. The expenses of the evaluations shall be borne by the Board. Where the applicant or licensee raises the issue of mental or physical competence or appeals a decision regarding mental or physical competence, the applicant or licensee shall be permitted to obtain an evaluation at the applicant or licensee's expense. If the Board suspects the objectivity or adequacy of the evaluation, the Board may compel an evaluation by its designated practitioners at its own expense.

(e)   Except as otherwise provided in this Article, the procedure for revocation, suspension, denial, limitations of the license, or other disciplinary, remedial, or rehabilitative actions shall be in accordance with the provisions of Chapter 150B of the General Statutes. The Board is required to provide the opportunity for a hearing under Chapter 150B to any applicant whose license or health services provider certification is denied or to whom licensure or health services provider certification is offered subject to any restrictions, probation, disciplinary action, remediation, or other conditions or limitations, or to any licensee before revoking, suspending, or restricting a license or health services provider certificate or imposing any other disciplinary action or remediation. If the applicant or licensee waives the opportunity for a hearing, the Board's denial, revocation, suspension, or other proposed action becomes final without a hearing having been conducted. Notwithstanding the provisions of this subsection, no applicant or licensee is entitled to a hearing for failure to pass an examination. In any proceeding before the Board, in any record of any hearing before the Board, in any complaint or notice of charges against any licensee or applicant for licensure, and in any decision rendered by the Board, the Board may withhold from public disclosure the identity of any clients who have not consented to the public disclosure of services provided by the licensee or applicant. The Board may close a hearing to the public and receive in closed session evidence involving or concerning the treatment of or delivery of services to a client who has not consented to the public disclosure of the treatment or services as may be necessary for the protection and rights of the client of the accused applicant or licensee and the full presentation of relevant evidence.

(f) All records, papers, and other documents containing information collected and compiled by or on behalf of the Board as a result of investigations, inquiries, or interviews conducted in connection with licensing or disciplinary matters shall not be considered public records within the meaning of Chapter 132 of the General Statutes. However, any notice or statement of charges against any licensee or applicant, or any notice to any licensee or applicant of a hearing in any proceeding, or any decision rendered in connection with a hearing in any proceeding shall be a public record within the meaning of Chapter 132 of the General Statutes, though the record may contain information collected and compiled as a result of the investigation, inquiry, or hearing. Any identifying information concerning the treatment of or delivery of services to a client who has not consented to the public disclosure of the treatment or services may be deleted. If any record, paper, or other document containing information collected and compiled by or on behalf of the Board, as provided in this section, is received and admitted in evidence in any hearing before the Board, it shall be a public record within the meaning of Chapter 132 of the General Statutes, subject to any deletions of identifying information concerning the treatment of or delivery of services to a client who has not consented to the public disclosure of treatment or services.

(g) A person whose license has been denied or revoked may reapply to the Board for licensure after one calendar year from the date of the denial or revocation.

(h) A licensee may voluntarily relinquish his or her license at any time. Notwithstanding any provision to the contrary, the Board retains full jurisdiction to investigate alleged violations of this Article by any person whose license is relinquished under this subsection and, upon proof of any violation of this Article by the person, the Board may take disciplinary action as authorized by this section.

(i) The Board may adopt rules deemed necessary to interpret and implement this section. (1983, c. 755, s. 1; 1987, c. 827, s. 1; 1993, c. 514, s. 1; 2009-367, s. 8.)

§ 90-341. Violation a misdemeanor.

Any person violating any provision of this Article is guilty of a Class 1 misdemeanor. (1983, c. 755, s. 1; 1993, c. 539, s. 651; 1994, Ex. Sess., c. 24, s. 14(c).)

§ 90-342. Injunction.

As an additional remedy, the Board may proceed in a superior court to enjoin and restrain any person from violating the prohibitions of this Article. The Board shall not be required to post bond in connection with such proceeding. (1983, c. 755, s. 1.)

§ 90-343. Disclosure.

Any individual, or employer of an individual, who is licensed under this Article may not charge a client or receive remuneration for professional counseling services unless, prior to the performance of those services, the client is furnished a copy of a Professional Disclosure Statement that includes the licensee's professional credentials, the services offered, the fee schedule, and other provisions required by the Board. (1993, c. 514, s. 1.)

§ 90-344. Third-party reimbursements.

Nothing in this Article shall be construed to require direct third-party reimbursement to persons licensed under this Article. (1993, c. 514, s. 1.)

§ 90-345. Criminal history record checks of applicants for licensure as professional counselors.

(a) Definitions. - The following definitions shall apply in this section:

(1) Applicant. - A person applying for licensure as a licensed professional counselor associate pursuant to G.S. 90-336(b) or licensed professional counselor pursuant to G.S. 90-336(c).

(2) Criminal history. - A history of conviction of a State or federal crime, whether a misdemeanor or felony, that bears on an applicant's fitness for licensure to practice professional counseling. The crimes include the criminal offenses set forth in any of the following Articles of Chapter 14 of the General Statutes: Article 5, Counterfeiting and Issuing Monetary Substitutes; Article 5A, Endangering Executive and Legislative Officers; Article 6, Homicide; Article 7A, Rape and Other Sex Offenses; Article 8, Assaults; Article 10, Kidnapping and Abduction; Article 13, Malicious Injury or Damage by Use of Explosive or Incendiary Device or Material; Article 14, Burglary and Other Housebreakings; Article 15, Arson and Other Burnings; Article 16, Larceny; Article 17, Robbery; Article 18, Embezzlement; Article 19, False Pretenses and Cheats; Article 19A, Obtaining Property or Services by False or Fraudulent Use of Credit Device or Other Means; Article 19B, Financial Transaction Card Crime Act; Article 20, Frauds; Article 21, Forgery; Article 26, Offenses Against Public Morality and Decency; Article 26A, Adult Establishments; Article 27, Prostitution; Article 28, Perjury; Article 29, Bribery; Article 31, Misconduct in Public Office; Article 35, Offenses Against the Public Peace; Article 36A, Riots, Civil Disorders, and Emergencies; Article 39, Protection of Minors; Article 40, Protection of the Family; Article 59, Public Intoxication; and Article 60, Computer-Related Crime. The crimes also include possession or sale of drugs in violation of the North Carolina Controlled Substances Act in Article 5 of Chapter 90 of the General Statutes and alcohol-related offenses including sale to underage persons in violation of G.S. 18B-302 or driving while impaired in violation of G.S. 20-138.1 through G.S. 20-138.5. In addition to the North Carolina crimes listed in this subdivision, such crimes also include similar crimes under federal law or under the laws of other states.

(b) The Board may request that an applicant for licensure, an applicant seeking reinstatement of a license, or a licensee under investigation by the Board for alleged criminal offenses in violation of this Article consent to a criminal history record check. Refusal to consent to a criminal history record check may constitute grounds for the Board to deny licensure to an applicant, deny reinstatement of a license to an applicant, or revoke the license of a licensee. The Board shall ensure that the State and national criminal history of an applicant is checked. The Board shall be responsible for providing to the North Carolina Department of Justice the fingerprints of the applicant or licensee to be checked, a form signed by the applicant or licensee consenting to the criminal record check and the use of fingerprints and other identifying information required by the State or National Repositories of Criminal Histories, and any additional information required by the Department of Justice in accordance with G.S. 114-19.26. The Board shall keep all information obtained pursuant to this section confidential. The Board shall collect any fees required by the Department of Justice and shall remit the fees to the Department of Justice for expenses associated with conducting the criminal history record check.

(c) If an applicant or licensee's criminal history record check reveals one or more convictions listed under subdivision (a)(2) of this section, the conviction shall not automatically bar licensure. The Board shall consider all of the following factors regarding the conviction:

(1) The level of seriousness of the crime.

(2) The date of the crime.

(3) The age of the person at the time of the conviction.

(4) The circumstances surrounding the commission of the crime, if known.

(5) The nexus between the criminal conduct of the person and the job duties of the position to be filled.

(6) The person's prison, jail, probation, parole, rehabilitation, and employment records since the date the crime was committed.

(7) The subsequent commission by the person of a crime listed in subdivision (a)(2) of this section.

If, after reviewing these factors, the Board determines that the applicant or licensee's criminal history disqualifies the applicant or licensee for licensure, the Board may deny licensure or reinstatement of the license of the applicant or revoke the license of the licensee. The Board may disclose to the applicant or licensee information contained in the criminal history record check that is relevant to the denial. The Board shall not provide a copy of the criminal history record check to the applicant or licensee. The applicant or licensee shall have the right to appear before the Board to appeal the Board's decision. However, an appearance before the full Board shall constitute an exhaustion of administrative remedies in accordance with Chapter 150B of the General Statutes.

(d)   Limited Immunity. - The Board, its officers, and employees, acting in good faith and in compliance with this section, shall be immune from civil liability for denying licensure or reinstatement of a license to an applicant or revoking a licensee's license based on information provided in the applicant or licensee's criminal history record check. (2009-367, s. 9; 2012-12, s. 2(II).)

§ 90-346. Reserved for future codification purposes.

§ 90-347. Reserved for future codification purposes.

§ 90-348. Reserved for future codification purposes.

§ 90-349. Reserved for future codification purposes.

Article 25.

Dietetics/Nutrition.

§ 90-350. Short title.

This Article shall be known as the Dietetics/Nutrition Practice Act. (1991, c. 668, s. 1.)

§ 90-351. Purpose.

It is the purpose of this Article to safeguard the public health, safety and welfare and to protect the public from being harmed by unqualified persons by providing for the licensure and regulation of persons engaged in the practice of dietetics/nutrition and by the establishment of educational standards for those persons. (1991, c. 668, s. 1.)

§ 90-352. Definitions.

As used in this Article, unless the context otherwise requires, the term:

(1) "Board" means the North Carolina Board of Dietetics/Nutrition.

(2) "Dietetics/nutrition" means the integration and application of principles derived from the science of nutrition, biochemistry, physiology, food, and management and from behavioral and social sciences to achieve and maintain a healthy status. The primary function of dietetic/nutrition practice is the provision of nutrition care services.

(3) "Licensed dietitian/nutritionist" means an individual licensed in good standing to practice dietetics/nutrition.

(4) "Nutrition care services" means any, part or all of the following:

a. Assessing the nutritional needs of individuals and groups, and determining resources and constraints in the practice setting.

b. Establishing priorities, goals, and objectives that meet nutritional needs and are consistent with available resources and constraints.

c. Providing nutrition counseling in health and disease.

d. Developing, implementing, and managing nutrition care systems.

e. Evaluating, making changes in, and maintaining appropriate standards of quality in food and nutrition services.

"Nutrition care services" does not include the retail sale of food products or vitamins. (1991, c. 668, s. 1.)

§ 90-353. Creation of Board.

(a) The North Carolina Board of Dietetics/Nutrition is created. The Board shall consist of seven members as follows:

(1) One member shall be a professional whose primary practice is clinical dietetics/nutrition;

(2) One member shall be a professional whose primary practice is community or public health dietetics/nutrition;

(3) One member shall be a professional whose primary practice is consulting in dietetics/nutrition;

(4) One member shall be a professional whose primary practice is in management of nutritional services;

(5) One member shall be an educator on the faculty of a college or university specializing in the field of dietetics/nutrition;

(6) Two members shall represent the public at large.

(b) Professional members of the Board shall:

(1) Be citizens of the United States and residents of this State;

(2) Have practiced in the field of dietetics/nutrition for at least five years; and

(3) Be licensed under this Article, except that initial appointees shall be licensed under this Article no later than March 31, 1992.

(c) The members of the Board appointed from the public at large shall be citizens of the United States and residents of this State and shall not be any of the following:

(1) A dietician/nutritionist.

(2) An agent or employee of a person engaged in the profession of dietetics/nutrition.

(3) A licensed health care professional or enrolled in a program to become prepared to be a licensed health care professional.

(4) An agent or employee of a health care institution, a health care insurer, or a health care professional school.

(5) A member of any allied health profession or enrolled in a program to become prepared to be a member of an allied health profession.

(6) The spouse of an individual who may not serve as a public member of the Board. (1991, c. 668, s. 1.)

§ 90-354. Appointments and removal of Board members, terms and compensation.

(a) The members of the Board shall be appointed as follows:

(1) The Governor shall appoint the professional member described in G.S. 90-353(a)(5) and the two public members described in G.S. 90-353(a)(6);

(2) The General Assembly upon the recommendation of the Speaker of the House of Representatives shall appoint the professional members described in G.S. 90-353(a)(1) and G.S. 90-353(a)(2) in accordance with G.S. 120-121, one of whom shall be a nutritionist with a masters or higher degree in a nutrition-related discipline; and

(3) The General Assembly upon the recommendation of the President Pro Tempore of the Senate shall appoint the professional members described in G.S. 90-353(a)(3) and G.S. 90-353(a)(4) in accordance with G.S. 120-121, one of whom shall be a nutritionist with a masters or higher degree in a nutrition-related discipline.

(b)   Members of the Board shall take office on the first day of July immediately following the expired term of that office and shall serve for a term of three years and until their successors are appointed and qualified.

(c)   No member shall serve on the Board for more than two consecutive terms.

(d)   The Governor may remove members of the Board, after notice and opportunity for hearing, for:

(1)   Incompetence;

(2)   Neglect of duty;

(3)   Unprofessional conduct;

(4)   Conviction of any felony;

(5)   Failure to meet the qualifications of this Article; or

(6)   Committing any act prohibited by this Article.

(e)   Any vacancy shall be filled by the appointing authority originally filling that position, except that any vacancy in appointments by the General Assembly shall be filled in accordance with G.S. 120-122.

(f)   Members of the Board shall receive no compensation for their services, but shall be entitled to travel, per diem, and other expenses authorized by G.S. 93B-5. (1991, c. 668, s. 1; 1995, c. 490, s. 16; 2001-342, s. 1.)

§ 90-355. Election of officers; meetings of Board.

(a)   The Board shall elect a chairman and a vice-chairman who shall hold office according to rules adopted by the Board.

(b)   The Board shall hold at least two regular meetings each year as provided by rules adopted by the Board. The Board may hold additional meetings upon the call of the chairman or any two Board members. A majority of the Board membership shall constitute a quorum. (1991, c. 668, s. 1; 2001-342, s. 2.)

§ 90-356. Power and responsibility of Board.

The Board shall:

(1)   Determine the qualifications and fitness of applicants for licenses, renewal of licenses, and reciprocal licenses;

(2)   Adopt rules necessary to conduct its business, carry out its duties, and administer this Article;

(3)   Adopt and publish a code of ethics;

(4)   Deny, issue, suspend, revoke, and renew licenses in accordance with this Article;

(5)   Conduct investigations, subpoena individuals and records, and do all other things necessary and proper to discipline persons licensed under this Article and to enforce this Article;

(6)   Employ professional, clerical, investigative or special personnel necessary to carry out the provisions of this Article, and purchase or rent office space, equipment and supplies;

(7)   Adopt a seal by which it shall authenticate its proceedings, official records, and licenses;

(8)   Conduct administrative hearings in accordance with Article 3A of Chapter 150B of the General Statutes when a "contested case" as defined in G.S. 150B-2(2) arises under this Article;

(9)   Establish reasonable fees for applications for examination; initial, provisional, and renewal licenses; and other services provided by the Board;

(10)   Submit an annual report to the Governor and General Assembly of all its official actions during the preceding year, together with any recommendations and findings regarding improvements of the practice of dietetics/nutrition;

(11) Publish and make available upon request the licensure standards prescribed under this Article and all rules adopted by the Board;

(12) Request and receive the assistance of State educational institutions or other State agencies;

(13) Approve educational curricula, clinical practice and continuing education requirements for persons seeking licensure under this Article. (1991, c. 668, s. 1; 2001-342, ss. 3, 4.)

§ 90-357. License requirements.

Each applicant for a license as a licensed dietitian/nutritionist shall meet the following requirements:

(1) Submit a completed application as required by the Board;

(2) Submit any fees required by the Board; and

(3) Either:

a. Provide evidence of current registration as a Registered Dietitian by the Commission on Dietetic Registration; or

b. 1. Have received a minimum of a baccalaureate degree from a regionally accredited college or university with a major course of study in human nutrition, foods and nutrition, dietetics, community nutrition, public health nutrition, or an equivalent major course of study, as approved by the Board. Regardless of the course of study, applicants must have successfully completed the Board's minimum course requirements in food sciences, social and behavioral sciences, chemistry, biology, human nutrition, diet therapy, advanced nutrition, and food systems management. Applicants who have obtained their education outside of the United States and its territories must have their academic degree validated by the Board as equivalent to a baccalaureate or masters degree conferred by a regionally accredited college or university in the United States; and

2. Have completed a planned, continuous program in approved clinical practice of not less than 900 hours under the supervision of a licensed dietitian/nutritionist as approved by the Board; and

3. Have passed an examination as defined by the Board; or

c. 1. Have received from a regionally accredited college or university a masters degree in human nutrition, nutrition education, foods and nutrition, public health nutrition or an equivalent major course of study as approved by the Board. Applicants who have obtained their education outside of the United States and its territories must have their academic degree validated by the Board as being equivalent to a masters degree conferred by a regionally accredited college or university in the United States; and

2. Have a documented supervised practice experience component in dietetic practice of not less than 900 hours under the supervision of a licensed health care provider; and

3. Have passed an examination as defined by the Board; or

d. Have received from a regionally accredited college or university a doctorate in human nutrition, nutrition education, foods and nutrition, public health nutrition, or an equivalent major course of study as approved by the Board, or have received a Doctor of Medicine. Regardless of the course of study, applicants must have successfully completed the Board's minimum course requirements in social and behavioral sciences, chemistry, biology, human nutrition, diet therapy and advanced nutrition. Applicants who have obtained their education outside of the United States and its territories must have their academic degree validated by the Board as being equivalent to a doctorate or Doctor of Medicine conferred by a regionally accredited college or university in the United States. (1991, c. 668, s. 1.)

§ 90-358. Notification of applicant following evaluation of application.

After evaluation of the application and of any other evidence submitted, the Board shall notify each applicant that the application and evidence submitted are satisfactory and accepted, or unsatisfactory and rejected. If rejected, the notice shall state the reasons for the rejection. (1991, c. 668, s. 1.)

§ 90-359. Examinations.

Competency examinations shall be administered at least twice each year to qualified applicants for licensing. The examinations may be administered by a national testing service. The Board shall prescribe or develop the examinations which may include an examination given by the Commission on Dietetic Registration of the American Dietetic Association or any other examination approved by two-thirds vote of the entire Board. (1991, c. 668, s. 1.)

§ 90-360. Granting license without examination.

The Board may grant, upon application and payment of proper fees, a license without examination to a person who at the time of application holds a valid license as a licensed dietitian/nutritionist issued by another state or any political territory or jurisdiction acceptable to the Board if in the Board's opinion the requirements for that license are substantially the same as the requirements of this Article. (1991, c. 668, s. 1.)

§ 90-361. Provisional licenses.

The Board may grant a provisional license for a period not exceeding 12 months to any individual who has successfully completed the educational and clinical practice requirements and has made application to take the examination required under G.S. 90-357. A provisional license shall allow the individual to practice as a dietitian/nutritionist under the supervision of a dietitian/nutritionist licensed in this State and shall be valid until revoked by the Board. (1991, c. 668, s. 1.)

§ 90-362. License as constituting property of Board; display requirement; renewal; inactive status.

(a)   A license issued by the Board is the property of the Board and must be surrendered to the Board on demand.

(b)   The licensee shall display the license certificate in the manner prescribed by the Board.

(c)   The licensee shall inform the Board of any change of the licensee's address.

(d)   The license shall be reissued by the Board annually upon payment of a renewal fee if the licensee is not in violation of this Article at the time of application for renewal and if the applicant fulfills current requirements of continuing education as established by the Board.

(e)   Each person licensed under this Article is responsible for renewing his license before the expiration date. The Board shall notify a licensee of pending license expiration at least 30 days in advance thereof.

(f)   The Board may provide for the late renewal of a license upon the payment of a late fee, but no such late fee renewal may be granted more than five years after a license expires.

(g)   Under procedures and conditions established by the Board, a licensee may request that his license be declared inactive. The licensee may apply for active status at any time and upon meeting the conditions set by the Board shall be declared in active status. (1991, c. 668, s. 1.)

§ 90-363. Suspension, revocation and refusal to renew license.

(a)   The Board may deny or refuse to renew a license, may suspend or revoke a license, or may impose probationary conditions on a license if the licensee or applicant for licensure has engaged in any of the following conduct:

(1)   Employment of fraud, deceit or misrepresentation in obtaining or attempting to obtain a license, or the renewal of a license;

(2)   Committing an act or acts of malpractice, gross negligence or incompetence in the practice of dietetics/nutrition;

(3)   Practicing as a licensed dietitian/nutritionist without a current license;

(4)   Engaging in conduct that could result in harm or injury to the public;

(5) Conviction of or a plea of guilty or nolo contendere to any crime involving moral turpitude;

(6) Adjudication of insanity or incompetency, until proof of recovery from the condition can be established;

(7) Engaging in any act or practice violative of any of the provisions of this Article or any rule adopted by the Board, or aiding, abetting or assisting any person in such a violation.

(b) Denial, refusal to renew, suspension, revocation or imposition of probationary conditions upon a license may be ordered by the Board after a hearing held in accordance with Chapter 150B of the General Statutes and rules adopted by the Board. An application may be made to the Board for reinstatement of a revoked license if the revocation has been in effect for at least one year. (1991, c. 668, s. 1.)

§ 90-364. Fees.

The Board shall establish fees in accordance with Chapter 150B of the General Statutes for the following purposes:

(1) For an initial application, a fee not to exceed one hundred dollars ($100.00).

(2) For examination or reexamination, a fee not to exceed two hundred dollars ($200.00).

(3) For issuance of a license, a fee not to exceed two hundred dollars ($200.00).

(4) For the renewal of a license, a fee not to exceed one hundred twenty-five dollars ($125.00).

(5) For the late renewal of a license, an additional late fee not to exceed one hundred dollars ($100.00).

(6) For a provisional license, a fee not to exceed one hundred dollars ($100.00).

(7) For copies of Board rules and licensure standards, charges not exceeding the actual cost of printing and mailing. (1991, c. 668, s. 1; 2001-342, s. 5.)

§ 90-365. Requirement of license.

After March 31, 1992, it shall be unlawful for any person who is not currently licensed under this Article to do any of the following:

(1) Engage in the practice of dietetics/nutrition.

(2) Use the title "dietitian/nutritionist".

(3) Use the words "dietitian," "nutritionist," or "licensed dietitian/nutritionist" alone or in combination.

(4) Use the letters "LD," "LN," or "LDN," or any facsimile or combination in any words, letters, abbreviations, or insignia.

(5) To imply orally or in writing or indicate in any way that the person is a licensed dietitian/nutritionist. (1991, c. 668, s. 1.)

§ 90-366. Violation a misdemeanor.

Any person who violates any provision of this Article shall be guilty of a Class 1 misdemeanor. Each act of such unlawful practice shall constitute a distinct and separate offense. (1991, c. 668, s. 1; 1993, c. 539, s. 652; 1994, Ex. Sess., c. 24, s. 14(c).)

§ 90-367. Injunctions.

The Board may make application to any appropriate court for an order enjoining violations of this Article, and upon a showing by the Board that any person has violated or is about to violate this Article, the court may grant an injunction, restraining order, or take other appropriate action. (1991, c. 668, s. 1.)

§ 90-368. Persons and practices not affected.

The requirements of this Article shall not apply to:

(1)   A health care professional duly licensed in accordance with Chapter 90 of the General Statutes.

(2)   A student or trainee, working under the direct supervision of a licensed dietitian/nutritionist while fulfilling an experience requirement or pursuing a course of study to meet requirements for licensure, for a limited period of time as determined by the Board.

(3)   A dietitian/nutritionist serving in the Armed Forces or the Public Health Service of the United States or employed by the Veterans Administration when performing duties associated with that service or employment.

(4)   A person aiding the practice of dietetics/nutrition if the person works under the direct supervision of a licensed dietitian/nutritionist and performs only support activities that do not require formal academic training in the basic food, nutrition, chemical, biological, behavioral, and social sciences that are used in the practice of dietetics.

(5)   An employee of the State, a local political subdivision, or a local school administrative unit or a person that contracts with the State, a local political subdivision, or a local school administrative unit while engaged in the practice of dietetics/nutrition within the scope of that employment.

(6)   A retailer who does not hold himself out to be a dietitian or nutritionist when that retailer furnishes nutrition information to customers on food, food materials, dietary supplements and other goods sold at his retail establishment in connection with the marketing and distribution of those goods at his retail establishment.

(7) A person who provides weight control services; provided the program has been reviewed by, consultation is available from, and no program change can be initiated without prior approval of:

a. A licensed dietitian/nutritionist;

b. A dietitian/nutritionist licensed in another state that has licensure requirements that are at least as stringent as under this Article; or

c. A dietitian registered by the Commission on Dietetic Registration of the American Dietetic Association.

(8) Employees or independent contractors of a hospital or health care facility licensed under Article 5 or Part A of Article 6 of Chapter 131E or Article 2 of Chapter 122C of the General Statutes.

(9) A person who does not hold himself out to be a dietitian or nutritionist when that person furnishes nutrition information on food, food materials, or dietary supplements. This Article does not prohibit that person from making explanations to customers about foods or food products in connection with the marketing and distribution of these products.

(10) An herbalist or other person who does not hold himself out to be a dietitian or nutritionist when the person furnishes nonfraudulent specific nutritional information and counseling about the reported or historical use of herbs, vitamins, minerals, amino acids, carbohydrates, sugars, enzymes, food concentrates, or other foods. (1991, c. 668, s. 1; 1995, c. 509, s. 135.2(s).)

§ 90-369. Third party reimbursement; limitation on modifications.

Nothing in this Article shall be construed to require direct third-party reimbursement to persons licensed under this Article. (1991, c. 668, s. 1; 2007-123, s. 1.)

§ 90-370. Costs.

The Board may assess the costs of disciplinary actions against a licensee or person found to be in violation of this Article or rules adopted by the Board. Costs recovered pursuant to this section shall be the property of the Board. (2009-271, s. 1.)

§ 90-371. Reserved for future codification purposes.

§ 90-372. Reserved for future codification purposes.

§ 90-373. Reserved for future codification purposes.

§ 90-374. Reserved for future codification purposes.

§ 90-375. Reserved for future codification purposes.

§ 90-376. Reserved for future codification purposes.

§ 90-377. Reserved for future codification purposes.

§ 90-378. Reserved for future codification purposes.

§ 90-379. Reserved for future codification purposes.

Article 26.

Fee-Based Practicing Pastoral Counselors.

§ 90-380. Title.

This Article shall be known as the "Fee-Based Practicing Pastoral Counselor Certification Act." (1991, c. 670.)

§ 90-381. Purpose.

It is the purpose of this Article to protect the public safety and welfare by providing for the certification and regulation of persons engaged in the practice of fee-based pastoral counseling and pastoral psychotherapy. (1991, c. 670.)

§ 90-382. Definitions.

The following definitions apply in this Article:

(1)   Accredited educational institution. - A college, university, or theological seminary chartered by the State and accredited by the appropriate regional association of colleges and secondary schools or by the appropriate association of theological schools and seminaries.

(2)   Board. - The North Carolina State Board of Examiners of Fee-Based Practicing Pastoral Counselors.

(3)   Fee-based pastoral counseling associate. - An individual, certified under this Article, who renders or offers professional pastoral counseling services only under qualified supervision in accordance with rules adopted by the Board.

(4)   Fee-based pastoral counselor. - A minister who receives fees from the practice of pastoral counseling.

(5)   Fee-based practice of pastoral counseling. - To render or offer for a fee or other compensation professional pastoral counseling services, whether to the general public or to organizations, either public or private; to individuals, singly or in groups; to couples, married or in other relationships; and to families.

(6)   Fee-based professional pastoral counseling services. - The application of pastoral care and pastoral counseling principles and procedures for a fee or other compensation with the purpose of understanding, anticipating, or influencing the behavior of individuals in order to assist in their attainment of maximum personal growth; optimal work, marital, family, church, school, social, and interpersonal relationships; and healthy personal adaptation. The application of pastoral care and pastoral psychotherapy principles and procedures includes sustaining, healing, shepherding, nurturing, guiding, and reconciling; interviewing, counseling, and using psychotherapy, diagnosing, preventing, and ameliorating difficulties in living; and resolving interpersonal and social conflict. Teaching, writing, the giving of public speeches or lectures, and

research concerned with pastoral care and counseling principles are not included in professional pastoral counseling services within the meaning of this Article.

(7) Minister. - A person who has been called, elected, or otherwise authorized by a church, denomination, or faith group through ordination, consecration or equivalent means, to exercise within and on behalf of the denomination or faith group specific religious leadership and service that furthers its purpose and mission and that differs from the religious service of the laity of the denomination or faith group.

(8) Pastoral counseling. - Used interchangeably with pastoral psychotherapy to mean a process in which a pastoral counselor utilizes insights and principles derived from the disciplines of theology and the behavioral sciences to help persons achieve wholeness and health.

(9) Pastoral psychotherapy. - The use of pastoral care and pastoral counseling methods in a professional relationship to assist a person in modifying feelings, attitudes, and behavior that are intellectually, socially, emotionally, or spiritually maladjustive, ineffectual, or that otherwise contribute to difficulties in living. (1991, c. 670.)

§ 90-383. Exemptions.

(a) Nothing in this Article shall be construed as limiting the ministry, activities, or services of a minister called, elected, or otherwise authorized by a church, denomination, or faith group to perform the ordinary duties or functions of the clergy.

(b) Nothing in this Article shall be construed as limiting the activities, services, or use of a title to designate a training status of a student, intern, or fellow preparing for the practice of pastoral care and counseling under qualified supervision in an accredited educational institution or service facility, provided that those activities and services constitute a part of the course of study.

(c) Nothing in this Article shall be construed to limit or restrict physicians, optometrists, or psychologists licensed to practice under the laws of North Carolina; or to restrict qualified members of other professional groups who render counseling and other helping services including counselors, social workers, and other similar professions; or to restrict qualified members of any other professional groups in the practice of their respective professions, provided they do not claim to the public by any title or description stating or implying that they are certified fee-based practicing pastoral counselors or certified fee-based pastoral counseling associates, or that they are certified to receive fees for the practice of pastoral counseling.

(d)   Except as otherwise provided in this Article, if a person exempt from the provisions of this Article becomes certified under this Article, he or she shall be required to comply with the requirements of this Article and rules adopted by the Board. (1991, c. 670.)

§ 90-384. Temporary certificates.

The Board may issue a temporary pastoral counseling certificate to any person who is otherwise qualified under this Article until the next annual examination is given. (1991, c. 670.)

§ 90-385. Creation of Board; appointment and removal of members; terms and compensation; powers.

(a)   The North Carolina State Board of Examiners of Fee-Based Practicing Pastoral Counselors is created. The Board shall consist of seven members as follows:

(1)   Three members appointed by the Governor, two of whom shall be certified fee-based practicing pastoral counselors and one of whom shall be a certified fee-based pastoral counseling associate.

(2)   Two members appointed by the General Assembly upon the recommendation of the Speaker of the House of Representatives, one of whom shall be a certified fee-based practicing pastoral counselor and one of whom shall be a public member who has no direct affiliation with the practice of pastoral counseling.

(3)   Two members appointed by the General Assembly upon the recommendation of the President Pro Tempore of the Senate, one of whom

shall be a certified fee-based practicing pastoral counselor and one of whom shall be a public member who has no direct affiliation with the practice of pastoral counseling.

Initial appointees shall be persons who meet the education and experience requirements for certification under this Article and shall be deemed certified upon appointment. In making appointments, consideration shall be given to adequate representation from the various fields and areas of the practice of pastoral counseling. Legislative appointments shall be made in accordance with G.S. 120-121.

(b) Of the members initially appointed, three members, including one certified fee-based practicing pastoral counselor appointed by the Governor, one certified fee-based pastoral counseling associate appointed by the Governor, and one public member who has no direct affiliation with the practice of pastoral counseling appointed by the General Assembly upon the recommendation of the President Pro Tempore of the Senate, shall serve for a term of two years. Two members, including one certified fee-based practicing pastoral counselor appointed by the General Assembly upon the recommendation of the Speaker of the House of Representatives and one public member who has no direct affiliation with the practice of pastoral counseling appointed by the General Assembly upon the recommendation of the Speaker of the House of Representatives, shall serve for a term of three years. Two members, including the certified fee-based practicing pastoral counselor appointed by the Governor and the certified fee-based practicing pastoral counselor appointed by the General Assembly upon the recommendation of the President Pro Tempore of the Senate, shall serve for a term of four years.

(c) After the initial terms specified in this section, each member shall be appointed to serve a term of four years or until a successor is appointed and qualified. A vacancy shall be filled by the appointing authority originally filling that position, except that any vacancy in appointments by the General Assembly shall be filled in accordance with G.S. 120-122. No person may be appointed more than once to fill an unexpired term nor to more than two consecutive terms.

(d) The Governor may remove any member of the Board for neglect of duty, malfeasance, conviction of a felony or conviction of a crime involving moral turpitude while in office, but for no other reason.

(e) Five Board members shall constitute a quorum. The Governor shall designate one Board member who is a certified fee-based practicing pastoral counselor to serve as chairperson during the term of his or her appointment to the Board. No person may serve as chairperson for more than four years. The Board shall specify the location of its principal office.

(f) The Board shall meet at least annually at a time set by the Board. The Board may hold additional meetings and conduct any proceeding or investigation necessary to its purposes and may empower its agents or counsel to conduct any investigation necessary to its purposes. The Board may order that any records concerning the provision of pastoral counseling services relevant to a complaint received by the Board or any inquiry or investigation conducted by or on behalf of the Board be produced for inspection and copying by representatives of the Board. The Board shall adopt an official seal, which shall be affixed to all certificates issued by the Board. The Board shall adopt rules necessary to conduct its business, carry out its duties, and administer this Article in accordance with Chapter 150B of the General Statutes.

(g) Board members shall receive no compensation for their services, but may be compensated for their expenses incurred in the performance of duties required by this Article, as provided in G.S. 138-6, from funds generated by examination fees or from contributions made to the Board. The Board may employ and compensate necessary personnel for the performance of its functions, within the limits of funds available to the Board. In no event shall the State be liable for expenses incurred by the Board in excess of the income derived from this Article. (1991, c. 670.)

§ 90-386. Annual report.

Within 90 days of the end of each fiscal year, beginning with fiscal year 1992-93, the Board shall submit to the Governor a report of the Board's activities since the preceding July 1, including the names of all fee-based practicing pastoral counselors and fee-based pastoral counseling associates to whom certificates have been granted under this Article during that fiscal year. (1991, c. 670.)

§ 90-387. Certification and examination.

(a) The Board shall issue a certificate to practice fee-based pastoral counseling to an applicant who:

(1) Pays an application fee of one hundred dollars ($100.00);

(2) Pays an examination fee set by the Board of not more than four hundred dollars ($400.00);

(3) Passes a Board examination in pastoral counseling;

(4) Submits evidence verified by oath and satisfactory to the Board that the applicant:

a. Is at least 21 years of age;

b. Is of good moral character;

c. Has received a masters of divinity or higher degree, or its equivalent, from an accredited educational institution;

d. Has received a masters or doctoral degree in pastoral counseling, or its equivalent, based on a planned and directed program of studies in pastoral counseling from an accredited educational institution; has completed satisfactorily one unit of full-time clinical pastoral education in a program accredited by the Association of Clinical Pastoral Education, or its equivalent; and has completed at least 1,375 hours of pastoral counseling while receiving a minimum of 250 hours of supervision during those hours of pastoral counseling;

e. Is a member of a recognized denomination or faith group that recognizes the applicant's status as a rabbi, priest, minister, or religious leader, as defined in the Federal Internal Revenue Code;

f. Has completed three years of full-time work as a rabbi, priest, minister, or religious leader, or its equivalent;

g. Has been ordained, or its equivalent as determined by the applicant's denomination or faith group, and has been endorsed to function as a pastoral counselor; and

h. Has not within the preceding six months failed an examination given by the Board.

(b) The Board shall issue a certificate to practice as a fee-based pastoral counseling associate to an applicant who:

(1) Pays an application fee of one hundred dollars ($100.00);

(2) Pays an examination fee set by the Board of not more than four hundred dollars ($400.00);

(3) Passes an examination in pastoral counseling satisfactory to the Board;

(4) Submits evidence verified by oath and satisfactory to the Board that the applicant:

a. Is at least 21 years of age;

b. Is of good moral character;

c. Has received a masters of divinity or higher degree, or its equivalent, from an accredited educational institution;

d. Is a member of a recognized denomination or faith group that recognizes the applicant's status as a rabbi, priest, minister, or religious leader;

e. Has completed three years of full-time work as a rabbi, priest, minister, or religious leader, or its equivalent;

f. Has been ordained, or its equivalent as determined by the applicant's denomination or faith group, and has been endorsed to function as a pastoral counselor;

g. Has not within the preceding six months failed an examination given by the Board; and

h. Has satisfactorily completed one unit of full-time clinical pastoral education in a program accredited by the American Association for Clinical Education, or its equivalent, and has completed at least 375 hours of pastoral counseling including a minimum of 125 hours of supervision of those pastoral counseling hours.

(c) A pastoral counseling associate may become a certified fee-based practicing pastoral counselor if the applicant complies with the requirements set forth in subsection (a) of this section and pays an examination fee set by the Board of not more than four hundred dollars ($400.00).

(d)   The examinations required by subsections (a) and (b) of this section shall be in a form and content prescribed by the Board and shall be oral and written. The examinations shall be administered at least annually at a time and place to be determined by the Board. (1991, c. 670, c. 761, s. 12.4.)

§ 90-388. Equivalent certification and memberships recognized.

(a)   The Board may grant a certificate as a fee-based practicing pastoral counselor to any person meeting the requirements of G.S. 90-387(a) who at the time of application is certified as a pastoral counselor by a board of another state whose standards, in the opinion of the Board, are at least equal to those required by this Article. This section applies only when the state grants similar privileges to residents of this State. To determine a candidate's qualifications, the Board may require a personal interview and any other documentation the Board deems necessary.

(b)   The Board may grant a certificate as a practicing pastoral counselor to any person who has been certified as a Fellow or Diplomate by the American Association of Pastoral Counselors if application is made by December 31, 1991. To determine a candidate's qualifications the Board may require a personal interview and any other documentation the Board deems necessary.

(c)   The Board may grant a certificate as a fee-based pastoral counseling associate to any person who has been certified as a member of the American Association of Pastoral Counselors if application is made by December 31, 1991. To determine a candidate's qualifications, the Board may require a personal interview and any other documentation the Board deems necessary. (1991, c. 670.)

§ 90-389. Renewal of certificate.

A certificate issued under this Article must be renewed annually on or before the first day of January of each year. Each application for renewal must be accompanied by a renewal fee set by the Board of not more than one hundred dollars ($100.00). If a certificate is not renewed on or before the first day of January of each year, an additional fee of not more than twenty-five dollars ($25.00) as set by the Board shall be charged for late renewal. The Board may establish requirements for continuing education for pastoral counselors and pastoral counseling associates certified in this State as an additional condition for renewal. (1991, c. 670.)

§ 90-390. Refusal, suspension, or revocation of a certificate.

(a)   A certificate applied for or issued under this Article may be refused, suspended, revoked, or otherwise limited as provided in subsection (e) of this section by the Board upon proof that the applicant or person to whom a certificate was issued:

(1)   Has been convicted of a felony;

(2)   Has been convicted of a misdemeanor involving moral turpitude, misrepresentation or fraud in dealing with the public, or an offense relevant to fitness to practice certified fee-based pastoral counseling;

(3)   Has engaged in fraud or deceit in securing or attempting to secure a certificate or the renewal of a certificate or has willfully concealed from the Board material information in connection with application for or renewal of a certificate under this Article;

(4)   Is a habitual drunkard or is addicted to deleterious habit-forming drugs;

(5)   Has made fraudulent or misleading statements pertaining to his education, licensure, professional credentials, or related to his qualification or fitness for the practice of pastoral counseling;

(6)   Has had a license for the practice of pastoral counseling in any other state or any other country suspended or revoked;

(7)   Has been guilty of unprofessional conduct as defined by the relevant code of ethics published by the American Association of Pastoral Counselors; or

(8)   Has violated any provision of this Article or the rules of the Board.

(b) A certificate issued under this Article shall be automatically suspended by the Board after failure to renew a certificate for a period of more than three months after the annual renewal date.

(c) Except as otherwise provided in this Article, the procedure for revocation, suspension, refusal, or other limitations of the certificate shall be in accordance with the provisions of Chapter 150B of the General Statutes. In any proceeding or record of any hearing before the Board, and in any complaint or notice of charges against any certified fee-based pastoral counselor or certified fee-based pastoral counseling associate and in any decision rendered by the Board, the Board shall endeavor to withhold from public disclosure the identity of any counselees or clients who have not consented to the public disclosure of treatment by the certified fee-based pastoral counselor or certified fee-based pastoral counseling associate. The Board may close a hearing to the public and receive in a closed session evidence concerning the treatment or delivery of pastoral counseling services to a counselee or a client who has not consented to public disclosure of treatment or services, as may be necessary for the protection of the counselee's or client's rights and the full presentation of relevant evidence. All records, papers, and documents containing information collected and compiled by or on behalf of the Board as a result of investigations, inquiries, or interviews conducted in connection with certification or disciplinary matters are not public records within the meaning of Chapter 132 of the General Statutes. However, any notice or statement of charges against any certified fee-based pastoral counselor or certified fee-based pastoral counseling associate, any notice to any certified fee-based pastoral counselor or certified fee-based pastoral counseling associate of a hearing in any proceeding, or any decision rendered in connection with a hearing in any proceeding is a public record within the meaning of Chapter 132 of the General Statutes, except that identifying information concerning the treatment or delivery of services to a counselee or client who has not consented to the public disclosure of such treatment or services may be deleted. Any record, paper, or other document containing information collected and compiled by or on behalf of the Board, as provided in this section, that is received and admitted in evidence in any hearing before the Board shall be a public record within the meaning of Chapter 132 of the General Statutes, subject to any deletions of identifying information concerning the treatment or delivery of pastoral counseling services to a counselee or client who has not consented to public disclosure of the treatment or services.

(d) The Board may reinstate a suspended certificate upon payment by an applicant of a fee of twenty dollars ($20.00), and may require that the applicant file a new application, submit to reexamination for reinstatement, and pay other authorized fees as required by the Board.

(e) Upon proof that a certified fee-based pastoral counselor or certified fee-based pastoral counseling associate certified under this Article has engaged in any of the prohibited actions specified in subsection (a) of this section, the Board may, in lieu of refusal, suspension, or revocation, do any one or more of the following:

(1) Issue a formal reprimand;

(2) Formally censure the certified fee-based pastoral counselor or certified fee-based pastoral counseling associate;

(3) Place the certified fee-based pastoral counselor or certified fee-based pastoral counseling associate on probation with any conditions the Board may deem advisable; or

(4) Limit or circumscribe the professional pastoral counseling services provided by the certified fee-based pastoral counselor or the certified fee-based pastoral counseling associate as the Board deems advisable.

(f) The Board may impose conditions of probation or restrictions on continued practice at the conclusion of a period of suspension or as a condition for the restoration of a revoked or suspended certificate. In lieu of or in connection with any disciplinary proceedings or investigation, the Board may enter into a consent order relating to the discipline, censure, proceeding costs, probation, or limitations on the practice of a certified fee-based pastoral counselor or certified fee-based pastoral counseling associate. (1991, c. 670, s. 1; 1993 (Reg. Sess., 1994), c. 570, s. 8.)

§ 90-391. Prohibited acts.

No person shall represent himself to be a certified fee-based practicing pastoral counselor or a certified fee-based pastoral counseling associate, or engage in or offer to engage in the practice of certified fee-based pastoral counseling, without a valid certificate issued under this Article. No person shall use these titles or descriptions, or any of their derivatives, in a manner that implies the person is certified under this Article. No called or elected pastor during his active full-time pastorate shall practice as a certified fee-based pastoral counselor even if certified under this Article. (1991, c. 670.)

§ 90-392. Disposition of fees.

The fees derived from the operation of this Article shall be used by the Board in carrying out its functions. The operations of the Board are subject to the oversight of the State Auditor pursuant to Article 5A of Chapter 147 of the General Statutes. (1991, c. 670.)

§ 90-393. Injunction for violations.

The Board may apply to superior court for an injunction to prevent violations of this Article or of any rules adopted by the Board, and the court has the authority to grant an injunction. (1991, c. 670.)

§ 90-394. Duplicate and replacement certificates.

A certified fee-based pastoral counselor may request that the Board issue a duplicate or replacement certificate for a fee set by the Board not to exceed fifty dollars ($50.00). Upon receipt of the request, a showing of good cause for the issuance of a duplicate or replacement certificate, and payment of the fee, the Board shall issue a duplicate or replacement certificate. (1991, c. 670, s. 1; 1991 (Reg. Sess., 1992), c. 1030, s. 23.)

§ 90-395. Practice of medicine and psychology not authorized.

Nothing in this Article shall authorize the practice of medicine as defined in Article 1 of this Chapter or the practice of psychology as defined in Article 18A of this Chapter. (1991, c. 670.)

§ 90-396. Repealed by Session Laws 1999-186, s. 1.1.

§§ 90-397 through 90-399. Reserved for future codification purposes.

Article 27.

Referral Fees and Payment for Certain Solicitations Prohibited.

§ 90-400. Definition.

As used in this Article, a health care provider is a person holding any license issued under this Chapter. (1991 (Reg. Sess., 1992), c. 858, s. 1.)

§ 90-401. Referral fees and payment for certain solicitations prohibited.

A health care provider shall not financially compensate in any manner a person, firm, or corporation for recommending or securing the health care provider's employment by a patient, or as a reward for having made a recommendation resulting in the health care provider's employment by a patient. No health care provider who refers a patient of that health care provider to another health care provider shall receive financial or other compensation from the health care provider receiving the referral as a payment solely or primarily for the referral. This section shall not be construed to prohibit a health care provider's purchase of advertising which does not entail direct personal contact or telephone contact of a potential patient. (1991 (Reg. Sess., 1992), c. 858, s. 1; 1993 (Reg. Sess., 1994), c. 689, s. 2.)

§ 90-401.1. Direct solicitation prohibited.

It shall be unlawful for a health care provider or the provider's employee or agent to initiate direct personal contact or telephone contact with any injured, diseased, or infirmed person, or with any other person residing in the injured, diseased, or infirmed person's household, for a period of 90 days following the injury or the onset of the disease or infirmity, if the purpose of initiating the contact, in whole or in part, is to attempt to induce or persuade the injured, diseased, or infirmed person to become a patient of the health care provider. This section shall not be construed to prohibit a health care provider's use of posted letters, brochures, or information packages to solicit injured, diseased, or infirmed persons, so long as such use does not entail direct personal contact with the person. (1993 (Reg. Sess., 1994), c. 689, s. 3.)

§ 90-402. Sanctions.

Violation of the provisions of this Article shall be grounds for the offending health care provider's licensing board to suspend or revoke the health care provider's license, to refuse to renew the health care provider's license, or to take any other disciplinary action authorized by law. (1991 (Reg. Sess., 1992), c. 858, s. 1; 1993 (Reg. Sess., 1994), c. 689, s. 4.)

§ 90-403. Reserved for future codification purposes.

§ 90-404. Reserved for future codification purposes.

Article 28.

Self-Referrals by Health Care Providers.

§ 90-405. Definitions.

As used in this Article, the term

(1)   "Board" means any of the following boards created in Chapter 90 of this Article relating respectively to the professions of medicine, dentistry, optometry, osteopathy, chiropractic, nursing, podiatry, psychology, physical therapy, occupational therapy, speech and language pathology and audiology.

(2)   "Department" means the Department of Health and Human Services of the State of North Carolina.

(3) "Designated health care services" means, and includes for purposes of this section, any health care procedure and service provided by a health care provider that is covered by or insured under any health benefit plan regulated by Chapter 58 of the General Statutes, any employee welfare benefit plan regulated by the Employee Retirement Income Security Act of 1974, any federal or State employee insurance program, Medicare or Medicaid.

(4) "Entity" means any individual, partnership, firm, corporation, or other business that provides health care services.

(5) "Fair market value" means the value of the rental property for commercial purposes not adjusted to reflect the additional value that one party (either the prospective lessee or lessor) would attribute to the property as a result of its proximity or convenience to sources of referrals or business.

(6) "Group practice" means a group of two or more health care providers legally organized as a partnership, professional corporation, or similar association:

a. In which each health care provider who is a member of the group provides services including consultation, diagnosis, or treatment, through the joint use of shared facilities, equipment, and personnel;

b. For which substantially all the services of the health care providers who are members of the group are provided through the group and are billed in the name of the group and amounts so received are treated as receipts of the group; and

c. In which the overhead expenses of and the income from the practice are distributed in accordance with methods previously determined by members of the group.

(7) "Health care provider" is any person who, pursuant to Chapter 90 of the General Statutes, is licensed, or is otherwise registered or certified to engage in the practice of any of the following: medicine, dentistry, optometry, osteopathy, chiropractic, nursing, podiatry, psychology, physical therapy, occupational therapy or speech and language pathology and audiology.

(8) "Immediate family member" means a health care provider's spouse or dependent minor child.

(9) "Investment interest" means an equity or debt security issued by an entity, or a lease or retained interest in real property held by an entity, including, without limitation, shares of stock in a corporation, units or other interests in a partnership, bonds, debentures, notes, leases, options or contracts related to real property or other equity interests or debt instruments. "Investment interest" and legal or beneficial interest shall not include any interest in:

a. Bonds or other debt instruments issued pursuant to the provisions of Chapter 159 of the General Statutes;

b. A written lease of real property entered into on or before January 1, 1990, for a term of five years or more or a written lease of real property for a term of one year or more, which fully describes the leased premises, the terms and conditions for the lease thereof, with the aggregate rental charge, set in advance, consistent with fair market value in arms-length transactions and not determined in a manner that takes into account the volume or value of any referrals or business otherwise generated between the parties to the lease;

c. An employee's stock purchase, savings, pension, profit sharing or other similar benefit plan in which the investor does not direct investments;

d. Investment interests (including shares of stock, bonds, debentures, notes or other debt instruments) in any corporation that is listed for trading on the New York Stock Exchange, the American Stock Exchange, or is a national market system security traded under automated interdealer quotation system operated by the National Association of Securities Dealers and has, at the end of the corporation's most recent fiscal year, total assets exceeding fifty million dollars ($50,000,000), provided that one of the following requirements is satisfied:

1. The investment interests are purchased in a nonissuer transaction as permitted by G.S. 78A-17(3); or

2. The investment interests are issued in a transaction terminating a health care provider's legal, beneficial, or investment interest in a privately held entity which such health care provider acquired before April 1, 1993, provided that such transaction is completed before July 1, 1995, and the health care provider liquidates the investment interests by July 1, 1997.

(10) "Investor" means an individual or entity owning a legal or beneficial ownership or investment interest, directly or indirectly (including without

limitation, through an immediate family member, trust, affiliate, or another entity related to the investor).

(11) "Referral" means any referral of a patient for designated health care services, including, without limitation:

a. The forwarding of a patient by one health care provider to another health care provider or to an entity that provides any designated health care service; or

b. The request or establishment of a plan of care by a health care provider, which includes the provision of designated health care services.

"Referral" does not mean any designated health care service or any referral to an entity for a designated health care service which is provided by, or provided under the personal supervision of, a sole health care provider or by a member of a group practice to the patients of that health care provider or group practice. (1993, c. 482, s. 1; 1995, c. 509, s. 46; 1997-443, s. 11A.118(a).)

§ 90-406. Self-referrals prohibited.

(a) A health care provider shall not make any referral of any patient to any entity in which the health care provider or group practice or any member of the group practice is an investor.

(b) No invoice or claim for payment shall be presented by any entity or health care provider to any individual, third-party payer, or other entity for designated health care services furnished pursuant to a referral prohibited under this Article.

(c) If any entity collects any amount pursuant to an invoice or claim presented in violation of this section, the entity shall refund such amount to the payor or individual, whichever is applicable, within 10 working days of receipt.

(d) Any health care provider or other entity that enters into an arrangement or scheme, such as a cross-referral arrangement that the health care provider or entity knows or should know is intended to induce referrals of patients for designated health care services to a particular entity and that, if the health care provider directly made referrals to such entity, would constitute a prohibited referral under this section, shall be in violation of this section. (1993, c. 482, s. 1.)

§ 90-407. Disciplinary action and penalties.

(a) Any violation of this Article shall constitute grounds for disciplinary action to be taken by the applicable Board pursuant to Chapter 90 of the General Statutes.

(b) Any health care provider who refers a patient in violation of G.S. 90-406(a), or any health care provider or entity who

(1) Presents or causes to be presented a bill or claim for service that the health care provider or entity knows or should know is prohibited by G.S. 90-406(b), or

(2) Fails to make a refund as required by G.S. 90-406(c),

shall be subject to a civil penalty of not more than twenty thousand dollars ($20,000) for each such bill or claim, to be recovered in an action instituted either in Wake County Superior Court, or any other county, by the Attorney General for the use of the State of North Carolina.

(c) Any health care provider or other entity that enters into an arrangement or scheme, such as cross-referral arrangement, that the health care provider or entity knows or should know is intended to induce referrals or patients for designated health care services to a particular entity and that, if the health care provider directly made referrals to such entity, would violate G.S. 90-406(d), shall be subject to a civil penalty of not more than seventy-five thousand dollars ($75,000) for each such circumvention arrangement or scheme, to be recovered in an action instituted either in Wake County Superior Court, or any other county, by the Attorney General for the use of the State of North Carolina. No civil penalty shall be assessed hereunder for any arrangement fully disclosed to the Attorney General in writing which receives a favorable determination by the Attorney General that, in his opinion, such arrangement is not a violation of G.S. 90-406, until a contrary determination is made in a court of law.

(d) The clear proceeds of civil penalties provided for in this section shall be remitted to the Civil Penalty and Forfeiture Fund in accordance with G.S. 115C-457.2. (1993, c. 482, s. 1; 1998-215, s. 74.)

§ 90-408. Exceptions for underserved areas.

(a) The provisions of G.S. 90-406 shall not apply to the referral by any health care provider to any entity in which such health care provider has a legal, beneficial, or investment interest upon receipt by such health care provider of a determination by the Department of Health and Human Services that:

(1) There is a demonstrated need in the county where the entity is located or is proposed to be located; and

(2) Alternative financing is not available on reasonable terms from other sources to develop such entity.

(b) The Department shall promulgate regulations governing the form and content of the applications to be filed by health care providers making application for exemption from G.S. 90-406, the business conduct of any such entity and the fair and reasonable access by all health care providers in such county to the entity. Any determination made by the Department under this section shall be applicable for a period of five years from the date of issuance.

(c) In all cases in which a health care provider refers a patient to a health care facility outside that health care provider's practice in which the health care provider has a legal, beneficial, or investment interest, the health care provider shall disclose to the patient the health care provider's investment interest. Patients shall be given a list of effective alternative facilities if any such facilities become reasonably available, informed that they have the option to use one of the alternative facilities, and assured that they will not be treated differently by the health care provider if they do not choose the health care provider's facility. (1993, c. 482, s. 1; 1997-443, s. 11A.118(a).)

§ 90-409. Reserved for future codification purposes.

Article 29.

Medical Records.

§ 90-410. Definitions.

As used in this Article:

(1) "Health care provider" means any person who is licensed or certified to practice a health profession or occupation under this Chapter or Chapters 90B or 90C of the General Statutes, a health care facility licensed under Chapters 131E or 122C of the General Statutes, and a representative or agent of a health care provider.

(2) "Medical records" means personal information that relates to an individual's physical or mental condition, medical history, or medical treatment, excluding X rays and fetal monitor records. (1993, c. 529, s. 4.3.)

§ 90-411. Record copy fee.

A health care provider may charge a reasonable fee to cover the costs incurred in searching, handling, copying, and mailing medical records to the patient or the patient's designated representative. The maximum fee for each request shall be seventy-five cents (75¢) per page for the first 25 pages, fifty cents (50¢) per page for pages 26 through 100, and twenty-five cents (25¢) for each page in excess of 100 pages, provided that the health care provider may impose a minimum fee of up to ten dollars ($10.00), inclusive of copying costs. If requested by the patient or the patient's designated representative, nothing herein shall limit a reasonable professional fee charged by a physician for the review and preparation of a narrative summary of the patient's medical record. This section shall only apply with respect to liability claims for personal injury, and claims for social security disability, except that charges for medical records and reports related to claims under Article 1 of Chapter 97 of the General Statutes shall be governed by the fees established by the North Carolina Industrial Commission pursuant to G.S. 97-26.1. This section shall not apply to Department of Health and Human Services Disability Determination Services requests for copies of medical records made on behalf of an applicant for Social Security or Supplemental Security Income disability. (1993, c. 529, s. 4.3; 1993 (Reg. Sess., 1994), c. 679, s. 5.5; 1995 (Reg. Sess., 1996), c. 742, s. 36; 1997-443, ss. 11.3, 11A.118(b).)

§ 90-412. Electronic medical records.

(a) Notwithstanding any other provision of law, any health care provider or facility licensed, certified, or registered under the laws of this State or any unit of State or local government may create and maintain medical records in an electronic format. The health care provider, facility, or governmental unit shall not be required to maintain a separate paper copy of the electronic medical record. A health care provider, facility, or governmental unit shall maintain electronic medical records in a legible and retrievable form, including adequate data backup.

(b) Notwithstanding any other provision of law, any health care provider or facility licensed, certified, or registered under the laws of this State or any unit of State or local government may permit authorized individuals to authenticate orders and other medical record entries by written signature, or by electronic or digital signature in lieu of a signature in ink. Medical record entries shall be authenticated by the individual who made or authorized the entry. For purposes of this section, "authentication" means identification of the author of an entry by that author and confirmation that the contents of the entry are what the author intended.

(c) The legal rights and responsibilities of patients, health care providers, facilities, and governmental units shall apply to records created or maintained in electronic form to the same extent as those rights and responsibilities apply to medical records embodied in paper or other media. This subsection applies with respect to the security, confidentiality, accuracy, integrity, access to, and disclosure of medical records. (1999-247, s. 2; 2007-248, s. 3.)

§ 90-413: Reserved for future codification purposes.

Article 29A.

North Carolina Health Information Exchange Act.

§ 90-413.1. Title.

This act shall be known and may be cited as the "North Carolina Health Information Exchange Act." (2011-337, s. 1.)

§ 90-413.2. Purpose.

This Article is intended to improve the quality of health care delivery within this State by facilitating and regulating the use of a voluntary, statewide health information exchange network for the secure electronic transmission of individually identifiable health information among health care providers, health plans, and health care clearinghouses in a manner that is consistent with the Health Insurance Portability and Accountability Act, Privacy Rule and Security Rule, 45 C.F.R. §§ 160, 164. (2011-337, s. 1.)

§ 90-413.3. Definitions.

The following definitions apply in this Article:

(1)   "Business associate" is as defined in 45 C.F.R. § 160.103.

(2)   "Business associate contract" means the documentation required by 45 C.F.R. § 164.502(e)(2) that meets the applicable requirements of 45 C.F.R. § 164.504(e).

(3)   "Covered entity" means any entity described in 45 C.F.R. § 160.103 or any other facility or practitioner licensed by the State to provide health care services.

(4)   "Disclose" or "disclosure" means the release, transfer, provision of access to, or divulging in any other manner an individual's protected health information through the HIE Network.

(5)   "Emergency medical condition" means a medical condition manifesting itself by acute symptoms of sufficient severity, including severe pain, such that the absence of immediate medical attention could reasonably be expected to result in (i) placing an individual's health in serious jeopardy, (ii) serious impairment to an individual's bodily functions, or (iii) serious dysfunction of any bodily organ or part of an individual.

(6) "HIE Network" means the voluntary, statewide health information exchange network overseen and administered by the NC HIE.

(7) "HIPAA" means the Health Insurance Portability and Accountability Act of 1996, P.L. 104-191, as amended.

(8) "Individual" is as defined in 45 C.F.R. § 160.103.

(9) "North Carolina Health Information Exchange" or "NC HIE" means the nonprofit corporation selected by the Governor to serve as the subrecipient of grant funds from or as the State-designated entity named by the State pursuant to section 3013 of the federal Health Information Technology for Economic and Clinical Health Act, P.L. 111-5, Div. A, Title XIII, section 13001, as amended.

(10) "Opt out" means an individual's affirmative decision to disallow his or her protected health information maintained by or on behalf of one or more specific covered entities from being disclosed to other covered entities through the HIE Network.

(11) "Protected health information" is as defined in 45 C.F.R. § 160.103.

(12) "Public health purposes" means the public health activities and purposes described in 45 C.F.R. § 164.512(b).

(13) "Qualified organization" means an entity designated by the NC HIE to contract with covered entities on the NC HIE's behalf to facilitate the participation of such covered entities in the HIE Network.

(14) "Research purposes" means research that meets the standard described in 45 C.F.R. § 164.512(i). (2011-337, s. 1.)

§ 90-413.3A. (Contingent effective date - see note) Required participation in NC HIE for some providers.

(a) The General Assembly makes the following findings:

(1) That controlling escalating health care costs of the Medicaid program is of significant importance to the State, its taxpayers, and its Medicaid recipients.

(2) That the State needs timely access to claims and clinical information in order to assess performance, pinpoint medical expense trends, identify beneficiary health risks, and evaluate how the State is spending Medicaid dollars.

(3) That making this clinical information available through the North Carolina Health Information Exchange will improve care coordination within and across health systems, increase care quality, enable more effective population health management, reduce duplication of medical services, augment syndromic surveillance, allow more accurate measurement of care services and outcomes, increase strategic knowledge about the health of the population, and facilitate health cost-containment.

(b) Any hospital, as defined in G.S. 131E-76(c), that has an electronic health record system shall connect to the NC HIE and submit individual patient demographic and clinical data on services paid for with Medicaid funds, based upon the findings set forth in subsection (a) of this section and notwithstanding the voluntary nature of the NC HIE under G.S. 90-413.2. The NC HIE shall give the Department of Health and Human Services real-time access to data and information contained in the NC HIE. (2013-363, s. 4.18(a); 2013-382, s. 14.1.)

§ 90-413.4. North Carolina Health Information Exchange; requirements.

(a) The NC HIE shall satisfy all of the following requirements:

(1) Oversee and administer the HIE Network in a manner that ensures all of the following:

a. Compliance with this Article.

b. Compliance with HIPAA and any rules adopted under HIPAA, including the Privacy Rule and Security Rule.

c. Compliance with the terms of any business associate contract the NC HIE or qualified organization enters into with a covered entity participating in the HIE Network.

d. Notice to the patient by the provider on the initial visit about the HIE Network, including information and education about the right of individuals on a continuing basis to opt out or rescind a decision to opt out.

e. Opportunity for all individuals to exercise on a continuing basis the right to opt out or rescind a decision to opt out.

f. Nondiscriminatory treatment by covered entities of individuals who exercise the right to opt out.

(2) Develop and enter into written participation agreements with covered entities that utilize the HIE Network. The participation agreements shall specify the terms and conditions governing participation in the HIE Network. The agreement shall also require compliance with policies developed by the NC HIE pursuant to this Article, or pursuant to applicable laws of the state of residence for entities located outside of North Carolina. In lieu of entering into a participation agreement directly with covered entities, the NC HIE may enter into participation agreements with qualified organizations, which in turn, enter into participation agreements with covered entities.

(3) Add, remove, disclose, and access protected health information through the HIE Network in accordance with this Article.

(4) Enter into a business associate contract with each of the covered entities participating in the HIE Network. In lieu of entering into a business associates contract directly with covered entities, the NC HIE may enter into business associates contracts with qualified organizations, which in turn, enter into business associates contracts with covered entities.

(5) Grant user rights to the HIE Network to business associates of covered entities participating in the HIE Network (i) at the request of the covered entities and (ii) at the discretion of the NC HIE upon consideration of the business associates' legitimate need for utilizing the HIE Network and privacy and security concerns.

(6) Facilitate and promote use of the HIE Network by covered entities.

(7) Periodically monitor compliance with this Article by covered entities participating in the HIE Network.

(b)   Nothing in this section shall be construed to restrict the NC HIE from exercising any of its corporate powers in a manner that is not inconsistent with this Article. (2011-337, s. 1.)

§ 90-413.5. Participation by covered entities.

(a)   Each covered entity that elects to participate in the HIE Network shall enter into a business associate contract and a written participation agreement with the NC HIE or qualified organization prior to disclosing or accessing any protected health information through the HIE Network.

(b)   Each covered entity that elects to participate in the HIE Network may authorize its business associates to disclose or access protected health information on behalf of the covered entity through the HIE Network in accordance with this Article and at the discretion of the NC HIE, as provided in G.S. 90-413.4(5).

(c)   Notwithstanding any State law or regulation to the contrary, each covered entity that elects to participate in the HIE Network may disclose an individual's protected health information through the HIE Network (i) to other covered entities for any purpose permitted by HIPAA, unless the individual has exercised the right to opt out and (ii) in order to facilitate the provision of emergency medical treatment to the individual, subject to the requirements set forth in G.S. 90-413.6(e).

(d)   Any health care provider who relies in good faith upon any information provided through the NC HIE or through a qualified organization in the health care provider's treatment of a patient shall not incur criminal or civil liability for damages caused by the inaccurate or incomplete nature of this information. (2011-337, s. 1.)

§ 90-413.6. Continuing right to opt out; effect of opt out; exception for emergency medical treatment.

(a)   Each individual has the right on a continuing basis to opt out or rescind a decision to opt out.

(b) The NC HIE or its designee shall enforce an individual's decision to opt out or rescind an opt out prospectively from the date the NC HIE or its designee receives notice of the individual's decision to opt out or rescind an opt out in the manner prescribed by the NC HIE. An individual's decision to opt out or rescind an opt out does not affect any disclosures made by the NC HIE or covered entities through the HIE Network prior to receipt by the NC HIE or its designee of the individual's notice to opt out or rescind an opt out.

(c) A covered entity may not deny treatment or benefits to an individual because of the individual's decision to opt out. However, nothing in this Article is intended to restrict a treating physician from otherwise appropriately terminating a relationship with a patient in accordance with applicable law and professional ethical standards.

(d) Except as otherwise permitted in subsection (e) of this section and G.S. 90-413.7(a)(3), the protected health information of an individual who has exercised the right to opt out may not be disclosed to covered entities through the HIE Network for any purpose.

(e) The protected health information of an individual who has exercised the right to opt out may be disclosed through the HIE Network in order to facilitate the provision of emergency medical treatment to the individual if all of the following criteria are met:

(1) The reasonably apparent circumstances indicate to the treating health care provider that (i) the individual has an emergency medical condition, (ii) a meaningful discussion with the individual about whether to rescind a previous decision to opt out is impractical due to the nature of the individual's emergency medical condition, and (iii) information available through the HIE Network could assist in the diagnosis or treatment of the individual's emergency medical condition.

(2) The disclosure through the HIE Network is limited to the covered entities providing diagnosis and treatment of the individual's emergency medical condition.

(3) The circumstances and extent of the disclosure through the HIE Network is recorded electronically in a manner that permits the NC HIE or its designee to periodically audit compliance with this subsection. (2011-337, s. 1.)

§ 90-413.7. Construction and applicability.

(a) Nothing in this Article shall be construed to do any of the following:

(1) Impair any rights conferred upon an individual under HIPAA, including all of the following rights related to an individual's protected health information:

    a. The right to receive a notice of privacy practices.

    b. The right to request restriction of use and disclosure.

    c. The right of access to inspect and obtain copies.

    d. The right to request amendment.

    e. The right to request confidential forms of communication.

    f. The right to receive an accounting of disclosures.

(2) Authorize the disclosure of protected health information through the HIE Network to the extent that the disclosure is restricted by federal laws or regulations, including the federal drug and alcohol confidentiality regulations set forth in 42 C.F.R. Part 2.

(3) Restrict the disclosure of protected health information through the HIE Network for public health purposes or research purposes, so long as disclosure is permitted by both HIPAA and State law.

(4) Prohibit the NC HIE or any covered entity participating in the HIE Network from maintaining in the NC HIE or qualified organization's computer system a copy of the protected health information of an individual who has exercised the right to opt out, as long as the NC HIE or the qualified organization does not access, use, or disclose the individual's protected health information for any purpose other than for necessary system maintenance or as required by federal or State law.

(b) This Article applies only to disclosures of protected health information made through the HIE Network, including disclosures made within qualified organizations. It does not apply to the use or disclosure of protected health information in any context outside of the HIE Network, including the redisclosure of protected health information obtained through the HIE Network. (2011-337, s. 1.)

§ 90-413.8. Penalties and remedies.

A covered entity that discloses protected health information in violation of this Article is subject to the following:

(1) Any civil penalty or criminal penalty, or both, that may be imposed on the covered entity pursuant to the Health Information Technology for Economic and Clinical Health (HITECH) Act, P.L. 111-5, Div. A, Title XIII, section 13001, as amended, and any regulations adopted under the HITECH Act.

(2) Any civil remedy under the HITECH Act or any regulations adopted under the HITECH Act that is available to the Attorney General or to an individual who has been harmed by a violation of this Article, including damages, penalties, attorneys' fees, and costs.

(3) Disciplinary action by the respective licensing board or regulatory agency with jurisdiction over the covered entity.

(4) Any penalty authorized under Article 2A of Chapter 75 of the General Statutes if the violation of this Article is also a violation of Article 2A of Chapter 75 of the General Statutes.

(5) Any other civil or administrative remedy available to a plaintiff by State or federal law or equity. (2011-337, s. 1.)

§ 90-414: Reserved for future codification purposes.

§ 90-415: Reserved for future codification purposes.

§ 90-416: Reserved for future codification purposes.

§ 90-417: Reserved for future codification purposes.

§ 90-418: Reserved for future codification purposes.

§ 90-419: Reserved for future codification purposes.

§ 90-420: Reserved for future codification purposes.

§ 90-421: Reserved for future codification purposes.

§ 90-422: Reserved for future codification purposes.

§ 90-423: Reserved for future codification purposes.

§ 90-424: Reserved for future codification purposes.

§ 90-425: Reserved for future codification purposes.

§ 90-426: Reserved for future codification purposes.

§ 90-427: Reserved for future codification purposes.

§ 90-428: Reserved for future codification purposes.

§ 90-429: Reserved for future codification purposes.

§ 90-430: Reserved for future codification purposes.

§ 90-431: Reserved for future codification purposes.

§ 90-432: Reserved for future codification purposes.

§ 90-433: Reserved for future codification purposes.

§ 90-434: Reserved for future codification purposes.

§ 90-435: Reserved for future codification purposes.

§ 90-436: Reserved for future codification purposes.

§ 90-437: Reserved for future codification purposes.

§ 90-438: Reserved for future codification purposes.

§ 90-439: Reserved for future codification purposes.

§ 90-440: Reserved for future codification purposes.

§ 90-441: Reserved for future codification purposes.

§ 90-442: Reserved for future codification purposes.

§ 90-443: Reserved for future codification purposes.

§ 90-444: Reserved for future codification purposes.

§ 90-445: Reserved for future codification purposes.

§ 90-446: Reserved for future codification purposes.

§ 90-447: Reserved for future codification purposes.

§ 90-448: Reserved for future codification purposes.

§ 90-449: Reserved for future codification purposes.

Article 30.

Practice of Acupuncture.

§ 90-450. Purpose.

It is the purpose of this Article to promote the health, safety, and welfare of the people of North Carolina by establishing an orderly system of acupuncture licensing and to provide a valid, effective means of establishing licensing requirements. (1993, c. 303, s. 1.)

§ 90-451. Definitions.

The following definitions apply in this Article:

(1)   Acupuncture. - A form of health care developed from traditional and modern Chinese medical concepts that employ acupuncture diagnosis and treatment, and adjunctive therapies and diagnostic techniques, for the promotion, maintenance, and restoration of health and the prevention of disease.

(2)   Board. - The Acupuncture Licensing Board.

(3)   Practice of acupuncture or practice acupuncture. - The insertion of acupuncture needles and the application of moxibustion to specific areas of the human body based upon acupuncture diagnosis as a primary mode of therapy. Adjunctive therapies within the scope of acupuncture may include massage, mechanical, thermal, electrical, and electromagnetic treatment and the recommendation of herbs, dietary guidelines, and therapeutic exercise. (1993, c. 303, s. 1.)

§ 90-452. Practice of acupuncture without license prohibited.

(a)   Unlawful Acts. - It is unlawful to engage in the practice of acupuncture without a license issued pursuant to this Article. It is unlawful to advertise or otherwise represent oneself as qualified or authorized to engage in the practice of acupuncture without having the license required by this Article. A violation of this subsection is a Class 1 misdemeanor.

(b)   Exemptions. - This section shall not apply to any of the following persons:

(1)   A physician licensed under Article 1 of this Chapter.

(2)   A student practicing acupuncture under the direct supervision of a licensed acupuncturist as part of a course of study approved by the Board.

(3)   A chiropractor licensed under Article 8 of this Chapter. (1993, c. 303, s. 1; 1994, Ex. Sess., c. 14, s. 48.)

§ 90-453. Acupuncture Licensing Board.

(a)   Membership. - The Acupuncture Licensing Board shall consist of nine members, three appointed by the Governor and six by the General Assembly. The six members appointed by the General Assembly shall be licensed to practice acupuncture in this State and shall not be licensed physicians under Article 1 of this Chapter. The persons initially appointed to those positions by the General Assembly need not be licensed at the time of selection but shall have met the qualifications under G.S. 90-455(a)(4) and (5). Of the Governor's three appointments, one shall be a layperson who is not employed in a health care profession; one shall be a physician licensed under Article 1 of this Chapter who has successfully completed 200 hours of Category I American Medical Association credit in medical acupuncture training as recommended by the American Academy of Medical Acupuncture; and one shall be licensed to practice acupuncture in this State. Of the members to be appointed by the General Assembly, three shall be appointed upon the recommendation of the Speaker of the House of Representatives, and three shall be appointed upon the recommendation of the President Pro Tempore of the Senate. The members appointed by the General Assembly must be appointed in accordance with G.S. 120-121.

Members serve at the pleasure of the appointing authority. Vacancies shall be filled by the original appointing authority and the term shall be for the balance of the unexpired term. A vacancy by a member appointed by the General Assembly must be filled in accordance with G.S. 120-122.

(b)   Terms. - The members appointed initially by the Governor shall each serve a term ending on June 30, 1994. Of the General Assembly's initial appointments upon the recommendation of the Speaker of the House of Representatives, one shall serve a term ending June 30, 1995, and the other shall serve a term ending June 30, 1996. Of the General Assembly's initial appointments upon the recommendation of the President Pro Tempore of the Senate, one shall serve a term ending June 30, 1995, and the other shall serve a term ending June 30, 1996. After the initial appointments, all members shall be appointed for terms of three years beginning on July 1. No person may serve more than two consecutive full terms as a member of the Board.

(c)   Meetings. - The Board shall meet at least once each year within 45 days after the appointment of the new members. At the Board's first meeting each year after the new members have been appointed, the members shall elect a chair of the Board and a secretary for the year. No person shall chair the Board for more than five consecutive years. The Board shall meet at other times as needed to perform its duties. A majority of the Board shall constitute a quorum for the transaction of business.

(d) Compensation. - Members of the Board are entitled to compensation and to reimbursement for travel and subsistence as provided in G.S. 93B-5. (1993, c. 303, s. 1; 2007-472, s. 1.)

§ 90-454. Powers and duties of Board.

The Board may:

(1) Deny, issue, suspend, and revoke licenses in accordance with rules adopted by the Board, and may collect fees, investigate violations of this Article, and otherwise administer the provisions of this Article.

(2) Sponsor or authorize other entities to offer continuing education programs, and approve continuing education requirements for license renewal.

(3) Establish requirements for, collect fees from, and approve schools of acupuncture in this State. The requirements shall be at least as stringent as the core curricula standards of the Council of Colleges of Acupuncture and Oriental Medicine.

(4) Sue to enjoin violations of G.S. 90-452. The court may issue an injunction even though no person has yet been injured as a result of the unauthorized practice.

(5) Adopt and use a seal to authenticate official documents of the Board.

(6) Employ and fix the compensation of personnel and professional advisors, including legal counsel, as may be needed to carry out its functions, and purchase, lease, rent, sell, or otherwise dispose of personal and real property for the operations of the Board.

(7) Expend funds as necessary to carry out the provisions of this Article from revenues and interest generated by fees collected under this Article.

(8) Adopt rules to implement this Article in accordance with Chapter 150B of the General Statutes.

(9) Establish practice parameters to become effective July 1, 1995. The practice parameters shall be applicable to general and specialty areas of practice. The Board shall review the parameters on a regular basis and shall require licensees to identify parameters being utilized, the plan of care, and treatment modalities utilized in accordance with the plan of care. (1993, c. 303, s. 1; 2005-379, s. 1.)

§ 90-455. Qualifications for license; renewal; inactive, suspended, expired, or lapsed license.

(a) Initial License. - To receive a license to practice acupuncture, a person shall meet all of the following requirements:

(1) Submit a completed application as required by the Board.

(2) Submit any fees required by the Board.

(3) Submit proof of successful completion of a licensing examination administered or approved by the Board.

(4) Provide documentary evidence of having met one of the following standards of education, training, or demonstrated experience:

a. Successful completion of a three-year postgraduate acupuncture college or training program approved by the Board.

b. Continuous licensure to practice acupuncture by an agency of another state or another state whose qualifications for licensure meet or exceed those of this State for at least 10 years before application for licensure in this State during which time no disciplinary actions were taken or are pending against the applicant and submitting proof to the Board that the applicant has fulfilled at least an average of 20 continuing education units in acupuncture or health care-related studies for each of the 10 years preceding application for licensure.

(5) Submit proof of successful completion of the Clean Needle Technique Course offered by the Council of Colleges of Acupuncture and Oriental Medicine.

(6) Be of good moral character.

(7) Is not currently or has not engaged in any practice or conduct that would constitute grounds for disciplinary action pursuant to G.S. 90-456.

(8) Submit a form signed by the applicant attesting to the intention of the applicant to adhere fully to the ethical standards adopted by the Board.

(b) Renewal of License. - The license to practice acupuncture shall be renewed every two years. Upon submitting all required declarations, documents, and fees required by the Board for renewal, the applicant's license shall remain in good standing for a period of up to 120 days during which time the Board shall meet to review and act upon the application for renewal. To renew a license, an applicant shall:

(1) Submit a completed application as required by the Board.

(2) Submit any fees required by the Board.

(3) Upon request by the Board, submit proof of completion of 40 hours of Board-approved continuing education units within each renewal period.

(c) Inactive License. - A licensed acupuncturist who is not actively engaged in the practice of acupuncture in this State and who does not wish to renew the license may direct the Board to place the license on inactive status. A license may remain on inactive status for a period not to exceed eight years from the date the license was placed on inactive status. Upon an applicant's proof of completion of 40 hours of Board-approved continuing education units, payment of all fees, a determination by the Board that the applicant is not engaged in any prohibited activities that would constitute the basis for discipline as set forth in G.S. 90-456, and has not engaged in any of those prohibited activities during the period of time the license has been on inactive status, the Board may activate the license of the applicant.

(d) Suspended License. - A suspended license is subject to the renewal requirements of this section and may be renewed as provided in this section. This renewal does not entitle the licensed person to engage in the licensed activity or in any other conduct or activity in violation of the order or judgment by which the license was suspended, until the license is reinstated. If a license revoked on disciplinary grounds is reinstated and requires renewal, the licensed person shall pay the renewal fee and any applicable late fee.

(e) Expired License. - A license that has expired as a result of failure to renew pursuant to subsection (b) of this section may be renewed no later than two years after its expiration. The date of renewal shall be the date the Board acts to approve the renewal. To apply for renewal of an expired license, the applicant shall:

(1) File an application for renewal on a form provided by the Board.

(2) Submit proof of completion of all continuing education requirements.

(3) Pay all accrued renewal fees, along with an expired license fee.

(f) Lapsed License. - A license that has lapsed as a result of not being renewed within two years after the license expired or not reactivated within eight years after the license lapsed is deemed inactive. A lapsed license may not be renewed, reactivated, or reinstated. A person with a lapsed license may apply to obtain a new license pursuant to subsection (a) of this section. (1993, c. 303, s. 1; 2005-379, s. 2.)

§ 90-456. Prohibited activities.

The Board may deny, suspend, or revoke a license, require remedial education, or issue a letter of reprimand, if a licensed acupuncturist or applicant:

(1) Engages in false or fraudulent conduct which demonstrates an unfitness to practice acupuncture, including any of the following activities:

a. Misrepresentation in connection with an application for a license or an investigation by the Board.

b. Attempting to collect fees for services which were not performed.

c. False advertising, including guaranteeing that a cure will result from an acupuncture treatment.

d. Dividing, or agreeing to divide, a fee for acupuncture services with anyone for referring a patient.

(2) Fails to exercise proper control over one's practice by any of the following activities:

a. Aiding an unlicensed person in practicing acupuncture.

b. Delegating professional responsibilities to a person the acupuncturist knows or should know is not qualified to perform.

c. Failing to exercise proper control over unlicensed personnel working with the acupuncturist in the practice.

(3) Fails to maintain records in a proper manner by any of the following:

a. Failing to keep written records describing the course of treatment for each patient.

b. Refusing to provide to a patient upon request records that have been prepared for or paid for by the patient.

c. Revealing personally identifiable information about a patient, without consent, unless otherwise allowed by law.

(4) Fails to exercise proper care for a patient, including either of the following:

a. Abandoning or neglecting a patient without making reasonable arrangements for the continuation of care.

b. Exercising, or attempting to exercise, undue influence within the acupuncturist/patient relationship by making sexual advances or requests for sexual activity or making submission to such conduct a condition of treatment.

(5) Displays habitual substance abuse or mental impairment so as to interfere with the ability to provide effective treatment.

(6) Is convicted of or pleads guilty or no contest to any crime which demonstrates an unfitness to practice acupuncture.

(7) Negligently fails to practice acupuncture with the level of skill recognized within the profession as acceptable under such circumstances.

(8) Willfully violates any provision of this Article or rule of the Board.

(9) Has had a license denied, suspended, or revoked in another jurisdiction for any reason which would be grounds for this action in this State. (1993, c. 303, s. 1.)

§ 90-457. Fees.

The Board may establish fees, not to exceed the following amounts:

(1) Application and an examination, one hundred dollars ($100.00).

(2) Issuance of a license, five hundred dollars ($500.00).

(3) Renewal of a license, three hundred dollars ($300.00).

(4) Renewal of a license, an additional late fee of two hundred dollars ($200.00).

(5) Duplicate license fee, twenty-five dollars ($25.00).

(6) Duplicate wall certificate fee, fifty dollars ($50.00).

(7) Labels for licensed acupuncturists, one hundred fifty dollars ($150.00).

(8) Returned check fee, forty dollars ($40.00).

(9) Licensure verification, forty dollars ($40.00).

(10) Name change, twenty-five dollars ($25.00).

(11) Continuing education program approval fee, fifty dollars ($50.00).

(12) Continuing education provider approval fee, two hundred dollars ($200.00).

(13) Initial school application fee, one thousand dollars ($1,000).

(14) Renewal school approval fee, seven hundred fifty dollars ($750.00).

(15) Inactive license renewal fee, fifty dollars ($50.00), payment due for each two-year extension. (1993, c. 303, s. 1; 2005-379, s. 3.)

§ 90-457.1. Continuing education.

(a) Applicants for license renewal shall complete all required continuing education units during the two calendar years immediately preceding the license renewal date.

(b) The Board shall set the minimum hours for study of specific subjects within the scope of practice of acupuncture. The Board shall set the maximum hours for subjects that have content relating to any health service and are relevant to the practice of acupuncture. In addition to formally organized courses, the Board may approve courses, such as personal training in nonaccredited programs and teaching diagnosis and treatment, as long as these courses have received prior approval by the Board.

(c) For purposes of this Article, one continuing education unit is defined as one contact hour or 50 minutes.

(d) The Board may choose to audit the records of any licensee who has reported and sworn compliance with the continuing education requirement. The audit of any licensee shall not take place more than every two years.

(e) Failure to comply with the continuing education requirements shall prohibit license renewal and result in the license reverting to expired status at the end of the renewal period.

(f) A licensee may apply to the Board for an extension of time to complete the portion of continuing education requirements that the licensee is unable to meet due to such unforeseeable events as military duty, family emergency, or prolonged illness. The Board may, at its discretion, grant an extension for a maximum of one licensing period. The Board shall receive the request no later than 30 days before the license renewal date. The applicant shall attest that the request is a complete and accurate statement, and the request shall contain the following:

(1) An explanation of the licensee's failure to complete the continuing education requirements.

(2) A list of continuing education courses and hours that the licensee has completed.

(3) The licensee's plan for satisfying the continuing education requirements. (2005-379, s. 4.)

§ 90-458. Use of titles and display of license.

The titles "Licensed Acupuncturist" or "Acupuncturist" shall be used only by persons licensed under this Article. Possession of a license under this Article does not by itself entitle a person to identify oneself as a doctor or physician. Each person licensed to practice acupuncture shall post the license in a conspicuous location at the person's place of practice. (1993, c. 303, s. 1.)

§ 90-459. Third-party reimbursements.

Nothing in this Article shall be construed to require direct third-party reimbursement to persons licensed under this Article. (1993, c. 303, s. 1.)

§ 90-460: Reserved for future codification purposes.

§ 90-461: Reserved for future codification purposes.

§ 90-462: Reserved for future codification purposes.

§ 90-463: Reserved for future codification purposes.

§ 90-464: Reserved for future codification purposes.

§ 90-465: Reserved for future codification purposes.

§ 90-466: Reserved for future codification purposes.

§ 90-467: Reserved for future codification purposes.

§ 90-468: Reserved for future codification purposes.

§ 90-469: Reserved for future codification purposes.

Article 31.

Institute of Medicine.

§ 90-470. Institute of Medicine.

(a) The persons appointed under the provisions of this section are declared to be a body politic and corporate under the name and style of the North Carolina Institute of Medicine, and by that name may sue and be sued, make and use a corporate seal and alter the same at pleasure, contract and be contracted with, and shall have and enjoy all the rights and privileges necessary for the purposes of this section. The corporation shall have perpetual succession.

(b) The purposes for which the corporation is organized are to:

(1) Be concerned with the health of the people of North Carolina;

(2) Monitor and study health matters;

(3) Respond authoritatively when found advisable;

(4) Respond to requests from outside sources for analysis and advice when this will aid in forming a basis for health policy decisions.

(c) The North Carolina Institute of Medicine shall be governed by a Board of Directors. The Board of Directors is authorized to establish and amend bylaws, to procure facilities, employ a director and staff, to solicit, receive and administer funds in the name of the North Carolina Institute of Medicine, and carry out other activities necessary to fulfill the purposes of this section.

(d) The Board of Directors shall select additional members of the North Carolina Institute of Medicine, so that the total membership will not exceed a number determined by the Board of Directors in its bylaws. The membership should be distinguished and influential leaders from the major health professions, the hospital industry, the health insurance industry, State and county government and other political units, education, business and industry, the universities, and the university medical centers.

(e)   The North Carolina Institute of Medicine may receive and administer funds from private sources, foundations, State and county governments, federal agencies, and professional organizations.

(f)   The director and staff of the North Carolina Institute of Medicine should be chosen from those well established in the field of health promotion and medical care.

(g)   The North Carolina Institute of Medicine is declared to be under the patronage and control of the State.

(h)   The General Assembly reserves the right to alter, amend, or repeal this Article. (1983, c. 923, s. 197; 1995, c. 297, s. 1; 2007-25, s. 1; 2013-360, s. 121.1(a); 2013-363, s. 4.1(a).)

§ 90-471. Board of Directors of the Institute of Medicine.

(a)   The Board of Directors of the North Carolina Institute of Medicine shall be appointed as follows:

(1)   Seven individuals appointed by the General Assembly on the recommendation of the Speaker of the House of Representatives.

(2)   Seven individuals appointed by the General Assembly on the recommendation of the President Pro Tempore of the Senate.

(3)   Seven individuals appointed by the Governor.

(b)   The members of the Board of Directors should be distinguished and influential leaders from the major health professions, the hospital industry, the health insurance industry, State and county government and other political units, education, business and industry, the universities, and the university medical centers.

(c) Terms on the Board of Directors shall be for four years, and no individual may serve more than two consecutive terms. (2013-360, s. 12I.1(b); 2013-363, s. 4.1(a).)

§ 90-472: Reserved for future codification purposes.

§ 90-473: Reserved for future codification purposes.

§ 90-474: Reserved for future codification purposes.

§ 90-475: Reserved for future codification purposes.

§ 90-476: Reserved for future codification purposes.

§ 90-477: Reserved for future codification purposes.

§ 90-478: Reserved for future codification purposes.

§ 90-479: Reserved for future codification purposes.

§ 90-480: Reserved for future codification purposes.

§ 90-481: Reserved for future codification purposes.

§ 90-482: Reserved for future codification purposes.

§ 90-483: Reserved for future codification purposes.

§ 90-484: Reserved for future codification purposes.

§ 90-485: Reserved for future codification purposes.

§ 90-486: Reserved for future codification purposes.

§ 90-487: Reserved for future codification purposes.

§ 90-488: Reserved for future codification purposes.

§ 90-489: Reserved for future codification purposes.

§ 90-490: Reserved for future codification purposes.

§ 90-491: Reserved for future codification purposes.

§ 90-492: Reserved for future codification purposes.

§ 90-493: Reserved for future codification purposes.

§ 90-494: Reserved for future codification purposes.

§ 90-495: Reserved for future codification purposes.

§ 90-496: Reserved for future codification purposes.

§ 90-497: Reserved for future codification purposes.

§ 90-498: Reserved for future codification purposes.

§ 90-499: Reserved for future codification purposes.

Article 32.

Employee Assistance Professionals.

§ 90-500. Definitions.

As used in this Article, unless the context requires otherwise:

(1)   "Board" means the Board of Employee Assistance Professionals.

(2)   "Certified employee assistance professional" means an employee assistance professional who is certified by the Employee Assistance Certification Commission and who has the necessary professional qualifications to provide the employee assistance program services listed in subdivision (2) of this section, which services can be worksite based and are designed to assist in the identification and resolution of productivity problems associated with employees impaired by personal concerns.

(3) "Consultation" means the act of giving expert advice on the role of an employee assistance professional in assisting troubled employees.

(4) "Employee Assistance Certification Commission" means the national body with the authority to certify employee assistance professionals based on experience and the passing of a national examination.

(5) "Employee assistance professional" means a person who provides the following services to the public in a program designed to assist in the identification and resolution of job performance problems in the workplace:

a. Expert consultation and training of appropriate persons in the identification and resolution of job performance issues related to the employees' personal concerns.

b. The confidential, appropriate, and timely assessment of problems.

c. Short-term problem resolution for issues that do not require clinical counseling or treatment.

d. Referrals for appropriate diagnosis, treatment, and assistance to certified or licensed professionals when clinical counseling or treatment is required.

e. Establishment of linkages between workplace and community resources that provide such services.

f. Follow-up services for employees and dependents who use such services. (1995 (Reg. Sess., 1996), c. 720, s. 1.)

§ 90-501. Board of Employee Assistance Professionals; members.

(a) The Board of Employee Assistance Professionals is created.

(b) The Board consists of five members to be appointed by the Governor. Members shall serve for terms of five years. All members must be residents of North Carolina.

(c) The following requirements shall apply to appointments to the Board:

(1) Two members shall be licensed employee assistance professionals who are privately employed.

(2) One member shall not be directly or indirectly engaged in the employee assistance profession.

(3) Two members shall be licensed employee assistance professionals.

(d) The licensed employee assistance professionals appointed pursuant to subdivision (1) or (3) of subsection (c) of this section must have been engaged in the active practice of being an employee assistance professional for no less than five years.

(e) The North Carolina Chapter of the Employee Assistance Professionals Association shall submit a list of at least three nominees for each appointment. The Governor may make appointments from this list.

(f) Any member of the Board shall be removed from the Board upon certification by the Board to the Governor that the member no longer satisfies the employment requirements set forth in subsection (c) of this section for appointment to the Board. The Governor shall appoint a replacement from a list of nominees submitted by the North Carolina Chapter of the Employee Assistance Professionals Association within 60 days of the Governor's receiving the list of nominees.

(g) Members shall serve until their successors are appointed and duly qualified. Any vacancy occurring on the Board shall be filled by the Governor appointing a member for the balance of the unexpired term. A Board member who has served a five-year term shall not be eligible for reappointment during the one-year period following the appointment of that member's successor.

(h) In making appointments to the Board, the Governor shall strive to ensure that at least one member serving on the Board is 60 years of age or older and that at least one member serving on the Board is a member of a racial minority.

(i) For each day engaged in the business of the Board, members shall receive compensation of fifty dollars ($50.00) and shall receive reimbursement for actual expenses.

(j) Annually, the members of the Board shall elect a chair and a secretary.

(k) The Board shall meet as frequently as is reasonably necessary to implement the provisions of this Article. Three or more members of the Board shall constitute a quorum for the purpose of transacting business.

(l) For administrative purposes, the Board shall be an independent entity. The Department of Health and Human Services shall provide staff to the Board to assist the Board in transacting its business. (1995 (Reg. Sess., 1996), c. 720, s. 1; 1997-443, s. 11A.118(a).)

§ 90-502. Powers and duties of the Board.

The Board shall:

(1) Approve educational programs and establish and prescribe the curricula and minimum standards for training required to prepare persons for licensure and licensure renewal under this Article.

(2) Adopt rules governing the issuance, renewal, suspension, and revocation of licenses.

(3) Establish minimum standards governing the activities and operations of licensed employee assistance professionals.

(4) Issue licenses.

(5) Establish and collect fees.

(6) Assess civil penalties as provided in this Article. (1995 (Reg. Sess., 1996), c. 720, s. 1.)

§ 90-503. License requirements.

(a) An applicant must satisfy all of the following requirements to be eligible to be licensed under this Article:

(1) Have obtained a masters degree.

(2) Have obtained a degree in any field of human services at either the undergraduate degree level or the masters degree level.

(3) Be certified by the Employee Assistance Certification Commission.

(4) Maintain certification by being recertified by the Employee Assistance Certification Commission every three years by either passing an examination or by completing continuing education in accordance with rules adopted by the Board.

(b) Notwithstanding the requirements of subsection (a) of this section, a person who has received a certification as an employee assistance professional from the Employee Assistance Certification Commission may apply until January 1, 2000, to the Board for licensure and shall receive a license as an employee assistance professional upon proof of such certification and upon payment of a fee in an amount established by the Board.

(c) Licenses must be obtained by each individual employee assistance professional. A company or organization shall not be issued a license.

(d) Any person desiring to be licensed under this Article as an employee assistance professional shall apply to the Board on a form approved by the Board. The applicant shall submit with the application form a fee in an amount established by the Board. The applicant shall complete the application, submitting all information the Board deems necessary to evaluate the applicant.

(e) Each license shall be valid for a period of up to three years. (1995 (Reg. Sess., 1996), c. 720, s. 1.)

§ 90-504. License renewals.

(a) Renewal of any license issued under the provisions of this Article may be accomplished by paying a fee in an amount established by the Board, submitting a renewal application, and otherwise complying with rules adopted by the Board.

(b) Any person licensed as an employee assistance professional shall renew his or her license according to rules adopted by the Board.

(c) If any licensee fails to renew his or her license within 60 days after the date the application becomes due, the license of that person shall be revoked automatically without further notice or hearing, unless the licensee specifically requests an extension. (1995 (Reg. Sess., 1996), c. 720, s. 1.)

§ 90-505. Requirements for persons licensed out-of-state.

An applicant who is currently certified by the Employee Assistance Certification Commission or licensed in another state and who:

(1) Is in good standing in another state;

(2) Meets the licensure requirements approved by the Board;

(3) Resides in this State, or resides outside the State and is employed by a service operating in this State; and

(4) Submits an application with a fee in an amount established by the Board

is eligible to apply for a license under this Article. (1995 (Reg. Sess., 1996), c. 720, s. 1.)

§ 90-506. Violations; enforcement; penalties.

(a) Whenever the Board has reason to believe that a violation of this Article, any rule adopted by the Board, or any order of the Board is occurring or about to occur, the Board may initiate any of the following enforcement measures:

(1) Commence a civil action in any court of the county in which the alleged offender resides or does business. The Board may seek and the court may grant any form of relief, including injunctive relief.

(2) If the activity involved appears to be a criminal offense, refer the matter to the appropriate district attorney for prosecution.

(3) For any person who fails to be licensed as required by this Article, the Board may assess a civil penalty against that person in an amount not to exceed fifty dollars ($50.00) per day for each violation.

(b) In assessing a penalty under subdivision (3) of subsection (a) of this section, the Board shall consider all of the following:

(1) Whether the amount of the penalty imposed will be a substantial economic deterrent to the violator.

(2) The circumstances leading to the violation.

(3) The severity of the violation and the risk of harm to the employee.

(4) Any economic benefits gained by the violator as a result of the violation.

(c) Civil penalties assessed by the Board pursuant to subdivision (3) of subsection (a) of this section are final 30 days after the date the assessment is served upon the alleged violation, unless the alleged violator seeks review by the Board within that time.

The clear proceeds of these civil penalties shall be remitted to the Civil Penalty and Forfeiture Fund in accordance with G.S. 115C-457.2. (1995 (Reg. Sess., 1996), c. 720, s. 1; 1998-215, s. 133.)

§ 90-507. Hearings.

Hearings before the Board on enforcement or disciplinary actions shall be conducted in accordance with Article 3A of Chapter 150B of the General Statutes. (1995 (Reg. Sess., 1996), c. 720, s. 1.)

§ 90-508. Representation as licensed professional.

No person shall, by verbal claim, advertisement, letterhead, card, or in any other way, represent that he or she is a licensed employee assistance professional unless that person possesses a valid license pursuant to this Article. Nothing in this Article shall prohibit an unlicensed person from providing the services described in G.S. 90-500(3) if that person refrains from representing that he or she is a licensed employee assistance professional. (1995 (Reg. Sess., 1996), c. 720, s. 1.)

§ 90-509. Other prohibited activities.

The Board may deny, suspend, or revoke any license, or otherwise discipline an applicant or holder of a license who the Board finds engaged in one or more of the following activities:

(1) Willfully or repeatedly violating any provision of this Article or any rule of the Board adopted pursuant to this Article.

(2) Fraudulently or deceptively procuring or attempting to procure a license, presenting evidence of qualification to the Board, or processing the examination to secure a license.

(3) Willfully failing to display a license.

(4) Fraudulently or deceptively misrepresenting or engaging in dishonest or illegal practices in or connected with the practice of employee assistance.

(5) Circulating knowingly untrue, fraudulent, misleading, or deceptive advertising.

(6) Engaging in gross malpractice, or a pattern of continued or repeated malpractice, ignorance, negligence, or incompetence in the course of the practice of employee assistance.

(7) Unprofessionally or unethically engaging in practices in connection with the practice of employee assistance, which activities are in violation of the standards of professional conduct prescribed by the Board.

(8) Engaging in conduct reflecting unfavorably upon the profession of employee assistance professionals.

(9) Willfully making any false statement as to material in any oath or affidavit when such statement is required by this Article.

(10) Being convicted of a felony five years prior to applying for a license or while licensed.

(11) Permitting or allowing another to use another person's license for the purpose of providing or offering employee assistance services.

(12) Engaging in practice under a false or assumed name, or impersonating another practitioner of a like, similar, or different name.

(13) Failing to inform clients fully about the limits of confidentiality in a given situation, the purposes for which information is obtained, and how it may be used.

(14) Referring a client to further obtain services from a source that would directly or indirectly financially profit the referring licensed employee assistance professional when these services are not in the best interest of the client.

(15) Denying a client's reasonable requests for access to any records concerning the client, or, when providing clients with access to records, failing to take due care to protect the confidences of other information contained in those records.

(16) Failing to obtain the informed consent of a client before taping, recording, or permitting third-party observation of the client's activities.

(17) Failing to clarify the nature and directions of an employee assistance professional's loyalties and responsibilities as mandated by law and as mandated by their contractual agreement with a company.

(18) Failing to fully inform consumers as to the purpose and nature of evaluative research, treatment, or educational training or failing to freely acknowledge that a client, student, or participant in research has freedom of choice with regard to his or her participation.

(19) Failing to attempt to terminate a consulting relationship when it is reasonably clear that the relationship is not benefiting the consumer. An employee assistance professional who finds that his or her services are being used by employers beyond their contractual agreement, or beyond their licensed qualification, in a way that is not beneficial to the participants, shall make his or her observations known to the responsible persons and propose modification or termination of the engagement. Upon request, the Board shall

advise and clarify in regard to such matters within a reasonable amount of time, and shall not revoke the employee assistance professional's license.

(20) Consenting through a contractual agreement to provide services such as prolonged therapy, that the employee assistance professional is not licensed to provide. (1995 (Reg. Sess., 1996), c. 720, s. 1.)

§ 90-510. Investigations; good faith reports of violations.

The Board may, on its own motion, investigate any report indicating that a licensee is or may be in violation of the provisions of this Article. Any person who in good faith reports to the Board any such information shall not be subject to suit for civil damages as a result of reporting this information. (1995 (Reg. Sess., 1996), c. 720, s. 1.)

§ 90-511. Employee assistance professional practice by members of other professional groups.

(a) Nothing in this Article shall be construed to prevent qualified members of other professional groups, as determined by the Board, including, but not limited to, licensed psychologists, licensed psychological associates, licensed clinical social workers, nurses, physicians, or members of the clergy, from doing or advertising that they perform the work of an employee assistance professional consistent with the accepted standards of their respective professions.

(b) Nothing in this Article shall be construed to prevent a staff member of a community mental health center from advertising, claiming, working, or in any other way representing that the member is an employee assistance professional consistent with the standards of a mental health center. (1995 (Reg. Sess., 1996), c. 720, s. 1.)

§ 90-512: Reserved for future codification purposes.

§ 90-513: Reserved for future codification purposes.

§ 90-514: Reserved for future codification purposes.

Article 33.

Industrial Hygiene.

§ 90-515. Definitions.

The following definitions apply in this Article:

(1) "American Board of Industrial Hygiene". - A nonprofit corporation incorporated in 1960 in Pennsylvania to improve the practice of the profession of Industrial Hygiene by certifying individuals who meet its education and experience standards and who pass its examination.

(2) "Certified Industrial Hygienist (CIH)". - A person who has met the education, experience, and examination requirements established by the American Board of Industrial Hygiene for a Certified Industrial Hygienist (CIH).

(3) "Industrial Hygiene". - The applied science devoted to the anticipation, evaluation, and control of contaminants and stressors that may cause sickness, impaired health and well-being, or significant discomfort and inefficiency among workers and the general public.

(4) "Industrial Hygienist". - A person who, through special studies and training in chemistry, physics, biology, and related sciences, has acquired competence in industrial hygiene. The special studies and training must have been sufficient to confer competence in the: (i) anticipation and recognition of environmental contaminants and stressors to which workers and other members of the public could be exposed in industrial operations, office buildings, homes, and the general community; (ii) assessment of the likely effects on the health and well-being of individuals exposed to these contaminants and stressors; (iii) quantification of levels of human exposure to these contaminants and stressors through scientific measurement techniques; and (iv) designation of methods to eliminate or to control these contaminants and stressors, or to reduce the level of human exposure to them.

(5) "Industrial Hygienist in Training (IHIT)". - A person who has met the education, experience, and examination requirements established by the American Board of Industrial Hygiene for an Industrial Hygienist in Training (IHIT). (1997-195, s. 1.)

§ 90-516. Unlawful acts.

(a) No person shall practice or offer to practice as a Certified Industrial Hygienist, use any advertisement, business card, or letterhead or make any other verbal or written communication that the person is a Certified Industrial Hygienist or acquiesce in such a representation unless that person is certified by the American Board of Industrial Hygiene.

(b) No person shall practice or offer to practice as an Industrial Hygienist in Training, use any advertisement, business card, or letterhead or make any other verbal or written communication that the person is an Industrial Hygienist in Training or acquiesce in such a representation unless that person is certified by the American Board of Industrial Hygiene.

(c) A violation of this Article shall be punished as a Class 2 misdemeanor.

(d) Any person, including the Attorney General, may apply to the superior court for injunctive relief to restrain a person who has violated this Article from continuing these illegal practices. The court may grant injunctive relief regardless of whether criminal prosecution or other action has been or may be instituted as a result of the violation. In the court's consideration of the issue of whether to grant or continue an injunction sought under this subsection, a showing of conduct in violation of the terms of this Article shall be sufficient to meet any requirement of general North Carolina injunction law for irreparable harm.

(e) The venue for actions brought under this Article is the superior court of any county in which the illegal or unlawful acts are alleged to have been committed or in the county where the defendant resides.

(f) Nothing in this Article shall be construed as authorizing a person certified in accordance with this Article to engage in the practice of engineering, nor to restrict or otherwise affect the rights of any person licensed to practice engineering under Chapter 89C of the General Statutes; provided, however, that no person shall use the title "Certified Industrial Hygienist" unless the person has complied with the provisions of this Article. (1997-195, s. 1.)

§ 90-517: Reserved for future codification purposes.

§ 90-518: Reserved for future codification purposes.

§ 90-519: Reserved for future codification purposes.

§ 90-520: Reserved for future codification purposes.

§ 90-521: Reserved for future codification purposes.

Article 34.

Athletic Trainers.

§ 90-522. Title; purpose.

(a)	This Article may be cited as the "Athletic Trainers Licensing Act".

(b)	The practice of athletic trainer services affects the public health, safety, and welfare. Licensure of the practice of athletic trainer services is necessary to ensure minimum standards of competency and to provide the public with safe athletic trainer services. It is the purpose of this Article to provide for the regulation of persons offering athletic trainer services. (1997-387, s. 1.)

§ 90-523. Definitions.

The following definitions apply in this Article:

(1)	Athletes.- Members of sports teams, including professional, amateur, and school teams; or participants in sports or recreational activities, including training and practice activities, that require strength, agility, flexibility, range of motion, speed, or stamina.

(2)	Athletic trainer. - A person who, under a written protocol with a physician licensed under Article 1 of Chapter 90 of the General Statutes and filed with the North Carolina Medical Board, carries out the practice of care, prevention, and rehabilitation of injuries incurred by athletes, and who, in carrying out these functions, may use physical modalities, including heat, light, sound, cold, electricity, or mechanical devices related to rehabilitation and treatment. A committee composed of two members of the North Carolina Medical Board and two members of the North Carolina Board of Athletic Trainer Examiners shall jointly define by rule the content, format, and minimum requirements for the written protocol required by this subdivision. The members shall be selected by their respective boards. The decision of this committee shall be binding on both Boards unless changed by mutual agreement of both Boards.

(3) Board. - The North Carolina Board of Athletic Trainer Examiners as created by G.S. 90-524.

(4) License. - A certificate that evidences approval by the Board that a person has successfully completed the requirements set forth in G.S. 90-528 entitling the person to perform the functions and duties of an athletic trainer. (1997-387, s. 1.)

§ 90-524. Board of Examiners created.

(a) The North Carolina Board of Athletic Trainer Examiners is created.

(b) Composition and Terms. - The Board shall consist of seven members who shall serve staggered terms. Four members shall be athletic trainers certified by the National Athletic Trainers' Association Board of Certification, Inc. One member shall be a licensed orthopedic surgeon, one member shall be a licensed family practice physician or pediatrician, and one member shall represent the public at large.

The initial Board members shall be selected on or before August 1, 1997, as follows:

(1) The General Assembly, upon the recommendation of the President Pro Tempore of the Senate, shall appoint two certified athletic trainers and an orthopedic surgeon. The certified athletic trainers shall serve for terms of three years, and the orthopedic surgeon shall serve for a term of one year.

(2) The General Assembly, upon the recommendation of the Speaker of the House of Representatives, shall appoint two certified athletic trainers and a family practice physician or pediatrician. The certified athletic trainers and the family practice physician or pediatrician shall serve for terms of two years.

(3) The Governor shall appoint for a three-year term a public member to the Board.

Upon the expiration of the terms of the initial Board members, each member shall be appointed for a term of three years and shall serve until a successor is appointed. No member may serve more than two consecutive full terms.

(c) Qualifications. - The athletic trainer members shall hold current licenses and shall reside or be employed in North Carolina. They shall have at least five years' experience as athletic trainers, including the three years immediately preceding appointment to the Board, and shall remain in active practice and in good standing with the Board as a licensee during their terms. The first athletic trainers appointed to the Board pursuant to this section shall be eligible for licensure under G.S. 90-529 and, upon appointment, shall immediately apply for a license.

(d) Vacancies. - A vacancy shall be filled in the same manner as the original appointment, except that all unexpired terms of Board members appointed by the General Assembly shall be filled in accordance with G.S. 120-122 and shall be filled within 45 days after the vacancy occurs. Appointees to fill vacancies shall serve the remainder of the unexpired term and until their successors have been duly appointed and qualified.

(e) Removal. - The Board may remove any of its members for neglect of duty, incompetence, or unprofessional conduct. A member subject to disciplinary proceedings as a licensee shall be disqualified from participating in the official business of the Board until the charges have been resolved.

(f) Compensation. - Each member of the Board shall receive per diem and reimbursement for travel and subsistence as provided in G.S. 93B-5.

(g) Officers. - The officers of the Board shall be a chair, who shall be a licensed athletic trainer, a vice-chair, and other officers deemed necessary by the Board to carry out the purposes of this Article. All officers shall be elected annually by the Board for one-year terms and shall serve until their successors are elected and qualified.

(h) Meetings. - The Board shall hold at least two meetings each year to conduct business and to review the standards and rules for improving athletic training services. The Board shall establish the procedures for calling, holding, and conducting regular and special meetings. A majority of Board members constitutes a quorum. (1997-387, s. 1.)

§ 90-525. Powers of the Board.

The Board shall have the power and duty to:

(1)   Administer this Article.

(2)   Issue interpretations of this Article.

(3)   Adopt, amend, or repeal rules as may be necessary to carry out the provisions of this Article.

(4)   Employ and fix the compensation of personnel that the Board determines is necessary to carry into effect the provisions of this Article and incur other expenses necessary to effectuate this Article.

(5)   Examine and determine the qualifications and fitness of applicants for licensure, renewal of licensure, and reciprocal licensure.

(6)   Issue, renew, deny, suspend, or revoke licenses and carry out any disciplinary actions authorized by this Article.

(7)   In accordance with G.S. 90-534, set fees for licensure, license renewal, and other services deemed necessary to carry out the purposes of this Article.

(8)   Conduct investigations for the purpose of determining whether violations of this Article or grounds for disciplining licensees exist.

(9)   Maintain a record of all proceedings and make available to licensees and other concerned parties an annual report of all Board action.

(10)   Develop standards and adopt rules for the improvement of athletic training services in the State.

(11)   Adopt a seal containing the name of the Board for use on all licenses and official reports issued by it. (1997-387, s. 1.)

§ 90-526. Custody and use of funds; contributions.

(a) All fees payable to the Board shall be deposited in the name of the Board in financial institutions designated by the Board as official depositories and shall be used to pay all expenses incurred in carrying out the purposes of this Article.

(b) The Board may accept grants, contributions, devises, and gifts that shall be kept in a separate fund and shall be used by it to enhance the practice of athletic trainers. (1997-387, s. 1; 2011-284, s. 65.)

§ 90-527. License required; exemptions from license requirement.

(a) On or after January 1, 1998, no person shall practice or offer to practice as an athletic trainer, perform activities of an athletic trainer, or use any card, title, or abbreviation to indicate that the person is an athletic trainer unless that person is currently licensed as provided by this Article.

(b) The provisions of this Article do not apply to:

(1) Licensed, registered, or certified professionals, such as nurses, physical therapists, and chiropractors if they do not hold themselves out to the public as athletic trainers.

(2) A physician licensed under Article 1 of Chapter 90 of the General Statutes.

(3) A person serving as a student-trainer or in a similar position under the supervision of a physician or licensed athletic trainer.

(4) An athletic trainer who is employed by, or under contract with, an organization, corporation, or educational institution located in another state and who is representing that organization, corporation, or educational institution at an event held in this State.

(5) Boxing trainers, if they do not hold themselves out to the public as athletic trainers. (1997-387, s. 1.)

§ 90-528. Application for license; qualifications; issuance.

(a) An applicant for a license under this Article shall make a written application to the Board on a form approved by the Board and shall submit to the Board an application fee along with evidence that demonstrates good moral character and graduation from an accredited four-year college or university in a course of study approved by the Board.

(b) The applicant shall also pass the examination administered by the National Athletic Trainers' Association Board of Certification, Inc.

(c) When the Board determines that an applicant has met all the qualifications for licensure and has submitted the required fee, the Board shall issue a license to the applicant. A license is valid for a period of one year from the date of issuance and may be renewed subject to the requirements of this Article. (1997-387, s. 1.)

§ 90-529. Athletic trainers previously certified.

The Board shall issue a license to practice as an athletic trainer to a person who applies to the Board on or before August 1, 1998, and furnishes to the Board on a form approved by the Board proof of good moral character, graduation from an accredited four-year college or university in a course of study approved by the Board, and a current certificate from the National Athletic Trainers' Association Board of Certification, Inc. (1997-387, s. 1.)

§ 90-530. Athletic trainers not certified.

(a) A person who has been actively engaged as an athletic trainer since August 1, 1994, and who continues to practice up to the time of application, shall be eligible for licensure without examination by paying the required fee and by demonstrating the following:

(1) Proof of good moral character.

(2) Proof of practice in this State since August 1, 1994.

(3) Proof of graduation from an accredited four-year college or university in a course of study approved by the Board.

(4) Fulfillment of any other requirements set by the Board.

An application made pursuant to this section shall be filed with the Board on or before August 1, 1998.

(b) A person is "actively engaged" as an athletic trainer if the person is a salaried employee of, or has contracted with, an educational institution, an industry, a hospital, a rehabilitation clinic, or a professional athletic organization or another bona fide athletic organization and the person performs the duties of an athletic trainer. (1997-387, s. 1.)

§ 90-531. Reciprocity with other states.

A license may be issued to a qualified applicant holding an athletic trainer license in another state if that state recognizes the license of this State in the same manner. (1997-387, s. 1.)

§ 90-532. License renewal.

Every license issued under this Article shall be renewed during the month of January. On or before the date the current license expires, any person who desires to continue practice shall apply for a license renewal and shall submit the required fee. Licenses that are not renewed shall automatically lapse. In accordance with rules adopted by the Board, a license that has lapsed may be reissued within five years from the date it lapsed. A license that has been expired for more than five years may be reissued only in a manner prescribed by the Board. (1997-387, s. 1.)

§ 90-533. Continuing education.

(a) As a condition of license renewal, a licensee must meet the continuing education requirements set by the Board. The Board shall determine the number of hours and subject matter of continuing education required as a condition of license renewal. The Board shall determine the qualifications of a provider of an educational program that satisfies the continuing education requirement.

(b)   The Board shall grant approval to a continuing education program or course upon finding that the program or course offers an educational experience designed to enhance the practice of athletic trainer, including the continuing education program of the National Athletic Trainers' Association.

(c)   If a continuing education program offers to teach licensees to perform advanced skills, the Board may grant approval for the program when it finds that the nature of the procedure taught in the program and the program facilities and faculty are such that a licensee fully completing the program can reasonably be expected to carry out those procedures safely and properly. (1997-387, s. 1.)

§ 90-534. Expenses and fees.

(a)   All salaries, compensation, and expenses incurred or allowed to carry out the purposes of this Article shall be paid by the Board exclusively out of the fees received by the Board as authorized by this Article or funds received from other sources. In no case shall any salary, expense, or other obligation of the Board be charged against the State treasury.

(b)   The schedule of fees shall not exceed the following:

(1)....... Issuance of a license.. $ 200.00

(2)....... License renewal... 75.00

(3)....... Reinstatement of lapsed license................................ 100.00

(4)   Reasonable charges for duplication services and material. (1997-387, s. 1; 2010-98, s. 1.)

§ 90-535. Hiring of athletic trainers by school units.

Local school administrative units may hire persons who are not licensed under this Article. The persons hired may perform the activities of athletic trainers in the scope of their employment but may not claim to be licensed under this Article. The persons hired may not perform the activities of athletic trainers outside the scope of this employment unless they are authorized to do so under G.S. 90-527(b). (1997-387, s. 1.)

§ 90-536. Disciplinary authority of the Board; administrative proceedings.

(a)　Grounds for disciplinary action against a licensee shall include the following:

(1)　Giving false information or withholding material information from the Board in procuring a license to practice as an athletic trainer.

(2)　Having been convicted of or pled guilty or no contest to a crime that indicates that the person is unfit or incompetent to practice as an athletic trainer or that indicates that the person has deceived or defrauded the public.

(3)　Having a mental or physical disability or using a drug to a degree that interferes with the person's fitness to practice as an athletic trainer.

(4)　Engaging in conduct that endangers the public health.

(5)　Being unfit or incompetent to practice as an athletic trainer by reason of deliberate or negligent acts or omissions regardless of whether actual injury to a patient is established.

(6)　Willfully violating any provision of this Article or rules adopted by the Board.

(7)　Having been convicted of or pled guilty or no contest to an offense under State or federal narcotic or controlled substance laws.

(b)　In accordance with Article 3A of Chapter 150B of the General Statutes, the Board may require remedial education, issue a letter of reprimand, restrict, revoke, or suspend any license to practice as an athletic trainer in North Carolina or deny any application for licensure if the Board determines that the applicant or licensee has committed any of the above acts or is no longer qualified to practice as an athletic trainer. The Board may reinstate a revoked license or remove licensure restrictions when it finds that the reasons for revocation or restriction no longer exist and that the person can reasonably be expected to practice as an athletic trainer safely and properly. (1997-387, s. 1.)

§ 90-537. Enjoining illegal practices.

If the Board finds that a person who does not have a license issued under this Article claims to be an athletic trainer or is engaging in practice as an athletic trainer in violation of this Article, the Board may apply in its own name to the Superior Court of Wake County for a temporary restraining order or other injunctive relief to prevent the person from continuing illegal practices. The court may grant injunctions regardless of whether criminal prosecution or other action has been or may be instituted as a result of a violation. (1997-387, s. 1.)

§ 90-538. Penalties.

A person who does not have a license issued under this Article who either claims to be an athletic trainer or engages in practice as an athletic trainer in violation of this Article is guilty of a Class 1 misdemeanor. Each act of unlawful practice constitutes a distinct and separate offense. (1997-387, s. 1.)

§ 90-539. Reports; immunity from suit.

A person who has reasonable cause to suspect misconduct or incapacity of a licensee, or who has reasonable cause to suspect that a person is in violation of this Article, shall report the relevant facts to the Board. Upon receipt of a charge, or upon its own initiative, the Board may give notice of an administrative hearing or may, after diligent investigation, dismiss unfounded charges. A person who, in good faith, makes a report pursuant to this section shall be immune from any criminal prosecution or civil liability resulting therefrom. (1997-387, s. 1.)

§ 90-540. No third-party reimbursement required.

Nothing in this Article shall be construed to require direct third-party reimbursement to persons licensed under this Article. (1997-387, s. 1.)

§§ 90-541 through 90-599. Reserved for future codification purposes.

Article 35.

Accident-Trauma Victim Identification.

§ 90-600. Short title.

This Article shall be known and may be cited as the Carolyn Sonzogni Act. (1997-443, s. 20.12(b).)

§ 90-601. Purpose.

The identification of accident-trauma victims is crucial to the timely notification of the next of kin of accident-trauma victims and to the recovery of organs and tissues for organ transplants. In recognition of these facts, it is the policy of this State and the purpose of this act to provide for the timely identification of accident-trauma victims by law enforcement, fire, emergency, rescue, and hospital personnel. (1997-443, s. 20.12(b).)

§ 90-602. Routine search for donor information; notification of hospital; definitions as provided in the Revised Uniform Anatomical Gift Act.

(a) For the purposes of this section, the terms "anatomical gift," "document of gift," "donor," and "refusal" have the same meaning as in G.S. 130A-412.4.

(a1) The following persons may make a reasonable search of an individual who the person reasonably believes is dead or near death for a document of gift or other information identifying the individual as a donor or as an individual who made a refusal:

(1) A law enforcement officer,

(2) A firefighter,

(3) A paramedic, or

(4) Another official emergency rescuer finding the individual.

If a document of gift or a refusal is located by a search under this subsection and the individual or deceased individual to whom it relates is taken to a hospital, the person conducting the search shall send the document of gift or refusal to the hospital or cause it to be sent.

(a2) If no other source of information is immediately available, a hospital shall make a reasonable search of an individual who the hospital reasonably believes is dead or near death, as soon as practical after the individual arrives at the hospital, for a document of gift or other information identifying the individual as a donor or as an individual who made a refusal.

(b) Any law enforcement officer or other person listed in subsection (a1) or (a2) of this section may conduct an administrative search of the accident-trauma victim's Division of Motor Vehicles driver record to ascertain whether the individual is a donor. If a document of gift or a refusal is located by a search under this subsection and the individual or deceased individual to whom it relates is taken to a hospital, the person conducting the search shall notify the hospital of the results or cause the hospital to be notified.

(c) A physical search pursuant to subsection (a1) or (a2) of this section shall be limited to those personal effects of the individual where a drivers license reasonably may be stored. Any information, document, tangible objects, or other items discovered during the search shall be used solely for the purpose of ascertaining the individual's identity, notifying the individual's next of kin, and determining whether the individual intends to make an anatomical gift, and in no event shall any such discovered material be admissible in any subsequent criminal or civil proceeding, unless obtained pursuant to a lawful search on other grounds.

(d) A hospital or other person with duties under this section is not subject to criminal or civil liability for failing to discharge those duties but may be subject to administrative sanctions.

(e) A person that acts under this section with due care, or attempts in good faith to do so, is not liable for the act in a civil action, criminal prosecution, or administrative proceeding. (1997-443, s. 20.12(b); 2008-153, s. 1.)

§ 90-603. Timely notification of next of kin.

A State or local law enforcement officer shall make a reasonable effort to notify the next of kin of an accident-trauma victim if the individual is hospitalized or dead. Whenever possible, the notification should be delivered in person and without delay after ensuring positive identification. If appropriate under the circumstances, the notification may be given by telephone in accordance with State and local law enforcement departmental policies. In addition to the notification of next of kin made by law enforcement personnel, other emergency rescue or hospital personnel may contact the next of kin, or the nearest organ procurement organization, in order to expedite decision making with regard to potential organ and tissue recovery. (1997-443, s. 20.12(b).)

§ 90-604. Use of body information tags.

(a) In order to provide the identifying information necessary to facilitate organ and tissue transplants, a body information tag shall be attached to or transmitted with the body of an accident-trauma victim by the following persons:

(1) A law enforcement officer, firefighter, paramedic, or other official emergency rescuer who believes the seriously injured individual to be near death; and

(2) Hospital personnel, after the individual has been pronounced dead.

(b) The body information tag shall include information identifying the accident-trauma victim, identifying whether the individual is an organ donor, and providing any information on the next of kin. The Division of Motor Vehicles shall be responsible for producing and distributing body information tags to all State and local law enforcement departments. In addition, the tags shall be distributed by the Division of Motor Vehicles to all State and local agencies employing firefighters, paramedics, and other emergency and rescue personnel. (1997-443, s. 20.12(b).)

§§ 90-605 through 90-619. Reserved for future codification purposes.

Article 36.

Massage and Bodywork Therapy Practice.

§ 90-620. Short title.

This Article shall be known as the North Carolina Massage and Bodywork Therapy Practice Act. (1998-230, s. 10.)

§ 90-621. Declaration of purpose.

The purpose of this Article is to ensure the protection of the health, safety, and welfare of the citizens of this State receiving massage and bodywork therapy services. This purpose is achieved by establishing education and testing standards that ensure competency in the practice of massage and bodywork therapy. Mandatory licensure of those engaged in the practice of massage and bodywork therapy assures the public that each individual has satisfactorily met the standards of the profession and continues to meet both the ethical and competency goals of the profession. (1998-230, s. 10; 2008-224, s. 1.)

§ 90-622. Definitions.

The following definitions apply in this Article:

(1) Accreditation. - Status granted to a postsecondary institution of higher learning that has met standards set by an accrediting agency recognized by the Secretary of the United States Department of Education. The accreditation for massage and bodywork schools may be institutional or programmatic in nature.

(1a) Board. - The North Carolina Board of Massage and Bodywork Therapy.

(2) Board-approved school. - Any massage and bodywork therapy school or training program in this State or another state that is not otherwise exempt from

Board approval, that has met the standards set forth in this Article, and been granted approval by the Board.

(2a) Criminal history record check. - A report resulting from a request made by the Board to the North Carolina Department of Justice for a history of conviction of a crime, whether a misdemeanor or felony, that bears on an applicant's fitness for licensure to practice massage and bodywork therapy.

(3) Massage and bodywork therapy. - Systems of activity applied to the soft tissues of the human body for therapeutic, educational, or relaxation purposes. The application may include:

a. Pressure, friction, stroking, rocking, kneading, percussion, or passive or active stretching within the normal anatomical range of movement.

b. Complementary methods, including the external application of water, heat, cold, lubricants, and other topical preparations.

c. The use of mechanical devices that mimic or enhance actions that may possibly be done by the hands.

(3a) Massage and bodywork therapy school. - Any educational institution that conducts a training program or curriculum for a tuition charge, which is intended to teach adults the knowledge, skills, and abilities necessary for the safe, effective, and ethical practice of massage and bodywork therapy.

(4) Massage and bodywork therapist. - A person licensed under this Article.

(5) Practice of massage and bodywork therapy. - The application of massage and bodywork therapy to any person for a fee or other consideration. (1998-230, s. 10; 2008-224, s. 2.)

§ 90-623. License required.

(a) A person shall not practice or hold out himself or herself to others as a massage and bodywork therapist without first applying for and receiving from the Board a license to engage in that practice.

(b) A person holds out himself or herself to others as a massage and bodywork therapist when the person adopts or uses any title or description including "massage therapist", "bodywork therapist", "masseur", "masseuse", "massagist", "somatic practitioner", "body therapist", "structural integrator", or any derivation of those terms that implies this practice.

(c) It shall be unlawful to advertise using the term "massage therapist" or "bodywork therapist" or any other term that implies a soft tissue technique or method in any public or private publication or communication by a person not licensed under this Article as a massage and bodywork therapist. Any person who holds a license to practice as a massage and bodywork therapist in this State may use the title "Licensed Massage and Bodywork Therapist". No other person shall assume this title or use an abbreviation or any other words, letters, signs, or figures to indicate that the person using the title is a licensed massage and bodywork therapist. An establishment employing or contracting with persons licensed under this Article may advertise on behalf of those persons.

(d) The practice of massage and bodywork therapy shall not include any of the following:

(1) The diagnosis of illness or disease.

(2) Medical procedures, chiropractic adjustive procedures, electrical stimulation, ultrasound, or prescription of medicines.

(3) The use of modalities for which a license to practice medicine, chiropractic, nursing, physical therapy, occupational therapy, acupuncture, or podiatry is required by law.

(4) Sexual activity, which shall mean any direct or indirect physical contact, by any person or between persons, which is intended to erotically stimulate either person, or which is likely to cause such stimulation and includes sexual intercourse, fellatio, cunnilingus, masturbation, or anal intercourse. As used in this subdivision, masturbation means the manipulation of any body tissue with the intent to cause sexual arousal. Sexual activity can involve the use of any device or object and is not dependent on whether penetration, orgasm, or ejaculation has occurred. (1998-230, s. 10; 2008-224, s. 3.)

§ 90-624. Exemptions.

Nothing in this Article shall be construed to prohibit or affect:

(1)   The practice of a profession by persons who are licensed, certified, or registered under other laws of this State and who are performing services within their authorized scope of practice.

(2)   The practice of massage and bodywork therapy by a person employed by the government of the United States while the person is engaged in the performance of duties prescribed by the laws and regulations of the United States.

(3)   The practice of massage and bodywork therapy by persons duly licensed, registered, or certified in another state, territory, the District of Columbia, or a foreign country when incidentally called into this State to teach a course related to massage and bodywork therapy or to consult with a person licensed under this Article.

(4)   Students enrolled in a Board-approved school while completing a clinical requirement for graduation that shall be performed under the supervision of a person licensed under this Article.

(5)   A person giving massage and bodywork therapy to members of that person's immediate family.

(6)   The practice of movement educators such as dance therapists or teachers, yoga teachers, personal trainers, martial arts instructors, movement repatterning practitioners, and other such professions.

(7)   The practice of techniques that are specifically intended to affect the human energy field.

(8)   A person employed by or contracting with a not-for-profit community service organization to perform massage and bodywork therapy on persons who are members of the not-for-profit community service organization and are of the same gender as the person giving the massage or bodywork therapy. (1998-230, s. 10; 2000-140, s. 93.)

§ 90-625. North Carolina Board of Massage and Bodywork Therapy.

(a) The North Carolina Board of Massage and Bodywork Therapy is created. The Board shall consist of seven members who are residents of this State and are as follows:

(1) Five members shall be massage and bodywork therapists who have been licensed under this Article and have been in the practice of massage and bodywork therapy for at least five of the last seven years prior to their serving on the Board. Consideration shall be given to geographical distribution, practice setting, clinical specialty, involvement in massage and bodywork therapy education, and other factors that will promote diversity of the profession on the Board. Two of the five members shall be appointed by the General Assembly, upon the recommendation of the Speaker of the House of Representatives, two shall be appointed by the General Assembly, upon the recommendation of the President Pro Tempore of the Senate, and one shall be appointed by the Governor.

(2) One member shall be a physician licensed pursuant to Article 1 of Chapter 90 of the General Statutes or a person once licensed as a physician whose license lapsed while the person was in good standing with the profession and eligible for licensure. The appointment shall be made by the Governor and may be made from a list provided by the North Carolina Medical Society.

(3) One member shall be a member of the general public who shall not be licensed under Chapter 90 of the General Statutes or the spouse of a person who is so licensed, or have any financial interest, directly or indirectly, in the profession regulated under this Article. The appointment shall be made by the Governor.

(b) Legislative appointments shall be made in accordance with G.S. 120-121. A vacancy in a legislative appointment shall be filled in accordance with G.S. 120-122.

(c) Each member of the Board shall serve for a term of three years, ending on June 30 of the last year of the term. A member shall not be appointed to serve more than two consecutive terms.

(d) The Board shall elect annually a chair and other officers as it deems necessary. The Board shall meet as often as necessary for the conduct of business but no less than twice a year. The Board shall establish procedures governing the calling, holding, and conducting of regular and special meetings. A majority of the Board shall constitute a quorum.

(e)   Each member of the Board may receive per diem and reimbursement for travel and subsistence as set forth in G.S. 93B-5.

(f)   Members may be removed by the official who appointed the member for neglect of duty, incompetence, or unprofessional conduct. A member subject to disciplinary proceedings as a licensee or other professional credential shall be disqualified from participating in the official business of the Board until the charges have been resolved by a determination that the misconduct does not rise to the level of disciplinary action resulting in the suspension or revocation of the member's professional credential. (1998-230, s. 10; 2008-224, s. 4.)

§ 90-626. Powers and duties.

The Board shall have the following powers and duties:

(1)   Represent the diversity within the profession at all times when making decisions and stay current and informed regarding the various branches of massage and bodywork therapy practice.

(2)   Evaluate the qualifications of applicants for licensure under this Article.

(3)   Issue, renew, deny, suspend, or revoke licenses under this Article.

(4)   Reprimand or otherwise discipline licensees under this Article.

(5)   Conduct investigations to determine whether violations of this Article exist or constitute grounds for disciplinary action against licensees under this Article.

(5a)   Approve and regulate massage and bodywork schools, not otherwise exempt from the requirements of Board approval, by formulating the criteria and standards for approval of massage and bodywork schools, investigating massage and bodywork schools applying for approval, issuing approvals to massage and bodywork schools that meet the standards established by the Board, providing periodic inspections of approved massage and bodywork schools, and requiring periodic reports of approved massage and bodywork schools.

(6) Conduct administrative hearings in accordance with Chapter 150B of the General Statutes when a contested case, as defined in G.S. 150B-2(2), arises under this Article.

(7) Employ professional, clerical, or other special personnel necessary to carry out the provisions of this Article and purchase or rent necessary office space, equipment, and supplies.

(8) Pursuant to the maximum amounts set by this Article and other specific authority authorizing fees, establish reasonable fees for applications for examination, certificates of licensure and renewal, approval of massage and bodywork therapy schools, and other services provided by the Board.

(9) Adopt, amend, or repeal any rules necessary to carry out the purposes of this Article and the duties and responsibilities of the Board, including rules related to the approval of massage and bodywork therapy schools, continuing education providers, examinations for licensure, the practice of advanced techniques or specialties, and massage and bodywork therapy establishments. Any rules adopted or amended shall take into account the educational standards of national bodywork and massage therapy associations and professional organizations.

(10) Appoint from its own membership one or more members to act as representatives of the Board at any meeting where such representation is deemed desirable.

(11) Maintain a record of all proceedings and make available to certificate holders and other concerned parties an annual report of the Board.

(12) Adopt a seal containing the name of the Board for use on all certificates and official reports issued by it.

(13) Provide a system for grievances to be presented and resolved.

(14) Assess civil penalties pursuant to G.S. 90-634.1.

(15) Assess the costs of disciplinary actions pursuant to G.S. 90-634.1(d).

The powers and duties set out in this section are granted for the purpose of enabling the Board to safeguard the public health, safety, and welfare against unqualified or incompetent practitioners and are to be liberally construed to accomplish this objective. (1998-230, s. 10; 2003-348, s. 3; 2008-224, ss. 6, 7.)

§ 90-627. Custody and use of funds.

All fees and other moneys collected and received by the Board shall be used for the purposes of implementing this Article. (1998-230, s. 10.)

§ 90-628. Expenses and fees.

(a) All salaries, compensation, and expenses incurred or allowed for the purposes of this Article shall be paid by the Board exclusively out of the fees received by the Board as authorized by this Article or from funds received from other sources. In no case shall any salary, expense, or other obligations of the Board be charged against the General Fund.

(b) The Board may impose the following fees up to the amounts listed below:

(1) Application for license... $20.00

(2) Initial license fee.. 150.00

(3) License renewal... 100.00

(4) Late renewal penalty.. 75.00

(5) Repealed by Session Laws 2008-224, s. 8, effective August 17, 2008.

(6) Duplicate license.. 25.00

(7) Repealed by Session Laws 2008-224, s. 8, effective August 17, 2008. (1998-230, s. 10; 2008-224, s. 8.)

§ 90-629. Requirements for licensure.

Upon application to the Board and the payment of the required fees, an applicant may be licensed as a massage and bodywork therapist if the applicant meets all of the following qualifications:

(1) Has obtained a high school diploma or equivalent.

(2) Is 18 years of age or older.

(3) Is of good moral character as determined by the Board.

(4) Has successfully completed a training program consisting of a minimum of 500 in-class hours of supervised instruction at a Board-approved school.

(5) Has passed a competency assessment examination that meets generally accepted psychometric principles and standards and is approved by the Board.

(6) Has submitted fingerprint cards in a form acceptable to the Board at the time the license application is filed and consented to a criminal history record check by the North Carolina Department of Justice. (1998-230, s. 10; 2008-224, s. 9.)

§ 90-629.1. Criminal history record checks of applicants for licensure.

(a) All applicants for licensure shall consent to a criminal history record check. Refusal to consent to a criminal history record check may constitute grounds for the Board to deny licensure to an applicant. The Board shall ensure that the State and national criminal history of an applicant is checked. The Board shall be responsible for providing to the North Carolina Department of Justice the fingerprints of the applicant to be checked, a form signed by the applicant consenting to the criminal record check and the use of fingerprints and other identifying information required by the State or National Repositories, and any additional information required by the Department of Justice. The Board shall keep all information obtained pursuant to this section confidential.

(b)   The cost of the criminal history record check and the fingerprinting shall be borne by the applicant.

(c)   If an applicant's criminal history record check reveals one or more criminal convictions, the conviction shall not automatically bar licensure. The Board shall consider all of the following factors regarding the conviction:

(1)   The level of seriousness of the crime.

(2)   The date of the crime.

(3)   The age of the person at the time of the conviction.

(4)   The circumstances surrounding the commission of the crime, if known.

(5)   The nexus between the criminal conduct of the person and the job duties of the position to be filled.

(6)   The person's prison, jail, probation, parole, rehabilitation, and employment records since the date the crime was committed.

If, after reviewing the factors, the Board determines that any of the grounds set forth in the subdivisions of G.S. 90-633(a) exist, the Board may deny licensure of the applicant. The Board may disclose to the applicant information contained in the criminal history record check that is relevant to the denial. The Board shall not provide a copy of the criminal history record check to the applicant. The applicant shall have the right to appear before the Board to appeal the Board's decision. However, an appearance before the full Board shall constitute an exhaustion of administrative remedies in accordance with Chapter 150B of the General Statutes.

(d)   The Board, its officers, and employees, acting in good faith and in compliance with this section, shall be immune from civil liability for denying licensure to an applicant based on information provided in the applicant's criminal history record check. (2008-224, s. 10.)

§ 90-630: Repealed by Session Laws 2008-224, s. 11, effective August 17, 2008.

§ 90-630.1. Licensure by endorsement.

(a) The Board may issue a license to a practitioner who is duly licensed, certified, or registered as a massage and bodywork therapist under the laws of another jurisdiction. The practitioner shall be eligible for licensure by endorsement if all of the following qualifications are met:

(1) The applicant meets the requirements of G.S. 90-629(1), (2), (3), and (6) and submits the required application and fees to the Board.

(2) The applicant currently holds a valid license, certificate, or registration as a massage and bodywork therapist in another jurisdiction, and that jurisdiction's requirements for licensure, certification, or registration as a massage and bodywork therapist are substantially equivalent to or exceed the requirements for licensure under this Article.

(3) The applicant is currently a practitioner in good standing, with no disciplinary proceeding or unresolved complaint pending in any jurisdiction at the time a license is to be issued in this State.

(4) The applicant passes a jurisprudence examination administered by the Board regarding laws and rules adopted by the Board for licensure under this Article.

(5) The applicant, including applicants credentialed in a foreign country, demonstrates satisfactory proof of proficiency in the English language.

(b) The Board may issue a license by endorsement to a practitioner from another state that does not license, certify, or register massage and bodywork therapists if all of the following qualifications are met:

(1) The applicant meets the requirements of G.S. 90-629(1), (2), (3), and (6) and submits the required application and fees to the Board.

(2) The applicant has passed a competency assessment examination that meets generally accepted psychometric principles and standards and is approved by the Board.

(3) The applicant has graduated from a massage and bodywork therapy school that: (i) offers a curriculum that meets or is substantially equivalent to the standards set forth in the Board's criteria for school approval; and (ii) is licensed or approved by the regulatory authority for schools of massage and bodywork therapy in the state, province, territory, or country in which it operates or is exempt by law.

(4) The applicant is currently a practitioner in good standing, with no disciplinary proceeding or unresolved complaint pending in any jurisdiction at the time a license is to be issued in this State.

(5) The applicant passes a jurisprudence examination administered by the Board regarding laws and rules adopted by the Board for licensure under this Article.

(6) The applicant, including an applicant credentialed in a foreign country, demonstrates satisfactory proof of proficiency in the English language.

(7) Notwithstanding the requirements of subdivisions (2) and (3) of this subsection, the applicant has other credentials, to be reviewed by the Board on a case-by-case basis, that are deemed by the Board to be substantially equivalent to the requirements in subdivisions (2) and (3) of this subsection.

(c) The Board shall maintain a list of jurisdictions whose regulatory standards for the practice of massage and bodywork therapy have been determined by the Board to be substantially equivalent to or to exceed the requirements for licensure under this Article. (2008-224, s. 12.)

§ 90-631. Massage and bodywork therapy schools.

(a) The Board shall establish rules for the approval of massage and bodywork therapy schools. These rules shall include:

(1) Basic curriculum standards that ensure graduates have the education and skills necessary to carry out the safe and effective practice of massage and bodywork therapy.

(2) Standards for faculty and learning resources.

(3) Requirements for reporting changes in instructional staff and curriculum.

(4) A description of the process used by the Board to approve a school.

Any school that offers a training program in massage and bodywork therapy, not otherwise exempt from the requirements of Board approval, shall submit an application for approval to the Board. If a massage and bodywork therapy school offers training programs at more than one physical location, each location shall constitute a separate massage and bodywork therapy school. The Board shall grant approval to a school, whether in this State or another state, that meets the criteria established by the Board. The Board shall maintain a list of approved schools and a list of community college programs operating pursuant to subsection (b) of this section.

(a1) The Board shall have general supervision over massage and bodywork therapy schools, not otherwise exempt from the requirements of Board approval, in this State for the purpose of protecting the health, safety, and welfare of the public by requiring that massage and bodywork therapy schools carry out their advertised promises and contracts made with their students and patrons and by requiring that approved massage and bodywork therapy schools maintain:

(1) Adequate, safe, and sanitary facilities.

(2) Sufficient and qualified instructional and administrative staff.

(3) Satisfactory programs of operation and instructions.

(b) A massage and bodywork therapy program operated by a North Carolina community college that is accredited by the Southern Association of Colleges and Schools is exempt from the approval process, licensure process, or both, established by the Board. The college shall certify annually to the Board that the program meets or exceeds the minimum standards for curriculum, faculty, and learning resources established by the Board. Students who complete the program shall qualify for licenses from the Board as if the program were approved, licensed, or both, by the Board.

(c) A massage and bodywork therapy program operated by a degree or diploma granting college or university that offers a degree or diploma in massage therapy and is accredited by any accrediting agency that is recognized by the United States Department of Education and is licensed by the North Carolina Community College System or The University of North Carolina Board of Governors is exempt from the approval process, licensure process, or both, established by the Board. The college or university shall certify annually to the Board that the program meets or exceeds the minimum standards for curriculum, faculty, and learning resources established by the Board. Students who complete the program shall qualify for licenses from the Board as if the program were approved, licensed, or both, by the Board. (1998-230, s. 10; 2005-276, s. 8.15(a); 2008-224, ss. 13, 14.)

§ 90-631.1. Massage and bodywork therapy school approval required.

Unless exempt from the Board approval process, no individual, association, partnership, corporation, or other entity shall open, operate, or advertise a massage and bodywork therapy school in this State unless it has first complied with all the requirements of this Article and rules adopted by the Board and has been approved by the Board. (2008-224, s. 15.)

§ 90-631.2. Authority to establish fees for massage and bodywork therapy school approval.

(a) The Board shall establish a schedule of fees for approvals and renewals granted and for inspections performed pursuant to this Article. The fees collected under this section are intended to cover the administrative costs of the approval programs. No fee for application approval or renewal of approval shall be refunded in the event the application is rejected or the approval suspended or revoked.

(b) Fees for Board approval of schools are as follows:

(1)   Request for Application Approval Package
$20.00

(2)   Initial application for approval (one program)
2,000.00

(3)   Initial application for approval of additional

programs (same location)   750.00

(4)   Inspection for initial approval or renewal (one program)
1,500.00

(5)   Inspection for initial approval or renewal of additional

programs (same location)   500.00

(6)   Renewal of approval (one program)
1,000.00

(7)   Renewal of approval (each additional program)
750.00

(c)   Renewal inspections shall not occur more frequently than every three years, unless necessary.

(d)   A school that is required to have more than one inspection in a fiscal year in order to investigate or verify areas of noncompliance with the standards for school approval shall pay a fee of one thousand five hundred dollars ($1,500) for each additional inspection. (2008-224, s. 15.)

§ 90-631.3. Grounds for suspension, revocation, or refusal of massage and bodywork therapy school approval; notice and hearing; judicial review.

(a)   The Board may deny, suspend, revoke, or refuse to approve a massage and bodywork therapy school for any of the following reasons:

(1)   The employment of fraud, deceit, or misrepresentation in obtaining or attempting to obtain approval of a massage and bodywork therapy school.(2)

Engaging in any act or practice in violation of any of the provisions of this Article or of any of the rules adopted by the Board, or aiding, abetting, or assisting any other person in the violation of the provisions of this Article or rules adopted by the Board.

(3)   Failure to require that its students must complete the minimum standards in order to graduate.

(4)   Operating a massage and bodywork therapy school without approval from this Board.

(5)   Engaging in conduct that could result in harm or injury to the public.

(6)   The employment of fraud, deceit, or misrepresentation when communicating with the general public, health care professionals, or other business professionals.

(7)   Falsely holding out a massage and bodywork therapy school as approved by this Board.

(8)   Failure to allow authorized representatives of the Board to conduct inspections of the massage and bodywork therapy school or refusing to make available to the Board, following written notice to the massage and bodywork therapy school, the requested information pertaining to the requirements for approval set forth in this Article.

(9)   Failure to notify the Board in writing within 30 days of any notification it receives from its accrediting agency or the United States Department of Education Office of Postsecondary Education of a show cause action, probation action, or denial of accreditation.

(10)   The applicant for or holder of massage and bodywork therapy school approval has pleaded guilty, entered a plea of nolo contendere, or has been found guilty of a crime involving moral turpitude by a judge or jury in any state or federal court.

(b)   A refusal to issue, refusal to renew, or suspension or revocation of massage and bodywork therapy school approval under this section shall be made in accordance with Chapter 150B of the General Statutes. (2008-224, s. 15.)

§ 90-632. License renewal and continuing education.

(a)   The license to practice under this Article shall be renewed every two years.

(b)   The continuing education requirement for the initial license renewal is as follows:

(1)   If the licensure period is two years or more, each licensee shall submit to the Board evidence of the successful completion of at least 24 hours of study, as approved by the Board, since the initial licensure application date in the practice of massage and bodywork therapy.

(2)   If the licensure period is less than two years, but more than one year, each licensee shall submit to the Board evidence of the successful completion of at least 12 hours of study, as approved by the Board, since the initial licensure application date in the practice of massage and bodywork therapy.

(c)   For subsequent license renewals, each licensee shall submit to the Board evidence of the successful completion of at least 24 hours of study, as approved by the Board, since the previous licensure renewal submission date in the practice of massage and bodywork therapy. (1998-230, s. 10; 2008-224, s. 16.)

§ 90-633. Disciplinary action.

(a)   The Board may deny, suspend, revoke, or refuse to license a massage and bodywork therapist or applicant for any of the following:

(1)   The employment of fraud, deceit, or misrepresentation in obtaining or attempting to obtain a license or the renewal of a license.

(2)   The use of drugs or intoxicating liquors to an extent that affects professional competency.

(3)   Conviction of an offense under any municipal, State, or federal narcotic or controlled substance law.

(4)   Conviction of a felony or other public offense involving moral turpitude.

(5) An adjudication of insanity or incompetency.

(6) Engaging in any act or practice in violation of any of the provisions of this Article or of any of the rules adopted by the Board, or aiding, abetting, or assisting any other person in the violation of these provisions or rules. For purposes of this subdivision, the phrase "aiding, abetting, or assisting any other person" does not include acts intended to inform the individual who is not in compliance with this Article of the steps necessary to comply with this Article or any rules adopted by the Board.

(7) The commission of an act of malpractice, gross negligence, or incompetency.

(8) Practice as a licensee under this Article without a valid certificate or renewal.

(9) Engaging in conduct that could result in harm or injury to the public.

(10) The employment of fraud, deceit, or misrepresentation when communicating with the general public, health care professionals, or other business professionals.

(11) Falsely holding out himself or herself as licensed or certified in any discipline of massage and bodywork therapy without successfully completing training approved by the Board in that specialty.

(12) The application of systems of activity by a massage and bodywork therapist during the course of therapy with the intent of providing sexual stimulation or otherwise pursuing sexual contact.

(b) The Board may reinstate a revoked license, revoke censure or other judgment, or remove other licensure restrictions if the Board finds that the reasons for revocation, censure, or other judgment or other licensure restrictions no longer exist and the massage and bodywork therapist or applicant can reasonably be expected to safely and properly practice as a massage and bodywork therapist. (1998-230, s. 10; 2008-224, s. 17.)

§ 90-634. Enforcement; injunctive relief.

(a)   It is unlawful for a person not licensed or exempted under this Article to engage in any of the following:

(1)   Practice of massage and bodywork therapy.

(2)   Advertise, represent, or hold out himself or herself to others to be a massage and bodywork therapist.

(3)   Use any title descriptive of any branch of massage and bodywork therapy, as provided in G.S. 90-623, to describe his or her practice.

(b)   A person who violates subsection (a) of this section shall be guilty of a Class 1 misdemeanor.

(b1)   Unless exempt from the approval process, it is unlawful for an individual, association, partnership, corporation, or other entity to open, operate, or advertise a massage and bodywork therapy school without first having obtained the approval required by G.S. 90-631.1.

(b2)   An individual, association, partnership, corporation, or other entity that violates subsection (b1) of this section shall be guilty of a Class 3 misdemeanor.

(c)   The Board may make application to superior court for an order enjoining a violation of this Article. Upon a showing by the Board that a person, association, partnership, corporation, or other entity has violated or is about to violate this Article, the court may grant an injunction, restraining order, or take other appropriate action. (1998-230, s. 10; 2008-224, s. 18; 2009-570, s. 12.)

§ 90-634.1. Civil penalties; disciplinary costs.

(a)   Authority to Assess Civil Penalties. - The Board may assess a civil penalty not in excess of one thousand dollars ($1,000) for the violation of any section of this Article or the violation of any rules adopted by the Board. The continuation of the same act for which the penalty is imposed shall not be the basis for an additional penalty unless the penalty is imposed against the same party who has repeated the same act for which the discipline has previously been imposed. The clear proceeds of any civil penalty assessed under this section shall be remitted to the Civil Penalty and Forfeiture Fund in accordance with G.S. 115C-457.2.

(b) Consideration Factors. - Before imposing and assessing a civil penalty, the Board shall consider the following factors:

(1) The nature, gravity, and persistence of the particular violation.

(2) The appropriateness of the imposition of a civil penalty when considered alone or in combination with other punishment.

(3) Whether the violation was willful and malicious.

(4) Any other factors that would tend to mitigate or aggravate the violations found to exist.

(c) Schedule of Civil Penalties. - The Board shall establish a schedule of civil penalties for violations of this Article and rules adopted by the Board.

(d) Transcriptions Costs. - The Board may assess the costs of transcriptions of a disciplinary hearing held by the Board or the Office of Administrative Hearings to include the recording of the hearing by a court reporter and transcription of the proceeding against a person found to be in violation of this Article or rules adopted by the Board. (2003-348, s. 4; 2008-224, s. 19.)

§ 90-635. Third-party reimbursement.

Nothing in this Article shall be construed to require direct third-party reimbursement to persons licensed under this Article. (1998-230, s. 10.)

§ 90-636. Regulation by county or municipality.

Nothing in this Article shall be construed to prohibit a county or municipality from regulating persons covered by this Article, however, a county or municipality may not impose regulations that are inconsistent with this Article. (1998-230, s. 10.)

§§ 90-637 through 90-639. Reserved for future codification purposes.

Article 37.

Health Care Practitioner Identification.

§ 90-640. Identification badges required.

(a)   For purposes of this section, "health care practitioner" means an individual who is licensed, certified, or registered to engage in the practice of medicine, nursing, dentistry, pharmacy, or any related occupation involving the direct provision of health care to patients.

(b)   When providing health care to a patient, a health care practitioner shall wear a badge or other form of identification displaying in readily visible type the individual's name and the license, certification, or registration held by the practitioner. If the identity of the individual's license, certification, or registration is commonly expressed by an abbreviation rather than by full title, that abbreviation may be used on the badge or other identification.

(c)   The badge or other form of identification is not required to be worn if the patient is being seen in the health care practitioner's office and, the name and license of the practitioner can be readily determined by the patient from a posted license, a sign in the office, a brochure provided to patients, or otherwise.

(d)   Each licensing board or other regulatory authority for health care practitioners may adopt rules for exemptions from wearing a badge or other form of identification, or for allowing use of the practitioner's first name only, when necessary for the health care practitioner's safety or for therapeutic concerns.

(e)   Violation of this section is a ground for disciplinary action against the health care practitioner by the practitioner's licensing board or other regulatory authority. (1999-320, s. 1.)

§§ 90-641 through 90-645. Reserved for future codification purposes.

Article 38.

Respiratory Care Practice Act.

§ 90-646. Short title.

This Article may be cited as the "Respiratory Care Practice Act". (2000-162, s. 1.)

§ 90-647. Purpose.

The General Assembly finds that the practice of respiratory care in the State of North Carolina affects the public health, safety, and welfare and that the mandatory licensure of persons who engage in respiratory care is necessary to ensure a minimum standard of competency. It is the purpose and intent of this Article to protect the public from the unqualified practice of respiratory care and from unprofessional conduct by persons licensed pursuant to this Article. (2000-162, s. 1.)

§ 90-648. Definitions.

The following definitions apply in this Article:

(1)   Board. - The North Carolina Respiratory Care Board.

(2)   Diagnostic testing. - Cardiopulmonary procedures and tests performed on the written order of a physician licensed under Article 1 of this Chapter that provide information to the physician to formulate a diagnosis of the patient's condition. The tests and procedures may include pulmonary function testing, electrocardiograph testing, cardiac stress testing, and sleep related testing.

(3)   Direct supervision. - The authority and responsibility to direct the performance of activities as established by policies and procedures for safe and appropriate completion of services.

(4)   Individual. - A human being.

(5) License. - A certificate issued by the Board recognizing the person named therein as having met the requirements to practice respiratory care as defined in this Article.

(6) Licensee. - A person who has been issued a license under this Article.

(7) Medical director. - An appointed physician who is licensed under Article 1 of this Chapter and a member of the entity's medical staff, and who is granted the authority and responsibility for assuring and establishing policies and procedures and that the provision of such is provided to the quality, safety, and appropriateness standards as recognized within the defined scope of practice for the entity.

(8) Person. - An individual, corporation, partnership, association, unit of government, or other legal entity.

(9) Physician. - A doctor of medicine licensed by the State of North Carolina in accordance with Article 1 of this Chapter.

(10) Practice of respiratory care. - As defined by the written order of a physician licensed under Article 1 of this Chapter, the observing and monitoring of signs and symptoms, general behavior, and general physical response to respiratory care treatment and diagnostic testing, including the determination of whether such signs, symptoms, reactions, behavior, or general response exhibit abnormal characteristics, and the performance of diagnostic testing and therapeutic application of:

a. Medical gases, humidity, and aerosols including the maintenance of associated apparatus, except for the purpose of anesthesia.

b. Pharmacologic agents related to respiratory care procedures, including those agents necessary to perform hemodynamic monitoring.

c. Mechanical or physiological ventilatory support.

d. Cardiopulmonary resuscitation and maintenance of natural airways, the insertion and maintenance of artificial airways under the direct supervision of a recognized medical director in a health care environment which identifies these services within the scope of practice by the facility's governing board.

e. Hyperbaric oxygen therapy.

f.   New and innovative respiratory care and related support activities in appropriately identified environments and under the training and practice guidelines established by the American Association of Respiratory Care.

The term also means the interpretation and implementation of a physician's written or verbal order pertaining to the acts described in this subdivision.

(11)   Respiratory care. - As defined by the written order of a physician licensed under Article 1 of Chapter 90, the treatment, management, diagnostic testing, and care of patients with deficiencies and abnormalities associated with the cardiopulmonary system.

(12)   Respiratory care practitioner. - A person who has been licensed by the Board to engage in the practice of respiratory care.

(13)   Support activities. - Procedures that do not require formal academic training, including the delivery, setup, and maintenance of apparatus. The term also includes giving instructions on the use, fitting, and application of apparatus, but does not include therapeutic evaluation and assessment. (2000-162, s. 1.)

§ 90-649. North Carolina Respiratory Care Board; creation.

(a)   The North Carolina Respiratory Care Board is created. The Board shall consist of 10 members as follows:

(1)   Two members shall be respiratory care practitioners.

(2)   Four members shall be physicians licensed to practice in North Carolina, and whose primary practice is Pulmonology, Anesthesiology, Critical Care Medicine, or whose specialty is Cardiothoracic Disorders.

(3)   One member shall represent the North Carolina Hospital Association.

(4)   One member shall represent the North Carolina Association of Medical Equipment Services.

(5)   Two members shall represent the public at large.

(b) Members of the Board shall be citizens of the United States and residents of this State. The respiratory care practitioner members shall have practiced respiratory care for at least five years and shall be licensed under this Article. The public members shall not be: (i) a respiratory care practitioner, (ii) an agent or employee of a person engaged in the profession of respiratory care, (iii) a health care professional licensed under this Chapter or a person enrolled in a program to become a licensed health care professional, (iv) an agent or employee of a health care institution, a health care insurer, or a health care professional school, (v) a member of an allied health profession or a person enrolled in a program to become a member of an allied health profession, or (vi) a spouse of an individual who may not serve as a public member of the Board. (2000-162, s. 1; 2003-384, s. 1.)

§ 90-650. Appointments and removal of Board members; terms and compensation.

(a) The members of the Board shall be appointed as follows:

(1) The Governor shall appoint the public members described in G.S. 90-649(a)(5).

(2) The General Assembly, upon the recommendation of the Speaker of the House of Representatives, shall appoint one of the respiratory care practitioner members described in G.S. 90-649(a)(1) and one of the physician members described in G.S. 90-649(a)(2) in accordance with G.S. 120-121.

(3) The General Assembly, upon the recommendation of the President Pro Tempore of the Senate, shall appoint one of the respiratory care practitioner members described in G.S. 90-649(a)(1) and one of the physician members described in G.S. 90-649(a)(2) in accordance with G.S. 120-121.

(4) The North Carolina Medical Society shall appoint one of the physician members described in G.S. 90-649(a)(2).

(5) The Old North State Medical Society shall appoint one of the physician members described in G.S. 96-649(a)(2).

(6) The North Carolina Hospital Association shall appoint the member described in G.S. 90-649(a)(3).

(7)   The North Carolina Association of Medical Equipment Services shall appoint the member described in G.S. 90-649(a)(4).

(b)   Members of the Board shall take office on the first day of November immediately following the expired term of that office and shall serve for a term of three years and until their successors are appointed and qualified. No member shall serve on the Board for more than two consecutive terms.

(c)   The Governor may remove members of the Board, after notice and an opportunity for hearing, for incompetence, neglect of duty, unprofessional conduct, conviction of any felony, failure to meet the qualifications of this Article, or committing any act prohibited by this Article.

(d)   Any vacancy shall be filled by the authority originally filling that position, except that any vacancy in appointments by the General Assembly shall be filled in accordance with G.S. 120-122. Appointees to fill vacancies shall serve the remainder of the unexpired term and until their successors have been duly appointed and qualified.

(e)   Members of the Board shall receive no compensation for their services but shall be entitled to travel, per diem, and other expenses authorized by G.S. 93B-5.

(f)   Individual members shall be immune from civil liability arising from activities performed within the scope of their official duties. (2000-162, s. 1.)

§ 90-651. Election of officers; meetings of the Board.

(a)   The Board shall elect a chair and a vice-chair who shall hold office according to rules adopted pursuant to this Article, except that all officers shall be elected annually by the Board for one-year terms and shall serve until their successors are elected and qualified.

(b)   The Board shall hold at least two regular meetings each year as provided by rules adopted pursuant to this Article. The Board may hold additional meetings upon the call of the chair or any two Board members. A majority of the Board membership shall constitute a quorum. (2000-162, s. 1.)

§ 90-652. Powers and duties of the Board.

The Board shall have the power and duty to:

(1) Determine the qualifications and fitness of applicants for licensure, renewal of licensure, and reciprocal licensure. The Board shall, in its discretion, investigate the background of an applicant to determine the applicant's qualifications with due regard given to the applicant's competency, honesty, truthfulness, and integrity. The Department of Justice may provide a criminal record check to the Board for a person who has applied for a license through the Board. The Board shall provide to the Department of Justice, along with the request, the fingerprints of the applicant, any additional information required by the Department of Justice, and a form signed by the applicant consenting to the check of the criminal record and to the use of the fingerprints and other identifying information required by the State or national repositories. The applicant's fingerprints shall be forwarded to the State Bureau of Investigation for a search of the State's criminal history record file, and the State Bureau of Investigation shall forward a set of the fingerprints to the Federal Bureau of Investigation for a national criminal history check. The Board shall keep all information pursuant to this subdivision privileged, in accordance with applicable State law and federal guidelines, and the information shall be confidential and shall not be a public record under Chapter 132 of the General Statutes. The Board shall collect any fees required by the Department of Justice and shall remit the fees to the Department of Justice for expenses associated with conducting the criminal history record check.

(2) Establish and adopt rules necessary to conduct its business, carry out its duties, and administer this Article.

(3) Adopt and publish a code of ethics.

(4) Deny, issue, suspend, revoke, and renew licenses in accordance with this Article.

(5) Conduct investigations, subpoena individuals and records, and do all other things necessary and proper to discipline persons licensed under this Article and to enforce this Article.

(6) Employ professional, clerical, investigative, or special personnel necessary to carry out the provisions of this Article and purchase or rent office space, equipment, and supplies.

(7)   Adopt a seal by which it shall authenticate its proceedings, official records, and licenses.

(8)   Conduct administrative hearings in accordance with Article 3A of Chapter 150B of the General Statutes.

(9)   Establish certain reasonable fees as authorized by this Article for applications for examination, licensure, provisional licensure, renewal of licensure, and other services provided by the Board.

(10)   Submit an annual report to the North Carolina Medical Board, the North Carolina Hospital Association, the North Carolina Society of Respiratory Care, the Governor, and the General Assembly of all the Board's official actions during the preceding year, together with any recommendations and findings regarding improvements of the practice of respiratory care.

(11)   Publish and make available upon request the licensure standards prescribed under this Article and all rules adopted pursuant to this Article.

(12)   Request and receive the assistance of State educational institutions or other State agencies.

(13)   Establish and approve continuing education requirements for persons seeking licensure under this Article. (2000-162, s. 1; 2003-384, s. 2; 2004-89, s. 1.)

§ 90-653. Licensure requirements; examination.

(a)   Each applicant for licensure under this Article shall meet the following requirements:

(1)   Submit a completed application as required by the Board.

(2)   Submit any fees required by the Board.

(3)   Submit to the Board written evidence, verified by oath, that the applicant has successfully completed the minimal requirements of a respiratory care education program as approved by the Commission for Accreditation of Allied

Health Educational Programs, or the Canadian Council on Accreditation for Respiratory Therapy Education.

(4) Submit to the Board written evidence, verified by oath, that the applicant has successfully completed the minimal requirements for Basic Cardiac Life Support as recognized by the American Heart Association, the American Red Cross, or the American Safety and Health Institute.

(5) Pass the entry-level examination given by the National Board for Respiratory Care, Inc.

(b) At least three times each year, the Board shall cause the examination required in subdivision (5) of subsection (a) of this section to be given to applicants at a time and place to be announced by the Board. Any applicant who fails to pass the first examination may take additional examinations in accordance with rules adopted pursuant to this Article. (2000-162, s. 1; 2003-384, s. 3.)

§ 90-654. Temporary license.

Upon application and payment of the required fees, the Board may grant a temporary license to a person who, at the time of application, submits notarized copies of the items required in G.S. 90-653(a)(3) through (a)(5) while awaiting official copies of the items from the issuing agency. The temporary license shall be valid for a period not to exceed 90 days from the date of application. (2000-162, s. 1; 2003-384, s. 4.)

§ 90-655. Licensure by reciprocity.

The Board may grant, upon application and the payment of proper fees, a license to a person who, at the time of application holds a valid license, certificate, or registration as a respiratory care practitioner issued by another state or a political territory or jurisdiction acceptable to the Board if, in the Board's determination, the requirements for that license, certificate, or registration are substantially the same as the requirements for licensure under this Article. (2000-162, s. 1.)

§ 90-656. Provisional license.

The Board may grant a provisional license for a period not exceeding 12 months to any applicant who has successfully completed the education requirements under G.S. 90-653(a)(3) and has made application to take the examination required under G.S. 90-653(a)(5). A provisional license allows the individual to practice respiratory care under the direct supervision of a respiratory care practitioner and in accordance with rules adopted pursuant to this Article. A license granted under this section shall contain an endorsement indicating that the license is provisional and stating the terms and conditions of its use by the licensee and shall state the date the license was granted and the date it expires. (2000-162, s. 1; 2003-384, s. 5.)

§ 90-657. Notification of applicant following evaluation of application.

After evaluation of the application and of any other evidence required from the applicant by the Board, the Board shall notify each applicant that the application and evidence submitted are satisfactory and accepted or unsatisfactory and rejected. If the application and evidence is rejected, the notice shall state the reasons for the rejection. (2000-162, s. 1.)

§ 90-658. License as property of the Board; display requirement; renewal; inactive status.

(a) A license issued by the Board is the property of the Board and shall be surrendered by the licensee to the Board on demand.

(b) The licensee shall display the license in the manner prescribed by the Board.

(c) The licensee shall inform the Board of any change of the licensee's address.

(d) The license shall be renewed by the Board annually upon the payment of a renewal fee if, at the time of application for renewal, the applicant is not in violation of this Article and has fulfilled the current requirements regarding continuing education as established by rules adopted pursuant to this Article.

(e) The Board shall notify a licensee at least 30 days in advance of the expiration of his or her license. Each licensee is responsible for renewing his or her license before the expiration date. Licenses that are not renewed automatically lapse.

(f) The Board may provide for the late renewal of an automatically lapsed license upon the payment of a late fee. No late fee renewal may be granted more than five years after a license expires.

(g) In accordance with rules adopted pursuant to this Article, a licensee may request that his or her license be declared inactive and may thereafter apply for active status. (2000-162, s. 1.)

§ 90-659. Suspension, revocation, and refusal to renew a license.

(a) The Board shall take the necessary actions to deny or refuse to renew a license, suspend or revoke a license, or to impose probationary conditions on a licensee or applicant if the licensee or applicant:

(1) Has engaged in any of the following conduct:

a. Employed fraud, deceit, or misrepresentation in obtaining or attempting to obtain a license or the renewal of a license.

b. Committed an act of malpractice, gross negligence, or incompetence in the practice of respiratory care.

c. Practiced respiratory care without a license.

d. Engaged in health care practices that are determined to be hazardous to public health, safety, or welfare.

(2) Was convicted of or entered a plea of guilty or nolo contendere to any crime involving moral turpitude.

(3)   Was adjudicated insane or incompetent, until proof of recovery from the condition can be established.

(4)   Engaged in any act or practice that violates any of the provisions of this Article or any rule adopted pursuant to this Article, or aided, abetted, or assisted any person in such a violation.

(b)   Denial, refusal to renew, suspension, or revocation of a license, or imposition of probationary conditions upon a licensee may be ordered by the Board after a hearing held in accordance with Article 3A of Chapter 150B of the General Statutes and rules adopted pursuant to this Article. An application may be made to the Board for reinstatement of a revoked license if the revocation has been in effect for at least one year. (2000-162, s. 1.)

§ 90-660. Expenses; fees.

(a)   All salaries, compensation, and expenses incurred or allowed for carrying out the purposes of this Article shall be paid by the Board exclusively out of the fees received by the Board as authorized by this Article or funds received from other sources. In no case shall any salary, expense, or other obligations of the Board be charged against the State.

(b)   All monies received by the Board pursuant to this Article shall be deposited in an account for the Board and shall be used for the administration and implementation of this Article. The Board shall establish fees in amounts to cover the cost of services rendered for the following purposes:

(1)   For an initial application, a fee not to exceed fifty dollars ($50.00).

(2)   For examination or reexamination, a fee not to exceed two hundred dollars ($200.00).

(3)   For issuance of any license, a fee not to exceed one hundred fifty dollars ($150.00).

(4)   For the renewal of any license, a fee not to exceed seventy-five dollars ($75.00).

(5) For the late renewal of any license, an additional late fee not to exceed seventy-five dollars ($75.00).

(6) For a license with a provisional or temporary endorsement, a fee not to exceed fifty dollars ($50.00).

(7) For copies of rules adopted pursuant to this Article and licensure standards, charges not exceeding the actual cost of printing and mailing.

(8) For official verification of licensure status, a fee not to exceed twenty dollars ($20.00).

(9) For approval of continuing education programs, a fee not to exceed one hundred fifty dollars ($150.00). (2000-162, s. 1; 2001-455, s. 7; 2003-384, s. 6; 2007-418, s. 1.)

§ 90-661. Requirement of license.

It shall be unlawful for any person who is not currently licensed under this Article to:

(1) Engage in the practice of respiratory care.

(2) Use the title "respiratory care practitioner".

(3) Use the letters "RCP", "RTT", "RT", or any facsimile or combination in any words, letters, abbreviations, or insignia.

(4) Imply orally or in writing or indicate in any way that the person is a respiratory care practitioner or is otherwise licensed under this Article.

(5) Employ or solicit for employment unlicensed persons to practice respiratory care. (2000-162, s. 1; 2003-384, s. 7.)

§ 90-662. Violation a misdemeanor.

Any person who violates any provision of this Article shall be guilty of a Class 1 misdemeanor. (2000-162, s. 1.)

§ 90-663. Injunctions.

The Board may apply to the superior court for an order enjoining violations of this Article, and upon a showing by the Board that any person has violated or is about to violate this Article, the court may grant an injunction or restraining order or take other appropriate action. (2000-162, s. 1.)

§ 90-664. Persons and practices not affected.

The requirements of this Article shall not apply to:

(1) Any person registered, certified, credentialed, or licensed to engage in another profession or occupation or any person working under the supervision of a person registered, certified, credentialed, or licensed to engage in another profession or occupation in this State who is performing work incidental to or within the practice of that profession or occupation and does not represent himself or herself as a respiratory care practitioner.

(2) A student or trainee working under the direct supervision of a respiratory care practitioner while fulfilling an experience requirement or pursuing a course of study to meet requirements for licensure in accordance with rules adopted pursuant to this Article.

(3) A respiratory care practitioner serving in the Armed Forces or the Public Health Service of the United States or employed by the Veterans Administration when performing duties associated with that service or employment.

(4) A person who performs only support activities as defined in G.S. 90-648(13). (2000-162, s. 1; 2011-183, s. 67.)

§ 90-665. Third-party reimbursement.

Nothing in this Article shall be construed to require direct third-party reimbursements to persons licensed under this Article. (2000-162, s. 1.)

§ 90-666. Civil penalties.

(a) Authority to Assess Civil Penalties. - In addition to taking any of the actions permitted under G.S. 90-659, the Board may assess a civil penalty not to exceed one thousand dollars ($1,000) for the violation of any section of this Article or any rules adopted by the Board. The clear proceeds of any civil penalty assessed under this section shall be remitted to the Civil Penalty and Forfeiture Fund in accordance with G.S. 115C-457.2.

(b) Consideration Factors. - Before imposing and assessing a civil penalty and fixing the amount of the penalty, the Board shall, as a part of its deliberations, consider the following factors:

(1) The nature, gravity, and persistence of the particular violation.

(2) The appropriateness of the imposition of a civil penalty when considered alone or in combination with other punishment.

(3) Whether the violation was willful and malicious.

(4) Any other factors that would tend to mitigate or aggravate the violations found to exist.

(c) Schedule of Civil Penalties. - The Board shall establish a schedule of civil penalties for violations of this Article. The schedule shall indicate for each type of violation whether the violation can be corrected. Penalties shall be assessed for the first, second, and third violations of specified sections of this Article and for specified rules.

(d) Costs. - The Board may assess the costs of disciplinary actions against a person found to be in violation of this Article or rules adopted by the Board. (2003-384, s. 8.)

§§ 90-667 through 90-670. Reserved for future codification purposes.

Article 39.

Safety Profession.

§ 90-671. Definitions.

The following definitions apply in this Article:

(1)   Associate Safety Professional (ASP). A person who has met the education, experience, and examination requirements established by the Board of Certified Safety Professionals for an Associate Safety Professional.

(2)   Board of Certified Safety Professionals (BCSP). A nonprofit corporation, incorporated in Illinois in 1969, established to improve the practice and educational standards of the profession of safety by certifying individuals who meet its education, experience, examination, and maintenance requirements.

(3)   Certified Safety Professional (CSP). A person who has met the education, experience, and examination requirements established by the Board of Certified Safety Professionals for a Certified Safety Professional. (2000-110, s. 1; 2000-140, s. 98.)

§ 90-672. Unlawful acts; injunctive relief; exclusion.

(a)   No person shall represent himself or herself as a Certified Safety Professional or Associate Safety Professional unless that person is certified by the Board of Certified Safety Professionals and has duly authorized the Board to file with the office of the Secretary of State all information required by G.S. 90-674.

(b)   A violation of this section constitutes an unfair trade practice under G.S. 75-1.1, and a court may impose a civil penalty against the defendant and shall be empowered to issue a restraining order to prevent further use of the title. (2000-110, s. 1; 2000-140, s. 98.)

§ 90-673. Exemptions and limitations.

(a) This Article does not apply to:

(1) A person who holds a license issued by a State board, commission, or other agency, is engaged in activities authorized by his or her license, and does not represent himself or herself as an Associate Safety Professional or Certified Safety Professional.

(2) A person who practices within the scope of safety, injury, or illness prevention and does not use the title "Associate Safety Professional" or "Certified Safety Professional", the initials "ASP" or "CSP", or otherwise represents himself or herself to the public as an Associate Safety Professional or Certified Safety Professional.

(3) A person who is licensed as an architect under Chapter 83A of the General Statutes or any person working under the supervision of a licensed architect.

(4) A person who is licensed as a professional engineer under Chapter 89C of the General Statutes or any person working under the supervision of a licensed professional engineer.

(b) Nothing in this Article shall permit the practice of engineering by persons who are not licensed under Chapter 89C of the General Statutes.

(c) Nothing in this Article shall permit the practice of architecture by persons not licensed under Chapter 83A of the General Statutes. (2000-110, s. 1; 2000-140, s. 98.)

§ 90-674. Certification registry.

The Board shall file with the Secretary of State the name, address, telephone number, and date of certification for all Associate Safety Professionals and Certified Safety Professionals. The Board shall remit a filing fee of thirty-five dollars ($35.00) to the Secretary of State with each certification filed. All fees paid to the Department shall be used to pay the costs incurred in administering and enforcing this Article. The Board may require this filing fee to be paid by the person whose certification is being filed. The Board shall promptly notify the Secretary of State when a person's certification is revoked or no longer in effect.

The Secretary of State shall maintain a registry of all current Associate Safety Professionals and Certified Safety Professionals as furnished by the Board. (2000-110, s. 1; 2000-140, s. 98.)

§§ 90-675 through 90-680. Reserved for future codification purposes.

Article 40.

Perfusionist Licensure Act.

§ 90-681. Legislative findings.

The General Assembly finds that the practice of perfusion is an area of health care that is continually evolving to include more sophisticated and demanding patient care activities. The General Assembly further finds that the practice of perfusion by unauthorized, unqualified, unprofessional, and incompetent persons is a threat to public health, safety, and welfare, and therefore it is necessary to establish minimum standards of education, training, and competency for persons engaged in the practice of perfusion. (2005-267, s. 1.)

§ 90-682. Definitions.

The following definitions apply in this Article:

(1) Certified clinical perfusionist. - A person who has successfully completed the examination process and has been issued a certificate by the American Board of Cardiovascular Perfusion or its successor organization.

(2) Committee. - The Perfusionist Advisory Committee of the North Carolina Medical Board.

(3) Extracorporeal circulation. - The diversion of a patient's blood through a heart-lung machine or a similar device that assumes the functions of the patient's heart, lungs, kidneys, liver, or other organs.

(4) Licensee. - A person who has been issued a license to practice perfusion under this Article.

(5) Medical Board. - The North Carolina Medical Board, as established under Article 1 of this Chapter.

(6) Perfusion protocols. - Perfusion-related policies and protocols developed or approved by a licensed health care facility or a physician through collaboration with administrators, licensed perfusionists, and other health care professionals.

(7) Practice of perfusion. - The performing of functions, under the supervision of a licensed physician, necessary for the support, treatment, measurement, or supplementation of the cardiovascular, circulatory, and respiratory systems or other organs, or a combination of those functions, and the ensuring of safe management of physiological function by monitoring and analyzing the parameters of the systems during any medical situation where it is necessary to support or replace the patient's cardiopulmonary or circulatory function. The term also includes the use of extracorporeal circulation, long-term cardiopulmonary support techniques, including extracorporeal carbon-dioxide removal and extracorporeal membrane oxygenation, and associated therapeutic and diagnostic technologies; counterpulsation, ventricular assistance, autotransfusion, blood conservation techniques, myocardial and organ preservation, extracorporeal life support, and isolated limb perfusion; the use of techniques involving blood management, advanced life support, and other related functions; and, in the performance of the acts described in this subdivision, (i) the administration of pharmacological and therapeutic agents, blood products, or anesthetic agents through the extracorporeal circuit or through an intravenous line as ordered by a physician; (ii) the performance and use of anticoagulation monitoring and analysis, physiologic monitoring and analysis, blood gas and chemistry monitoring and analysis, hematological monitoring and analysis, hypothermia, hyperthermia, hemoconcentration and hemodilution, and hemodialysis in conjunction with perfusion service; and (iii) the observation of signs and symptoms related to perfusion services, the determination of whether the signs and symptoms exhibit abnormal characteristics, and the implementation of appropriate reporting, perfusion protocols, or changes in or the initiation of emergency procedures. (2005-267, s. 1; 2007-525, s. 5.)

§ 90-682.1. Medical Board approval required.

(a) The Committee shall report to the Medical Board all actions taken by the Committee pursuant to this Article, except for actions taken by the Committee pursuant to G.S. 90-684. No action by the Committee is effective unless the action is approved by the Medical Board. The Medical Board may also rescind or supersede, in whole or in part, any action taken by the Committee in carrying out the provisions of this Article, except for actions taken by the Committee pursuant to G.S. 90-684. In rescinding or superseding an action by the Committee, the Board may remand the matter back to the Committee with instructions to perform some act consistent with this Article or Article 1 of Chapter 90. Members of the Medical Board may be selected by the President of the Board to participate in the matter that is the subject of the Order remanding the matter back to the Committee.

(b) The Board may waive any requirements of this Article consistent with G.S. 90-12.5. (2005-267, s. 1; 2007-346, s. 7; 2007-525, s. 6.)

§ 90-683. License required; exemptions.

(a) On or after July 1, 2006, no person shall practice or offer to practice perfusion as defined in this Article, use the title "licensed perfusionist" or "provisional licensed perfusionist", use the letters "LP" or "PLP", or otherwise indicate or imply that the person is a licensed perfusionist or a provisionally licensed perfusionist unless that person is currently licensed as provided in this Article.

(b) The provisions of this Article shall not apply to:

(1) Any person registered, certified, credentialed, or licensed to engage in another profession or occupation or any person working under the supervision of a person registered, certified, credentialed, or licensed to engage in another profession or occupation in this State if the person is performing work incidental to the practice of that profession or occupation and the person does not represent himself or herself as a licensed perfusionist or a provisionally licensed perfusionist.

(2) A student enrolled in an accredited perfusion education program if perfusion services performed by the student are an integral part of the student's

course of study and are performed under the direct supervision of a licensed perfusionist.

(3) A perfusionist employed by the United States government when performing duties associated with that employment.

(4) A person performing autotransfusion or blood conservation techniques under the direct supervision of a licensed physician. (2005-267, s. 1.)

§ 90-684. Perfusion Advisory Committee.

(a) Composition and Terms. - The North Carolina Perfusion Advisory Committee is created. The Committee shall consist of seven members who shall serve staggered terms. The initial Committee members shall be selected on or before October 1, 2005, as follows:

(1) The North Carolina Medical Board shall appoint three licensed perfusionists, two of whom shall serve a term of three years and one of whom shall serve a term of two years.

(2) The North Carolina Medical Board shall appoint one physician who is licensed under Article 1 of Chapter 90 of the General Statutes and is a cardiothoracic surgeon or a cardiovascular anesthesiologist, who shall serve a term of two years.

(3) The North Carolina Hospital Association shall appoint two hospital administrators, one of whom shall serve a term of two years and one of whom shall serve a one-year term.

(4) The Governor shall appoint one public member who shall serve a one-year term.

Upon the expiration of the terms of the initial Committee members, members shall be appointed by the appointing authorities designated in subdivisions (1) through (4) of this subsection for a term of three years and shall serve until a successor is appointed. No member may serve more than two consecutive full terms.

(b) Qualifications. - Members of the Committee shall be citizens of the United States and residents of this State. The perfusionist members shall hold current licenses from the Committee and shall remain in good standing with the Committee during their terms. Public members of the Committee shall not be: (i) trained or experienced in the practice of perfusion, (ii) an agent or employee of a person engaged in the practice of perfusion, (iii) a health care professional licensed under this Chapter or a person enrolled in a program to become a licensed health care professional, (iv) an agent or employee of a health care institution, a health care insurer, or a health care professional school, (v) a member of an allied health profession or a person enrolled in a program to become a member of an allied health profession, or (vi) a spouse of an individual who may not serve as a public member of the Committee.

(c) Vacancies. - Any vacancy shall be filled by the authority originally filling that position. Appointees to fill vacancies shall serve the remainder of the unexpired term and until their successors have been duly appointed and qualified.

(d) Removal. - The Committee may remove any of its members for neglect of duty, incompetence, or unprofessional conduct. A member subject to disciplinary proceedings in his or her capacity as a licensed perfusionist shall be disqualified from participating in the official business of the Committee until the charges have been resolved.

(e) Compensation. - Each member of the Committee shall receive per diem and reimbursement for travel and subsistence as provided in G.S. 93B-5.

(f) Officers. - The officers of the Committee shall be a chair, a vice-chair, and other officers deemed necessary by the Committee to carry out the purposes of this Article. All officers shall be elected annually by the Committee for two-year terms and shall serve until their successors are elected and qualified. The chair of the Committee shall be a licensed perfusionist.

(g) Meetings. - The Committee shall hold its first meeting within 30 days after the appointment of its members and shall hold at least two meetings each year to conduct business and to review the standards and rules previously adopted by the Committee. The Committee shall establish the procedures for calling, holding, and conducting regular and special meetings. A majority of Committee members constitutes a quorum.

(h) Qualified Immunity. - The Committee and its members and staff shall not be held liable in any civil or criminal proceeding for exercising, in good faith, the powers and duties authorized by law. A person, partnership, firm, corporation, association, authority, or other entity acting in good faith without fraud or malice shall be immune from civil liability for (i) reporting, investigating, or providing an expert medical opinion to the Committee regarding the acts and omissions of a licensee or applicant that violates the provisions of G.S. 90-691(a) or any other provision of law relating to the fitness of a licensee or applicant to practice perfusion and (ii) initiating or conducting proceedings against a licensee or applicant if a complaint is made or action is taken in good faith without fraud or malice. A person shall not be held liable in any civil proceeding for testifying before the Committee in good faith and without fraud or malice in any proceeding involving a violation of G.S. 90-961(a) or any other law relating to the fitness of an applicant or licensee to practice perfusion, or for making a recommendation to the Committee in the nature of peer review, in good faith and without fraud and malice. (2005-267, s. 1; 2007-525, s. 7.)

§ 90-685. Powers of the Committee.

The Committee shall have the power and duty to:

(1) Administer this Article.

(2) Issue interpretations of this Article.

(3) Adopt, amend, or repeal rules as may be necessary to carry out the provisions of this Article.

(4) Employ and fix the compensation of personnel that the Committee determines is necessary to carry into effect the provisions of this Article and incur other expenses necessary to effectuate this Article.

(4a) Establish the standards for qualifications and fitness of applicants for licensure, provisional licensure, licensure renewal, and reciprocal licensure.

(5) Determine the qualifications and fitness of applicants for licensure, provisional licensure, licensure renewal, and reciprocal licensure.

(6)   Issue, renew, deny, suspend, or revoke licenses, order probation, issue reprimands, and carry out any other disciplinary actions authorized by this Article.

(7)   Set fees for licensure, provisional licensure, reciprocal licensure, licensure renewal, and other services deemed necessary to carry out the purposes of this Article.

(8)   Establish continuing education requirements for licensees.

(9)   Establish a code of ethics for licensees.

(10)   Maintain a current list of all persons who have been licensed under this Article.

(11)   Conduct investigations for the purpose of determining whether violations of this Article or grounds for disciplining licensees exist.

(12)   Maintain a record of all proceedings and make available to all licensees and other concerned parties an annual report of all Committee action.

(13)   Adopt a seal containing the name of the Committee for use on all official documents and reports issued by the Committee.

(14)   Summon and issue subpoenas for the appearance of any witnesses deemed necessary to testify concerning any matter to be heard before or inquired into by the Committee.

(15)   Order that any patient records, documents, or other material concerning any matter to be heard before or inquired into by the Committee shall be produced before the Committee or made available for inspection, notwithstanding any other provisions of law providing for the application of any physician-patient privilege with respect to such records, documents, or other material. The Committee shall withhold from public disclosure the identity of a patient, including information relating to dates and places of treatment, or any other information that would tend to identify the patient, unless the patient or the representative of the patient expressly consents to the disclosure.

(16)   Order a licensee whose health and effectiveness have been significantly impaired by alcohol, drug addiction, or mental illness to attend and successfully

complete a treatment program as deemed necessary and appropriate. (2005-267, s. 1; 2007-525, s. 8.)

§ 90-685.1. Confidentiality of Committee investigative information.

(a)   All records, papers, investigative files, investigative reports, other investigative information, and other documents containing information in the possession of or received or gathered by the Committee or its members or employees as a result of investigations, inquiries, or interviews conducted in connection with a licensing, complaint, or disciplinary matter shall not be considered public records within the meaning of Chapter 132 of the General Statutes and are privileged, confidential, and not subject to discovery, subpoena, or other means of legal compulsion for release to any person other than the Committee, its employees, or agents involved in the application for license or discipline of a license holder, except as provided in subsection (b) of this section. For purposes of this subsection, investigative information includes information relating to the identity of, and a report made by, a perfusionist, or other person performing an expert review for the Committee.

(b)   The Committee shall provide the licensee or applicant with access to all information in its possession that the Committee intends to offer into evidence in presenting its case in chief at the contested hearing on the matter, subject to any privilege or restriction set forth by rule, statute, or legal precedent, upon written request from a licensee or applicant who is the subject of a complaint or investigation, or from the licensee's or applicant's counsel, unless good cause is shown for delay. The Committee is not required to provide any of the following:

(1)   A Committee investigative report.

(2)   The identity of a nontestifying complainant.

(3)   Attorney-client communications, attorney work product, or other materials covered by a privilege recognized by the Rules of Civil Procedure or the Rules of Evidence. (2007-525, s. 9.)

§ 90-686. Qualifications for licensure.

(a) An applicant shall be licensed to practice perfusion if the applicant meets all of the following qualifications:

(1) Is at least 18 years old.

(2) Completes an application on a form provided by the Committee.

(3) Successfully completes a perfusion education program approved by the Committee.

(4) Pays the required fee under G.S. 90-689.

(5) Is a certified clinical perfusionist.

(b) All persons licensed under this section shall practice perfusion under the supervision of a physician licensed under Article 1 of Chapter 90 of the General Statutes. (2005-267, s. 1.)

§ 90-687. Reciprocity.

The Committee may grant, upon application and payment of proper fees, a license to a person who has been licensed to practice perfusion in another state or territory of the United States whose standards of competency are substantially equivalent to those provided in this Article or holds a current certificate as a certified clinical perfusionist. (2005-267, s. 1.)

§ 90-688. Provisional license.

The Committee may grant a provisional license for a period not exceeding 12 months to any applicant who has successfully completed an approved perfusion education program and pays the required fee under G.S. 90-689. A provisional license shall allow the individual to practice perfusion under the supervision and direction of a licensed perfusionist and in accordance with rules adopted pursuant to this Article. A license granted under this section shall contain an endorsement indicating that the license is provisional and stating the terms and conditions of its use by the licensee and shall state the date the license was granted and the date it expires. Provisional licenses shall be renewed in accordance with the provisions of G.S. 90-690. (2005-267, s. 1.)

§ 90-689. Expenses; fees.

(a) All fees shall be payable to the Medical Board and deposited in the name of the Medical Board in financial institutions designated by the Medical Board as official depositories. These fees shall be used to carry out the purposes of this Article.

(b) All salaries, compensation, and expenses incurred or allowed to carry out the purposes of this Article shall be paid by the Medical Board exclusively out of the fees received by the Medical Board as authorized by this Article or funds received from other sources. In no case shall any salary, expense, or other obligation authorized by this Article be charged against the State treasury.

(c) The Committee, upon the approval of the Medical Board, shall establish fees not exceeding the following amounts:

(1)	License application	$350.00
(2)	Biennial renewal of license	$350.00
(3)	Late renewal of license	$100.00
(4)	Provisional license	$175.00
(5)	Copies of rules	Cost.

(2005-267, s. 1.)

§ 90-690. Renewal of licenses.

(a) All licenses to practice perfusion shall expire two years after the date they were issued. The Committee shall send a notice of expiration to each licensee at his or her last known address at least 30 days prior to the expiration of his or her license. All applications for renewal of unexpired licenses shall be filed with the Committee and accompanied by proof satisfactory to the Committee that the applicant has completed the continuing education requirements established by the Committee and the renewal fee as required by G.S. 90-689.

(b) An application for renewal of a license that has been expired for less than three years shall be accompanied by proof satisfactory to the Committee that the applicant has current certification as defined by G.S. 90-682(1), has satisfied the continuing education requirements established by the Committee and has paid the renewal and late fees required by G.S. 90-689. A license that has been expired for more than three years shall not be renewed, but the applicant may apply for a new license by complying with the current requirements for licensure under this Article. (2005-267, s. 1; 2007-525, s. 10.)

§ 90-690.1. Maintenance of certification to maintain licensure.

(a) After December 31, 2007, all licensed perfusionists who are licensed under this Article shall maintain certification as defined in G.S. 90-682(1) in order to maintain licensure. If certification shall lapse at any time, the Committee may initiate disciplinary action under G.S. 90-691, or upon a finding consistent with G.S. 150B-3(c), may order the summary suspension of the perfusionist's license.

(b) The provisions of this section shall not apply to perfusionists who were licensed under Section 2 of S. L. 2005-267. (2007-525, s. 11.)

§ 90-691. Disciplinary authority.

(a) The Committee may place on probation with or without conditions, impose limitations and conditions on, publicly reprimand, assess monetary redress, issue public letters of concern, require satisfactory completion of treatment programs or remedial or educational training, deny, refuse to renew, suspend, or revoke an application or license if the applicant or licensee:

(1) Gives false information or withholds material information from the Committee in procuring or attempting to procure a license.

(2) Gives false information or withholds material information from the Committee during the course of an investigation conducted by the Committee.

(3) Has been convicted of or pled guilty or no contest to a crime that indicates the person is unfit or incompetent to practice perfusion as defined in this Article or that indicates the person has deceived, defrauded, or endangered the public.

(4) Has a habitual substance abuse or mental impairment that interferes with his or her ability to provide appropriate care as established by this Article or rules adopted by the Committee. The Committee is empowered and authorized to require a licensee to submit to a mental or physical examination by persons designated by the Committee before or after charges may be presented against the licensee, and the results of the examination shall be admissible in evidence in a hearing before the Committee.

(5) Has demonstrated gross negligence, incompetency, or misconduct in the practice of perfusion as defined in this Article. The Committee may, upon reasonable grounds, require a licensee to submit to inquiries or examinations, written or oral, as the Committee deems necessary to determine the professional qualifications of the licensee.

(6) Has had an application for licensure or a license to practice perfusion in another jurisdiction denied, suspended, or revoked for reasons that would be grounds for similar action in this State.

(7) Has willfully violated any provision of this Article or rules adopted by the Committee.

(8) Has allowed his or her certification to lapse.

(b) The taking of any action authorized under subsection (a) of this section may be ordered by the Committee after a hearing is held in accordance with Article 3A of Chapter 150B of the General Statutes. The Committee may reinstate a revoked license if it finds that the reasons for revocation no longer exist and that the person can reasonably be expected to perform the services authorized under this Article in a safe manner. (2005-267, s. 1; 2007-525, s. 12.)

§ 90-692. Enjoining illegal practices.

The Committee may apply to the superior court for an order enjoining violations of this Article. Upon a showing by the Committee that any person has violated this Article, the court may grant injunctive relief. (2005-267, s. 1.)

§ 90-693. Civil penalties; disciplinary costs.

(a)   Authority to Assess Civil Penalties. - The Committee may assess a civil penalty not in excess of one thousand dollars ($1,000) for the violation of any section of this Article or the violation of any rules adopted by the Committee. The clear proceeds of any civil penalty assessed under this section shall be remitted to the Civil Penalty and Forfeiture Fund in accordance with G.S. 115C-457.2.

(b)   Consideration Factors. - Before imposing and assessing a civil penalty, the Committee shall consider the following factors:

(1)   The nature, gravity, and persistence of the particular violation.

(2)   The appropriateness of the imposition of a civil penalty when considered alone or in combination with other punishment.

(3)   Whether the violation was willful and malicious.

(4)   Any other factors that would tend to mitigate or aggravate the violations found to exist.

(c)   Schedule of Civil Penalties. - The Committee shall establish a schedule of civil penalties for violations of this Article and rules adopted by the Committee.

(d)   Costs. - The Committee may assess the costs of disciplinary actions against a person found to be in violation of this Article or rules adopted by the Committee. (2005-267, s. 1.)

§ 90-694. Third-party reimbursement.

Nothing in this Article shall be construed to require direct third-party reimbursements to persons licensed under this Article. (2005-267, s. 1.)

§ 90-695. Reserved for future codification purposes.

§ 90-696. Reserved for future codification purposes.

§ 90-697. Reserved for future codification purposes.

§ 90-698. Reserved for future codification purposes.

§ 90-699. Reserved for future codification purposes.

§ 90-700. Reserved for future codification purposes.

Article 41.

Pathology Services Billing.

§ 90-701. Billing of anatomic pathology services.

(a) It shall be unlawful for any person licensed to practice medicine, podiatry, or dentistry in this State to bill a patient, entity, or person for anatomic pathology services in an amount in excess of the amount charged by the clinical laboratory for performing the service unless the licensed practitioner discloses conspicuously on the itemized bill or statement, or in writing by a separate itemized disclosure statement:

(1) The amounts charged by the laboratory for the anatomic pathology service;

(2) Any other charge that has been included in the bill; and

(3) The name of the licensed practitioner performing or supervising the anatomic pathology service.

The disclosure required under this subsection shall be printed in a 10-point or higher font size.

(b) It shall be unlawful for any hospital licensed in this State to bill a patient, entity, or person for anatomic pathology services in an amount in excess of the amount charged by the clinical laboratory for performing the service unless the hospital discloses conspicuously on the itemized bill or statement, or in writing by a separate itemized disclosure statement:

(1) The amounts charged by the laboratory for the professional anatomic pathology services;

(2) Any other charge that has been included in the bill; and

(3) The name of the licensed practitioner performing or supervising the anatomic pathology service.

The disclosure required under this subsection shall be printed in a 10-point or higher font size.

(c) A bill for anatomic pathology services submitted to a patient, entity, or person for payment shall disclose the name and address of the laboratory performing the professional component of the service.

(d) The requirements of subsections (a) and (b) of this section shall not apply to:

(1) A licensed practitioner performing or supervising anatomic pathology services, or

(2) A hospital or physician group practice where a physician employee or physician under contract to a hospital or a physician group practice is providing or supervising anatomic pathology services and is compensated by the hospital or physician group practice for the services.

(e) As used in this section, the term "anatomic pathology services" means:

(1) Histopathology or surgical pathology meaning the gross and microscopic examination and histologic processing of organ tissue performed by a physician or under the supervision of a physician;

(2) Cytopathology meaning the examination of cells from fluids, aspirates, washings, brushings, or smears, including the Pap test examination performed by a physician or under the supervision of a physician;

(3) Hematology meaning the microscopic evaluation of bone marrow aspirates and biopsies performed by a physician or under the supervision of a physician, and peripheral blood smears when the attending or treating physician or technologist requests that a blood smear be reviewed by a pathologist;

(4) Subcellular pathology and molecular pathology; and

(5) Blood-banking services performed by pathologists.

(f) Nothing in this section shall be construed to require the disclosure of the terms or conditions of a contract for the provision of anatomic pathology services between a managed care organization and a hospital or between a managed care organization and a physician's practice.

(g) The requirements of subsections (a) and (b) of this section shall not apply to a referring laboratory providing anatomic pathology services for services performed by that laboratory in instances where one or more samples must be sent for a second medical opinion on a specimen.

(h) Nothing in this section shall be construed as a prohibition on a physician requesting the anatomic pathology services of more than one clinical laboratory for a second medical opinion on a specimen.

(i) Each intentional failure to disclose in violation of subsections (a), (b), or (c) of this section is a separate Class 3 misdemeanor offense punishable by a fine of two hundred fifty dollars ($250.00).

(j) The respective State licensing boards having jurisdiction over practitioners subject to this section may revoke, suspend, or deny renewal of the license of a practitioner who violates this section. Each State licensing board having jurisdiction may take disciplinary action on a finding by the board of intentional violation or an ongoing pattern of violations in the absence of a misdemeanor conviction.

(k) Not later than six months from the effective date of this section, the respective State licensing boards having jurisdiction, and the Division of Health Service Regulation, shall communicate the requirements of this section to all licensed practitioners and licensed facilities subject to this section. (2005-415, ss. 1, 1.1; 2007-182, s. 1.)

§ 90-702: Reserved for future codification purposes.

§ 90-703: Reserved for future codification purposes.

§ 90-704: Reserved for future codification purposes.

§ 90-705: Reserved for future codification purposes.

§ 90-706: Reserved for future codification purposes.

§ 90-707: Reserved for future codification purposes.

§ 90-708: Reserved for future codification purposes.

§ 90-709: Reserved for future codification purposes.

§ 90-710: Reserved for future codification purposes.

§ 90-711: Reserved for future codification purposes.

§ 90-712: Reserved for future codification purposes.

§ 90-713: Reserved for future codification purposes.

§ 90-714: Reserved for future codification purposes.

§ 90-715: Reserved for future codification purposes.

§ 90-716: Reserved for future codification purposes.

§ 90-717: Reserved for future codification purposes.

§ 90-718: Reserved for future codification purposes.

§ 90-719: Reserved for future codification purposes.

§ 90-720: Reserved for future codification purposes.

Article 42.

Polysomnography Practice Act.

§ 90-721. Definitions.

The following definitions apply in this Article:

(1) Board. - The Board of Registered Polysomnographic Technologists (BRPT), a member of the National Organization of Certification Associations and accredited by the National Commission for Certifying Agencies (NCCA), the accreditation body of the National Organization for Competency Assurance (NOCA).

(2) Direct supervision. - An act whereby a registered polysomnographic technologist who is providing supervision is present in the area where the polysomnographic procedure is being performed and immediately available to furnish assistance and direction throughout the performance of the procedure.

(3) General supervision. - The authority and responsibility to direct the performance of activities as established by policies and procedures for safe and appropriate completion of polysomnography services whereby the physical presence of a licensed physician is not required during the performance of the polysomnographic procedure, but the licensed physician must be available for assistance, if needed.

(4) Licensed physician. - A physician licensed to practice medicine under Article 1 of Chapter 90 of the General Statutes.

(5) Medical Board. - The North Carolina Medical Board established under G.S. 90-2.

(6) Polysomnography. - The allied health specialty involving the process of attended and unattended monitoring, analysis, and recording of physiological data during sleep and wakefulness to assist in the assessment of sleep and wake disorders and other sleep disorders, syndromes, and dysfunctions that are sleep-related, manifest during sleep, or disrupt normal sleep and wake cycles and activities.

(7) Registered polysomnographic technologist. - A person who is credentialed by the Board as a "Registered Polysomnographic Technologist" (RPSGT).

(8) Student. - A person who is enrolled in a polysomnography educational program approved by the Board as an acceptable pathway to meet eligibility requirements for credentialing. (2009-434, s. 1.)

§ 90-722. Practice of polysomnography.

(a) Practice. - The "practice of polysomnography" means the performance of any of the following tasks:

(1) Monitoring and recording physiological data during the evaluation of sleep-related disorders, including sleep-related respiratory disturbances, by applying the following techniques, equipment, or procedures:

a. Positive airway pressure (PAP) devices, such as continuous positive airway pressure (CPAP), and bilevel and other approved devices, providing forms of pressure support used to treat sleep disordered breathing on patients using a mask or oral appliance; provided, the mask or oral appliance does not attach to an artificial airway or extend into the trachea.

b. Supplemental low flow oxygen therapy, up to eight liters per minute, utilizing nasal cannula or administered with continuous or bilevel positive airway pressure during a polysomnogram.

c. Capnography during a polysomnogram.

d. Cardiopulmonary resuscitation.

e. Pulse oximetry.

f. Gastroesophageal pH monitoring.

g. Esophageal pressure monitoring.

h. Sleep staging, including surface electroencephalography, surface electrooculagraphy, and surface submental or masseter electromyography.

i. Surface electromyography.

j. Electrocardiography.

k. Respiratory effort monitoring, including thoracic and abdominal movement.

l. Plethysmography blood flow monitoring.

m. Snore monitoring.

n. Audio and video monitoring.

o. Body movement.

p. Nocturnal penile tumescence monitoring.

q. Nasal and oral airflow monitoring.

r. Body temperature monitoring.

s. Actigraphy.

(2) Observing and monitoring physical signs and symptoms, general behavior, and general physical response to polysomnographic evaluation and determining whether initiation, modification, or discontinuation of a treatment regimen is warranted based on protocol and physician's order.

(3) Analyzing and scoring data collected during the monitoring described in subdivisions (1) and (2) of this subsection for the purpose of assisting a licensed physician in the diagnosis and treatment of sleep and wake disorders.

(4) Implementing a written or verbal order from a licensed physician that requires the practice of polysomnography.

(5) Educating a patient regarding polysomnography and sleep disorders.

(b) Limitations. - The practice of polysomnography shall be performed under the general supervision of a licensed physician. The practice of polysomnography shall take place in a hospital, a stand-alone sleep laboratory or sleep center, or a patient's home. However, the scoring of data and education of patients may take place in settings other than a hospital, stand-alone sleep laboratory or sleep center, or patient's home. (2009-434, s. 1.)

§ 90-723. Unlawful acts.

(a) Unlawful Act. - On or after January 1, 2012, it shall be unlawful for a person to do any of the following unless the person is listed with the Medical Board as provided in this Article:

(1) Practice polysomnography.

(2) Represent, orally or in writing, that the person is credentialed to practice polysomnography.

(3) Use the title "Registered Polysomnographic Technologist" or the initials "RPSGT."

(b) Violations. - A violation of this section is a Class 1 misdemeanor. Complaints and investigations of violations of this Article shall be directed to and conducted by the Board. The court may issue injunctions or restraining orders to prevent further violations under this Article. (2009-434, s. 1.)

§ 90-724. Exemptions.

The provisions of this Article do not apply to any of the following:

(1) A person registered, certified, credentialed, or licensed to engage in another profession or occupation or any person working under the supervision of a person registered, certified, credentialed, or licensed to engage in another profession or occupation in this State if the person is performing work incidental to or within the scope of practice of that profession or occupation and the person does not represent himself or herself as a registered polysomnographic technologist.

(2) An individual employed by the United States government when performing duties associated with that employment.

(3) Research investigation that monitors physiological parameters during sleep or wakefulness, provided that the research investigation has been approved and deemed acceptable by an institutional review board, follows conventional safety measures required for the procedures, and the information is not obtained or used for the practice of clinical medicine.

(4) A physician licensed to practice medicine under Article 1 of Chapter 90 of the General Statutes or a physician assistant or nurse practitioner licensed to perform medical acts, tasks, and functions under Article 1 of Chapter 90 of the General Statutes.

(5) A student actively enrolled in a polysomnography education program if:

a. Polysomnographic services and post-training experience are performed by the student as an integral part of the student's course of study;

b. The polysomnographic services are performed under the direct supervision of a registered polysomnographic technologist; and

c. The student adheres to post-training examination guidelines established by the Board. (2009-434, s. 1.)

§ 90-725. Listing requirements.

(a) Annual Listing. - A person may not practice polysomnography under this Article unless the person is listed with the Medical Board. In order to be listed with the Medical Board, a person must annually submit on or before September 1 of each year all of the following information to the Medical Board in the manner prescribed by the Medical Board:

(1) The person's full legal name.

(2) The person's complete address and telephone number.

(3) Evidence that the person is currently credentialed in good standing by the Board as a Registered Polysomnographic Technologist (RPSGT).

(4) The date the person was credentialed by the Board to practice polysomnography.

(5) A nonrefundable listing fee of fifty dollars ($50.00).

(b) Listing. - The Medical Board must maintain a listing of polysomnographic technologists that have submitted proof of credentials under this section. The Board must promptly notify the Medical Board, by mail or electronic means, when a person's credential is revoked or no longer in effect. Upon receipt of this notification, the Medical Board must remove the person's name from the list. (2009-434, s. 1.)

Chapter 90A.

Sanitarians and Water and Wastewater Treatment Facility Operators.

Article 1.

Sanitarians.

§§ 90A-1 through 90A-19: Repealed by Session Laws 1981 (Regular Session, 1982), c. 1274, s. 1.

Article 2.

Certification of Water Treatment Facility Operators.

§ 90A-20. Purpose.

It is the purpose of this Article to protect the public health and to conserve and protect the water resources of the State; to protect the public investment in water treatment facilities; to provide for the classifying of public water treatment facilities; to require the examination of water treatment facility operators and the certification of their competency to supervise the operation of water treatment facilities; and to establish the procedures for such classification and certification. Further, it is the purpose of this Article to provide for the certification of personnel operating the distribution portion of a water treatment facility. (1969, c. 1059, s. 2; 1989, c. 227, s. 1.)

§ 90A-20.1. Definitions.

In this Article, unless the context clearly requires otherwise, the following definitions apply:

(1) "Board" or "Board of Certification" means the Water Treatment Facility Operators Board of Certification.

(2) "Operator" means a person who operates, maintains or inspects water treatment facilities.

(3) "Operator in responsible charge" means a person designated by the owner of the water treatment facility to be responsible for the total operation and maintenance of the facility.

(4) "Public water system" means a system for the provision of piped water for human consumption as defined in G.S. 130A-313(10).

(5) "Unit of local government" means a county, city, consolidated city-county, sanitary district or other local political subdivision, authority or agency of local government.

(6) "Water treatment facility" means any facility or facilities used or available for use in the collection, treatment, testing, storage, pumping, or distribution of water for a public water system. (1989, c. 227, s. 2.)

§ 90A-21. Water Treatment Facility Operators Board of Certification.

(a) Board Membership. - There is hereby established within the Department of Environment and Natural Resources a Water Treatment Facility Operators Board of Certification (hereinafter termed the "Board of Certification") composed of eight members to be appointed by the Governor as follows:

(1) One member who is currently employed as a water treatment facility operator;

(2) One member who is manager of a North Carolina municipality using a surface water supply;

(3) One member who is manager of a North Carolina municipality using a treated groundwater supply;

(4)   One member who is employed as a director of utilities, water superintendent, or equivalent position with a North Carolina municipality;

(5)   One member employed by a private water utility or private industry and who is responsible for the operation or supervision of a water supply and treatment facility;

(6)   One member who is a faculty member of a four-year college or university whose major field is related to water supply;

(7)   One member employed by the Department of Environment and Natural Resources and working in the field of water supply;

(8)   One member not certified or regulated under this Article, who shall represent the interest of the public at large.

(b)   Terms of Office. - All members serving on the Board on June 30, 1981, shall complete their respective terms. No member appointed to the Board on or after July 1, 1981, shall serve more than two complete consecutive three-year terms, except that the member employed by the Department of Environment and Natural Resources may serve more than two consecutive terms, and except that each member shall serve until his successor is appointed and qualifies. The Governor may remove any member for good cause shown and shall appoint members to fill unexpired terms. The Governor shall appoint the public member not later than July 1, 1981.

(c)   Powers and Responsibilities. - The Board of Certification shall establish all rules, regulations and procedures with respect to the certification program and advise and assist the Secretary of Environment and Natural Resources in its administration.

(d)   Compensation. - Members of the Board of Certification who are officers or employees of State agencies or institutions shall receive subsistence and travel allowances at the rates authorized by G.S. 138-5.

(e)   Officers. - The Board shall elect a chairman and all other necessary officers to serve one-year terms. A majority of the members of the Board shall constitute a quorum for the transaction of business.

(f)   Annual Report. - The Board shall report annually to the Governor a full statement of its disciplinary and enforcement programs and activities during the year, together with such recommendations as it may deem expedient. (1969, c. 1059, s. 2; 1973, c. 476, s. 128; 1981, c. 616, ss. 1-5; 1989, c. 727, s. 219(7); 1997-443, s. 11A.24.)

§ 90A-22. Classification of water treatment facilities; notification of users.

(a) On or before July 1, 1982, the Board of Certification, with the advice and assistance of the Secretary of Environment and Natural Resources, shall classify all surface water treatment facilities and all facilities for treating groundwater supplies that are used, or intended for use, as part of a public water supply system with due regard for the size of the facility, its type, character of water to be treated, other physical conditions affecting the treatment of the water, and with respect to the degree of skill, knowledge, and experience that the operator responsible for the water treatment facility must have to supervise successfully the operation of the facilities so as to adequately protect the public health.

(b) The Board shall notify users of such facilities when any classification of a facility by the Board would result in a certified operator's not being required to supervise the operation of that facility. Any user so notified may demand a hearing on the Board's decision, and that hearing and any appeal therefrom shall be conducted in accordance with Articles 3 and 4 of Chapter 150B of the General Statutes. (1969, c. 1059, s. 2; 1973, c. 476, s. 128; 1981, c. 616, s. 6; 1987, c. 827, ss. 1, 230; 1989, c. 727, s. 219(8); 1997-443, s. 11A.25.)

§ 90A-23. Grades of certificates.

The Board of Certification, with the advice and assistance of the Secretary of Environment and Natural Resources, shall establish grades of certification for water treatment facility operators corresponding to the classification of water treatment facilities. (1969, c. 1059, s. 2; 1973, c. 476, s. 128; 1989, c. 227, s. 3; c. 727, s. 219(9); 1997-443, s. 11A.26.)

§ 90A-24. Operator qualifications and examination.

The Board of Certification, with the advice and assistance of the Secretary of Environment and Natural Resources shall establish minimum requirements of education, experience and knowledge for each grade of certification for water treatment facility operators, and shall establish procedures for receiving applications for certification, conducting examinations and making investigations of applicants as may be necessary and appropriate to the end that prompt and fair consideration be given every application and the water treatment facilities of the State may be adequately supervised by certified operators. (1969, c. 1059, s. 2; 1973, c. 476, s. 128; 1989, c. 727, s. 219(10); 1997-443, s. 11A.27.)

§ 90A-25. Issuance of certificates.

(a) The Board shall issue a certificate to an applicant who meets the requirements for certification and pays the required fee. The certificate shall state the grade of certification appropriate for the classification of water treatment facilities the applicant is qualified to operate.

(b) Certificates may be issued, without examination, in a comparable grade to any person who holds a certificate in any state, territory or possession of the United States, if in the judgment of the Board of Certification the requirements for operators under which the person's certificate was issued do not conflict with the provisions of this Article, and are of a standard not lower than that specified under rules and regulations adopted under this Article.

(c) Certificates in an appropriate grade will be issued to operators who, on July 1, 1969, hold certificates of competency issued under the voluntary certification program now being administered through the Department of Environment and Natural Resources with the cooperation of the North Carolina Water Works Operators Association, the North Carolina Section of the American Water Works Association, and the North Carolina League of Municipalities.

(d) Certificates in an appropriate grade will be issued without examination to any person or persons certified by the governing board in the case of a city, town, county, sanitary district, or other political subdivision, or by the owner in the case of a private utility or industry, to have been in responsible charge of its water treatment facilities on the date the Board of Certification notifies the governing board, or owner, of the classification of its water treatment facility, provided the facility was classified before July 1, 1981, and provided the application for such certification is made within one year of the date of notification. A certificate so issued will be valid for use by the holder only in the water treatment facility in which he was employed at the time of his certification. No certificate shall be issued under this subsection to any operator of any water treatment facility classified by the board on or after July 1, 1981.

(e) Temporary certificates in any grade may be issued without examination to any person employed as a water treatment facility operator when the Board of Certification finds that the supply of certified operators, or persons with training necessary to certification, is inadequate. Temporary certificates shall be valid for only one year. Temporary certificates may be issued with such special conditions or requirements relating to the place of employment of the person holding the certificate, his supervision on a consulting or advisory basis, or other matters as the Board of Certification may deem necessary to protect the public health. No temporary certificate may be renewed more than one time either by any operator at the same grade level or by any operator for employment at the same water treatment facility. (1969, c. 1059, s. 2; 1973, c. 476, s. 128; 1981, c. 616, ss. 7, 8; 1989, c. 727, s. 18; 1991, c. 321, s. 1; 1997-443, s. 11A.28.)

§ 90A-25.1. Renewal of certificate.

A certificate expires on December 31 of the year in which it is issued or renewed. The Board, with the advice and assistance of the Secretary of Environment and Natural Resources, may establish minimum continuing education requirements that an applicant must meet to renew a certificate. The Board shall renew a certificate if the applicant meets the continuing education requirements imposed as a condition for renewal, pays the required renewal fee plus any renewal fees in arrears, and, if the application is late, pays the late penalty. (1991, c. 321, s. 2; 1997-443, s. 11A.29.)

§ 90A-26. Revocation or suspension of certificate.

The Board of Certification, in accordance with the procedure set forth in Chapter 150B of the General Statutes of North Carolina, may issue a reprimand to an operator, or suspend or revoke the certificate of an operator, when it finds any of the following:

(1) The operator has practiced fraud or deception.

(2) The operator failed to use reasonable care, judgment, knowledge, or ability in the performance of an operator's duties.

(3) The operator is incompetent or unable to properly perform the duties of an operator.

(4) The operator has failed to comply with the requirements for certification or renewal of certification. (1969, c. 1059, s. 2; 1973, c. 1331, s. 3; 1981, c. 616, s. 9; 1987, c. 827, s. 1; 1991, c. 321, s. 3.)

§ 90A-27. Application fee.

The Board may establish a schedule of fees for the issuance or renewal of a certificate to cover the costs of administering the certification programs. The fee for issuing or renewing a certificate may not exceed fifty dollars ($50.00). The Board may impose a penalty not to exceed thirty dollars ($30.00) for the late renewal of a certificate. (1969, c. 1059, s. 2; 1981, c. 562, s. 1; 1991, c. 321, s. 4.)

§ 90A-28. Promotion of training and other powers.

The Board of Certification and the Secretary of Environment and Natural Resources may take all necessary and appropriate steps in order to effectively and fairly achieve the purposes of this Article, including, but not limited to, the providing of training for operators and cooperating with educational institutions and private and public associations, persons, or corporations in the promotion of training for water treatment facility personnel. (1969, c. 1059, s. 2; 1973, c. 476, s. 128; 1989, c. 727, s. 219(11); 1997-443, s. 11A.30.)

§ 90A-29. Certified operators required.

(a) On and after July 1, 1971, every person, corporation, company, association, partnership, unit of local government, State agency, federal agency, or other legal entity owning or having control of a water treatment facility shall have the obligation of assuring that the operator in responsible charge of such facility is duly certified by the Board of Certification under the provisions of this Article.

(b)   No person, after July 1, 1971, shall perform the duties of an operator, in responsible charge of a water treatment facility, without being duly certified under the provisions of this Article. (1969, c. 1059, s. 2; 1981, c. 616, s. 10; 1989, c. 227, s. 4.)

§ 90A-30. Penalties; remedies; contested cases.

(a)   Upon the recommendation of the Board of Certification, the Secretary of Environment and Natural Resources or a delegated representative may impose an administrative, civil penalty on any person, corporation, company, association, partnership, unit of local government, State agency, federal agency, or other legal entity who violates G.S. 90A-29(a). Each day of a continued violation shall constitute a separate violation. The penalty shall not exceed one hundred dollars ($100.00) for each day such violation continues. No penalty shall be assessed until the person alleged to be in violation has been notified of the violation.

The clear proceeds of penalties imposed pursuant to this section shall be remitted to the Civil Penalty and Forfeiture Fund in accordance with G.S. 115C-457.2.

(b)   Any person wishing to contest a penalty issued under this section shall be entitled to an administrative hearing and judicial review conducted according to the procedures outlined in Articles 3 and 4 of Chapter 150B of the General Statutes.

(c)   The Secretary may bring a civil action in the superior court of the county in which the violation is alleged to have occurred to recover the amount of the administrative penalty whenever an owner or person in control of a water treatment facility

(1)   Who has not requested an administrative hearing fails to pay the penalty within 60 days after being notified of such penalty, or

(2) Who has requested an administrative hearing fails to pay the penalty within 60 days after service of a written copy of the decision as provided in G.S. 150B-36.

(d) Notwithstanding any other provision of law, this section imposes the only penalty or sanction, civil or criminal, for violations of G.S. 90A-29(a) or for the failure to meet any other legal requirement for a water system to have a certified operator in responsible charge. (1981, c. 616, s. 11; 1987, c. 827, s. 231; 1989, c. 227, s. 5; c. 727, s. 219(12); 1989 (Reg. Sess., 1990), c. 1024, s. 18; 1997-443, s. 11A.31; 1998-215, s. 45.)

§ 90A-31. Commercial water treatment operation firms.

(a) Every person, corporation, company, association, partnership, unit of local government, State agency, federal agency, or other legal entity owning or having control of a water treatment facility may contract with a responsible commercial water treatment facility operation firm for operational and other services of that firm. The owner with the firm's consent may designate an employee of that contracting firm as the operator in responsible charge. This designee and other licensed employees of the firm shall be responsible for the total operation and maintenance of the water treatment facility, and shall be limited as to the number of facilities, distance between facilities, and frequency of visits as can reasonably be handled during the ordinary course of business as well as during emergencies. Contractual firms shall not be limited as to the number of facilities, distance between facilities, location of office or other internal management procedures.

(b) Any operator in responsible charge shall obtain certification from the Water Treatment Facility Operators Board of Certification and shall comply with all of the requirements specified in Chapter 90A and the rules and reasonable standards of the Board, applicable to all operators in responsible charge, designed to assure satisfactory operation of water treatment facilities. (1985, c. 550, s. 1; 1989, c. 227, s. 6.)

§ 90A-32. Certification of distribution operators.

The Board of Certification shall have the authority to establish certification programs for personnel who operate the distribution portion of a water treatment facility. The Board may provide for voluntary of mandatory certification and may provide requirements for training, education, and experience of personnel to be certified. The owner of a water treatment facility shall have three years to obtain certification or the services of appropriately certified distribution personnel after the effective date of mandatory certification. (1989, c. 227, s. 7.)

§ 90A-33: Reserved for future codification purposes.

§ 90A-34: Reserved for future codification purposes.

Article 3.

Certification of Water Pollution Control System Operators and Animal Waste Management System Operators.

Part 1. Certification of Water Pollution Control System Operators.

§ 90A-35. Purpose.

It is the purpose of this Article to protect the public health and to conserve and protect the quality of the water resources of the State and maintain the quality of receiving waters as assigned by the North Carolina Environmental Management Commission; to protect the public investment in water pollution control systems; to provide for the classification of water pollution control systems; to require the examination of water pollution control system operators and the certification of their competency to supervise the operation of such systems; and to establish procedures for such classification and certification. (1969, c. 1059, s. 3; 1973, c. 1262, s. 23; 1991, c. 623, ss. 1, 3; 1995 (Reg. Sess., 1996), c. 626, s. 6(a).)

§ 90A-36. Repealed by Session Laws 1973, c. 1262, s. 44.

§ 90A-37. Classification of water pollution control systems.

The Commission, with the advice and assistance of the Secretary of Environment and Natural Resources, shall classify all water pollution control systems. In making the classification, the Commission shall give due regard, among other factors, to the size of the system, the nature of the wastes to be treated or removed from the wastewater, the treatment process to be employed, and the degrees of skill, knowledge and experience that the operator of the water pollution control system must have to supervise the operation of the system so as to adequately protect the public health and maintain the water quality standards of the receiving waters as assigned by the North Carolina Environmental Management Commission. (1969, c. 1059, s. 3; 1973, c. 1262, s. 23; 1977, c. 771, s. 4; 1979, c. 554, ss. 1, 2; 1989, c. 727, s. 218(23); 1991, c. 623, ss. 1, 4; 1997-443, s. 11A.119(a).)

§ 90A-38. Grades of certificates.

(a) The Commission, with the advice and assistance of the Secretary of Environment and Natural Resources, shall establish grades and types of certification for water pollution control system operators corresponding to the classification of water pollution control systems. The grades of certification shall be ranked so that a person holding a certification in the highest grade is thereby affirmed competent to operate water pollution control systems of that type in the highest classification and any water pollution control system of that type in a lower classification; a person holding a certification in the next highest grade is affirmed as competent to operate water pollution control systems in the next-to-the-highest classification of that type and any lower classification of that type; and in a like manner through the range of grades of certification and classification of water pollution control systems.

(b) No certificate shall be required under this Article to operate a conventional septic tank system. For purposes of this section, "conventional septic tank system" means a subsurface sanitary sewage system consisting of a settling tank and a subsurface disposal field without a pump or other appurtenances. (1969, c. 1059, s. 3; 1973, c. 1262, s. 23; 1977, c. 771, s. 4; 1979, c. 554, s. 2; 1989, c. 727, s. 218(24); 1991, c. 623, ss. 1, 5; 1997-443, s. 11A.119(a).)

§ 90A-39. Operator qualifications and examination.

The Commission, with the advice and assistance of the Secretary of Environment and Natural Resources, shall establish minimum requirements of education, experience, and knowledge for each grade of certification for water pollution control facility operators and shall establish procedures for receiving applications for certification, conducting examinations, and making investigations of applicants as may be necessary and appropriate to the end that prompt and fair consideration be given every applicant and that the water pollution control systems within the State may be adequately supervised by certified operators. (1969, c. 1059, s. 3; 1973, c. 1262, s. 23; 1977, c. 771, s. 4; 1979, c. 554, s. 2; 1989, c. 727, s. 218(25); 1991, c. 623, ss. 1, 6; 1997-443, s. 11A.119(a).)

§ 90A-40. Issuance of certificates.

(a)   An applicant, upon meeting satisfactorily the appropriate requirements, shall be issued a suitable certificate by the Commission designating the level of his competency. Once issued, a certificate shall be valid unless:

(1)   The certificate holder voluntarily surrenders the certificate to the Commission;

(2)   The certificate is replaced by one of a higher grade;

(3)   The certificate is revoked by the Commission for cause; or

(4)   The certificate holder fails to pay the annual renewal fee when due.

(b)   A certificate may be issued in an appropriate grade without examination to any person who is properly registered on the "National Association of Boards of Certification" reciprocal registry and who meets all other requirements of rules adopted under this Article.

(c)   Repealed by Session Laws 1987, c. 582, s. 2.

(d)   Repealed by Session Laws 1991, c. 623, s. 7.

(e) Temporary certificates in an appropriate grade may be issued without examination to any person employed as a water pollution control system operator when the Commission finds that the supply of certified operators or persons with training and experience necessary for certification is inadequate. Temporary certificates shall be valid for only one year, but may be renewed. Temporary certificates may be issued with such special conditions or requirements relating to the place of employment of the person holding the certificate, his supervision on a consulting or advisory basis, or other matters as the Commission may deem necessary to protect the public health and maintain the water quality standards of the receiving waters as assigned by the North Carolina Environmental Management Commission.

(f) Certificates in an appropriate grade and type may be issued without examination to water pollution control system operators who on 1 January 1992 hold certificates of competency issued under the voluntary certification program administered by the North Carolina Water Pollution Control Association. (1969, c. 1059, s. 3; 1973, c. 476, s. 128; c. 1262, s. 23; 1979, c. 554, ss. 2-4; 1987, c. 582, ss. 1, 2; 1991, c. 623, ss. 1, 7.)

§ 90A-41. Revocation of certificate.

The Commission, in accordance with the procedure set forth in Chapter 150B of the General Statutes, may suspend or revoke a certificate or may issue a written reprimand to an operator if it finds that the operator has practiced fraud or deception; that reasonable care, judgment, or the application of his knowledge or ability was not used in the performance of his duties; or that the operator is incompetent or unable to properly perform his duties. (1969, c. 1059, s. 3; 1973, c. 1331, s. 3; 1979, c. 554, s. 2; 1987, c. 827, s. 1; 1991, c. 623, ss. 1, 8.)

§ 90A-42. Fees.

(a) The Commission, in establishing procedures for implementing the requirements of this Article, shall impose the following schedule of fees:

(1) Examination including Certificate, $85.00;

(2) Temporary Certificate, $200.00;

(3) Temporary Certification Renewal, $300.00;

(4) Conditional Certificate, $75.00;

(5) Repealed by Session Laws 1987, c. 582, s. 3.

(6) Reciprocity Certificate, $100.00;

(6a) Voluntary Conversion Certificate, $50.00;

(7) Annual Renewal, $50.00;

(8) Replacement of Certificate, $20.00;

(9) Late Payment of Annual Renewal, $50.00 penalty in addition to all current and past due annual renewal fees plus one hundred dollars ($100.00) penalty per year for each year for which annual renewal fees were not paid prior to the current year; and

(10) Mailing List Charges - The Commission may provide mailing lists of certified water pollution control system operators and of water pollution control system operators to persons who request such lists. The charge for such lists shall be twenty-five dollars ($25.00) for each such list provided.

(b) The Water Pollution Control System Account is established as a nonreverting account within the Department. Fees collected under this section shall be credited to the Account and applied to the costs of administering this Article. (1969, c. 1059, s. 3; 1979, c. 554, s. 5; 1981, c. 361, ss. 1-4; 1987, c. 582, s. 3; 1989, c. 372, s. 7; 1989 (Reg. Sess., 1990), c. 850, s. 1; 1991, c. 623, ss. 1, 9; 1991 (Reg. Sess., 1992), c. 1039, s. 1; 1998-212, s. 29A.11(e); 2007-323, s. 30.3(c).)

§ 90A-43. Promotion of training and other powers.

The Commission and the Secretary of Environment and Natural Resources are authorized to take all necessary and appropriate steps in order to effectively and fairly achieve the purposes of this Article, including, but not limited to, the providing of training for water pollution control system operators and cooperating with educational institutions and private and public associations, persons, or corporations in the promotion of training for water pollution control system personnel. (1969, c. 1059, s. 3; 1973, c. 1262, s. 23; 1977, c. 771, s. 4; 1979, c. 554, s. 2; 1989, c. 727, s. 218(26); 1991, c. 623, ss. 1, 10; 1997-443, s. 11A.119(a).)

§ 90A-44. Certified operators required.

No person, firm, or corporation, municipal or private, owning or having control of a water pollution control system for which a certified operator is required under rules adopted by the Commission shall allow such system to be operated by any person who does not hold a currently valid certificate in an appropriate grade and type issued by the Commission. No person shall perform the duties of a water pollution control system operator in responsible charge without being duly certified under the provisions of this Article. No person shall perform the duties of a water pollution control system operator who has not paid all fees required under this Article. (1969, c. 1059, s. 3; 1979, c. 554, s. 2; 1991, c. 623, s. 11.)

§ 90A-45. Commercial water pollution control system operating firms.

(a) Any person, firm, or corporation, municipal or private, owning or having control of a water pollution control system may contract with a responsible commercial water pollution control system operating firm for operational and other services of that firm. Such firm shall designate an employee as the operator in responsible charge of the water pollution control system. Such employee and any other employees who have been duly certified under this Article shall be responsible for the total operation and maintenance of the water pollution control system. Commercial water pollution control system operating firms shall not be limited as to the number of systems, distance between systems, location of office or residence, or other internal management procedures.

(b) Any employee designated by the firm as operator in responsible charge must hold an appropriate certificate issued by the Commission and must comply with all of the requirements of this Article and rules adopted by the Commission.

(c) The Commission may adopt rules requiring that any commercial water pollution control system operating firm file an annual report with the Commission as to the operation of such system. (1983, c. 489, s. 1; 1991, c. 623, ss. 1, 12.)

§ 90A-46. Definitions.

The following definitions shall apply throughout this Article:

(1) "Commercial water pollution control system operating firm" means a person who contracts to operate a water pollution control system for any person who holds a permit for a water pollution control system, other than an employee of the permittee.

(2) "Commission" means the Water Pollution Control System Operators Certification Commission.

(3) "Waste" has the same meaning as in G.S. 143-213.

(4) "Operator" means a person who holds a currently valid certificate as a water pollution control system operator issued by the Commission under rules adopted pursuant to this Article.

(5) "Operator in responsible charge" means the person designated by a person owning or having control of a water pollution control system as the operator of record of the water pollution control system and who has primary responsibility for the operation of such system.

(6) "Water pollution control system" means a system for the collection, treatment, or disposal of waste for which a permit is required under rules adopted by either the North Carolina Environmental Management Commission or the Commission for Public Health. (1991, c. 623, s. 13; 2007-182, s. 2.)

§ 90A-46.1. Expiration and renewal of certificates; continuing education requirements.

A certificate issued under this Part expires on 31 December of the year in which it is issued or renewed. The Commission may establish minimum continuing education requirements that an applicant must meet to renew a certificate. The Commission shall renew a certificate if the applicant meets the continuing education requirement and pays the required renewal fee, any renewal fee in arrears, and any late application penalty. (1997-496, s. 1.)

Part 2. Certification of Animal Waste Management System Operators.

§ 90A-47. Purpose.

The purpose of this Part is to reduce nonpoint source pollution in order to protect the public health and to conserve and protect the quality of the State's water resources, to encourage the development and improvement of the State's agricultural land for the production of food and other agricultural products, and to require the examination of animal waste management system operators and certification of their competency to operate or supervise the operation of those systems. (1995 (Reg. Sess., 1996), c. 626, s. 6(b).)

§ 90A-47.1. Definitions.

(a) As used in this Part:

(1) "Animal waste" means liquid residuals resulting from an animal operation that are collected, treated, stored, or applied to the land through an animal waste management system.

(2) "Application" means laying, spreading on, irrigating, or injecting animal waste onto land.

(3) "Commission" means the Water Pollution Control System Operators Certification Commission.

(4) "Operator in charge" means a person who holds a currently valid certificate to operate an animal waste management system and who has primary responsibility for the operation of the system.

(5) "Owner" means the person who owns or controls the land used for agricultural purposes or the person's lessee or designee.

(b) The definitions set out in G.S. 143-215.10B, other than the definition of "animal waste", apply to this Part. (1995 (Reg. Sess., 1996), c. 626, s. 6(b).)

§ 90A-47.2. Certified operator in charge required; qualifications for certification.

(a) No owner or other person in control of an animal operation having an animal waste management system shall allow the system to be operated by a person who does not hold a valid certificate as an operator in charge of an animal waste management system issued by the Commission. No person shall perform the duties of an operator in charge of an animal waste management system without being certified under the provisions of this Part. Other persons may assist in the operation of an animal waste management system so long as they are directly supervised by an operator in charge who is certified under this Part.

(b) The owner or other person in control of an animal operation may contract with a certified animal waste management system operator in charge to provide for the operation of the animal waste management system at that animal operation. The Commission may adopt rules requiring that any certified animal waste management system operator in charge who contracts with one or more owners or other persons in control of an animal operation file an annual report with the Commission as to the operation of each system at which the services of the operator in charge are provided. (1995 (Reg. Sess., 1996), c. 626, s. 6(b).)

§ 90A-47.3. Qualifications for certification; training; examination.

(a) The Commission shall develop and administer a certification program for animal waste management system operators in charge that provides for receipt of applications, training and examination of applicants, and investigation of the qualifications of applicants.

(b) The Commission, in cooperation with the Division of Water Resources of the Department of Environment and Natural Resources, and the Cooperative Extension Service, shall develop and administer a training program for animal waste management system operators in charge. An applicant for initial certification shall complete 10 hours of classroom instruction prior to taking the examination. In order to remain certified, an animal waste management system operator in charge shall complete six hours of approved additional training during each three-year period following initial certification. A certified animal waste management system operator in charge who fails to complete approved additional training within 30 days of the end of the three-year period shall take and pass the examination for certification in order to renew the certificate. (1995 (Reg. Sess., 1996), c. 626, s. 6(b); 1996, 2nd Ex. Sess., c. 18, s. 27.34(c); 1997-443, s. 11A.119(a); 2013-413, s. 57(c).)

§ 90A-47.4. Fees; certificate renewals.

(a) An applicant for certification under this Part shall pay a fee of twenty-five dollars ($25.00) for the examination and the certificate.

(b) The certificate shall be renewed annually upon payment of a renewal fee of ten dollars ($10.00). A certificate holder who fails to renew the certificate and pay the renewal fee within 30 days of its expiration shall be required to take and pass the examination for certification in order to renew the certificate. (1995 (Reg. Sess., 1996), c. 626, s. 6(b); 1998-212, s. 29A.11(f).)

§ 90A-47.5. Suspension; revocation of certificate.

(a) The Commission, in accordance with the provisions of Chapter 150B of the General Statutes, may suspend or revoke the certificate of any operator in charge who:

(1) Engages in fraud or deceit in obtaining certification.

(2) Fails to exercise reasonable care, judgment, or use of the operator's knowledge and ability in the performance of the duties of an operator in charge.

(3) Is incompetent or otherwise unable to properly perform the duties of an operator in charge.

(b) In addition to revocation of a certificate, the Commission may levy a civil penalty, not to exceed one thousand dollars ($1,000) per violation, for willful violation of the requirements of this Part.

The clear proceeds of civil penalties levied pursuant to this subsection shall be remitted to the Civil Penalty and Forfeiture Fund in accordance with G.S. 115C-457.2. (1995 (Reg. Sess., 1996), c. 626, s. 6(b); 1998-215, s. 46.)

§ 90A-47.6. Rules.

The Commission shall adopt rules to implement the provisions of this Part. (1995 (Reg. Sess., 1996), c. 626, s. 6(b).)

§ 90A-48. Reserved for future codification purposes.

§ 90A-49. Reserved for future codification purposes.

Article 4.

Registrations of Environmental Health Specialists.

§ 90A-50. State Board of Environmental Health Specialist Examiners.

(a) There is hereby created a State Board of Environmental Health Specialist Examiners to register qualified environmental health specialists to practice within the State. Each registered sanitarian and registered sanitarian intern shall be a registered environmental health specialist or a registered environmental health specialist intern as applicable.

(b) It is the sole purpose of this Article to safeguard the health, safety, and general welfare of the public from adverse environmental factors and to register those environmental health professionals practicing as registered environmental health specialists or registered environmental health specialist interns who are qualified by education, training, and experience to work in the public sector in the field of environmental health within the scope of practice as defined in this

Article. (1959, c. 1271, s. 2; 1973, c. 476, s. 128; 1981 (Reg. Sess., 1982), c. 1274, s. 2; 2009-443, s. 1(b).)

§ 90A-51. Definitions.

The words and phrases defined below shall when used in this Article have the following meaning unless the context clearly indicates otherwise:

(1) "Board" means the Board of Environmental Health Specialist Examiners.

(2) "Certificate of registration" means a document issued by the Board as evidence of registration and qualification to practice as a registered environmental health specialist or a registered environmental health specialist intern under this Article. The certificate shall bear the designation "Registered Environmental Health Specialist" or "Registered Environmental Health Specialist Intern" and show the name of the person, date of issue, serial number, seal, and signatures of the members of the Board.

(2a) "Environmental health practice" means the provision of environmental health services, including administration, organization, management, education, enforcement, and consultation regarding environmental health services provided to or for the public. These services are offered to prevent environmental hazards and promote and protect the health of the public in the following areas: food, lodging, and institutional sanitation; on-site wastewater treatment and disposal; public swimming pool sanitation; childhood lead poisoning prevention; well permitting and inspection; tattoo parlor sanitation; and all other areas of environmental health requiring the delegation of authority by the Division of Public Health of the Department of Health and Human Services to State and local environmental health professionals to enforce rules adopted by the Commission for Public Health. The definition also includes local environmental health professionals enforcing rules of local boards of health for on-site wastewater systems and wells.

(2b) "Environmental health specialist" means a public health professional who meets the educational requirements under this Article and has attained specialized training and acceptable environmental health field experience effectively to plan, organize, manage, provide, execute, and evaluate one or more of the many diverse elements comprising the field of environmental health practice.

(3) Repealed by Session Laws 2009-443, s. 2, effective August 7, 2009.

(4) "Registered environmental health specialist" means an environmental health specialist registered in accordance with the provisions of this Article.

For purposes of this Article the following are not included within the definition of "registered environmental health specialist" unless the person is working as an environmental health specialist:

a. A person teaching, lecturing, or engaging in research.

b. A person who is a sanitary engineer, public health engineer, public health engineering assistant, registered professional engineer, industrial hygienist, health physicist, chemist, epidemiologist, toxicologist, geologist, hydrogeologist, waste management specialist, or soil scientist.

c. A public health officer or public health department director.

d. A person who holds a North Carolina license to practice medicine, veterinary medicine, or nursing.

e. Laboratory personnel when performing or supervising the performance of sanitation related laboratory functions.

(5) "Registered environmental health specialist intern" means a person who possesses the necessary educational qualifications as prescribed in G.S. 90A-53, but who has not completed the experience and specialized training requirements in the field of public health sanitation as required for registration. (1959, c. 1271, s. 1; 1981 (Reg. Sess., 1982), c. 1274, s. 2; 1989, c. 545, s. 1; 2009-443, s. 2; 2011-145, s. 13.3(ii).)

§ 90A-52. Practice without certificate unlawful.

(a) In order to safeguard life, health and the environment, it shall be unlawful for any person to practice as an environmental health specialist or an environmental health specialist intern in the State of North Carolina or use the title "registered environmental health specialist" or "registered environmental health specialist intern" unless the person shall have obtained a certificate of registration from the Board. No person shall offer services as a registered environmental health specialist or registered environmental health specialist intern or use, assume or advertise in any way any title or description tending to convey the impression that the person is a registered environmental health specialist or registered environmental health specialist intern unless the person is the holder of a current certificate of registration issued by the Board.

(b)   Notwithstanding the provisions of subsection (a) of this section, a person may practice as an environmental health specialist intern for a period not to exceed three years from the date of the initial registration, provided the person has obtained a temporary certificate of registration from the Board. (1959, c. 1271, s. 12; 1981 (Reg. Sess., 1982), c. 1274, s. 2; 2009-443, s. 3.)

§ 90A-53. Qualifications and examination for registration as an environmental health specialist or environmental health specialist intern.

(a)   The Board shall issue a certificate to a qualified person as a registered environmental health specialist or a registered environmental health specialist intern. A certificate as a registered environmental health specialist or a registered environmental health specialist intern shall be issued to any person upon the Board's determination that the person:

(1)   Has made application to the Board on a form prescribed by the Board and paid a fee not to exceed one hundred dollars ($100.00);

(2)   Is of good moral and ethical character and has signed an agreement to adhere to the Code of Ethics adopted by the Board;

(3)   Meets any of the following combinations of education and practice experience standards:

a.   Graduated from a baccalaureate or postgraduate degree program that is accredited by the National Environmental Health Science and Protection Accreditation Council (EHAC) and has one or more years of experience in the field of environmental health practice; or

b.   Graduated from a baccalaureate or postgraduate degree program that is accredited by an accrediting organization recognized by the United States Department of Education, Council for Higher Education Accreditation (CHEA) and meets both of the following:

1. Earned a minimum of 30 semester hours or its equivalent in the physical or biological sciences; and

2. Has two or more years of experience in the field of environmental health practice.

c. Graduated from a baccalaureate program rated as acceptable by the Board and meets both of the following:

1. Earned a minimum of 30 semester hours or its equivalent in the physical or biological sciences; and

2. Has two or more years of experience in the field of environmental health practice.

(4) Has satisfactorily completed a course in specialized instruction and training approved by the Board in the practice of environmental health;

(5) Repealed by Session Laws 2009-443, s. 4, effective August 7, 2009.

(6) Has passed an examination administered by the Board designed to test for competence in the subject matters of environmental health sanitation. The examination shall be in a form prescribed by the Board and may be oral, written, or both. The examination for applicants shall be held annually or more frequently as the Board may by rule prescribe, at a time and place to be determined by the Board. A person shall not be registered if such person fails to meet the minimum grade requirements for examination specified by the Board. Failure to pass an examination shall not prohibit such person from being examined at subsequent times and places as specified by the Board; and

(7) Has paid a fee set by the Board not to exceed the cost of purchasing the examination and an administrative fee not to exceed one hundred fifty dollars ($150.00).

(b) The Board may issue a certificate to a person serving as a registered environmental health specialist intern without the person meeting the full requirements for experience of a registered environmental health specialist for a period not to exceed three years from the date of initial registration as a registered environmental health specialist intern, provided, the person meets the educational requirements in G.S. 90A-53 and is in the field of environmental health practice. (1959, c. 1271, s. 6; 1981 (Reg. Sess., 1982), c. 1274, s. 2; 1989, c. 545, s. 2; 1993, c. 233, ss. 1-3; 2009-443, s. 4.)

§ 90A-54: Repealed by Session Laws 2009-443, s. 5, effective August 7, 2009.

§ 90A-55. State Board of Environmental Health Specialist Examiners; appointment and term of office.

(a) Board Membership. - The Board shall consist of 12 members who shall serve staggered terms: the Secretary of Health and Human Services, or the Secretary's duly authorized representative, one public-spirited citizen, one environmental sanitation educator from an accredited college or university, one local health director, a representative of the Division of Public Health of the Department of Health and Human Services, and seven practicing environmental health specialists who qualify by education and experience for registration under this Article, six of whom shall represent the Western, Piedmont, and Eastern Regions of the State as described more specifically in the rules adopted by the Board.

(b) Term of Office. - Each member of the State Board of Environmental Health Specialist Examiners shall be appointed by the Governor for a term of four years. As the term of each current member expires, the Governor shall appoint a successor in accordance with the provisions of this section. If a vacancy occurs on the Board for any other reason than the expiration of a member's term, the Governor shall appoint a successor for the remainder of the unexpired term. No person shall serve as a member of the Board for more than two consecutive four-year terms.

(c) The Environmental Health Section of the North Carolina Public Health Association, Inc., shall submit a recommended list of Board member candidates to the Governor for the Governor's consideration in appointments, except for the two representatives of the Department of Health and Human Services recommended by the Secretary of Health and Human Services and the local health director recommended by the North Carolina Local Health Directors Association.

(d) The Governor may remove an appointee member for misconduct in office, incompetency, neglect of duty, or other sufficient cause. (1959, c. 1271, s. 2; 1973, c. 476, s. 128; 1981 (Reg. Sess., 1982), c. 1274, s. 2; 1989, c. 727,

s. 23; 1997-443, s. 11A.32; 2005-386, s. 1.1; 2009-443, s. 6; 2011-145, s. 13.3(jj), (kk).)

§ 90A-56. Compensation of Board members; expenses; employees.

Members of the Board may receive compensation and be reimbursed for travel expenses in accordance with G.S. 93B-5. Notwithstanding G.S. 93B-5(a), the per diem for eligible Board members shall not exceed fifty dollars ($50.00). The Board may employ necessary personnel for the performance of its functions and fix the compensation therefor, within the limits of funds available to the Board. The total expenses of the administration of this Article shall not exceed the total income therefrom and none of the expenses of said Board or the compensation or expenses of any officer thereof or any employee shall ever be paid or payable out of the treasury of the State of North Carolina; and neither the Board nor any officer or employee thereof shall have any power or authority to make or incur any expense, debt, or other financial obligation binding upon the State of North Carolina. (1981 (Reg. Sess., 1982), c. 1274, s. 2; 1991 (Reg. Sess., 1992), c. 1011, s. 5; 2009-443, s. 7.)

§ 90A-57. Election of officers; meetings; regulations.

(a) The Board shall annually elect a chair, vice-chair, and a secretary-treasurer from among its membership. The officers may serve more than one term. The Board shall meet annually in the City of Raleigh, at a time set by the Board, and it may hold additional meetings and conduct business at any place in the State. Seven members of the Board shall constitute a quorum to do business. The Board may designate any member to conduct any proceeding, hearing, or investigation necessary to its purpose, but any final action requires a quorum of the Board. The Board is authorized to adopt such rules and regulations as may be necessary for the efficient operation of the Board.

(b) The Board shall have an official seal and each member shall be empowered to administer oaths in taking of testimony upon any matters pertaining to the function of the Board. (1959, c. 1271, s. 3; 1981 (Reg. Sess., 1982), c. 1274, s. 2; 2009-443, s. 8.)

§ 90A-58. Applicability of Chapter 93B.

The Board shall be subject to the provisions of Chapter 93B of the General Statutes of North Carolina. (1959, c. 1271, s. 5; 1981 (Reg. Sess., 1982), c. 1274, s. 2.)

§ 90A-59. Record of proceedings; register of applications; registry of registered environmental health specialists and environmental health specialist interns.

(a)   The Board shall keep a record of its proceedings.

(b)   The Board shall maintain records for registration, which shall include:

(1)   The place of residence, name and age of each applicant;

(2)   The name and address of the employer of each applicant;

(3)   The date of application;

(3a)   The date of employment;

(4)   Complete information of educational and experience qualifications;

(4a)   A signed Code of Ethics;

(5)   The action taken by the Board;

(6)   The serial number of the certificate of registration issued to the applicant;

(7)   The date on which the Board reviewed and acted upon the application;

(7a)   Information on continuing education required to maintain registration; and

(8)   Such other pertinent information as may be deemed necessary by the Board.

(c) The Board shall maintain a current registry of all environmental health specialists and environmental health specialist interns in the State of North Carolina that have been registered in accordance with the provisions of this Article.

(d) Records of the Board are public records as defined in Chapter 132 of the General Statutes of North Carolina. However, college transcripts, examinations, and medical information submitted to the Board shall not be considered public records. (1981 (Reg. Sess., 1982), c. 1274, s. 2; 1987, c. 282, s. 11; 2009-443, s. 9.)

§ 90A-60: Repealed by Session Laws 2009-443, s. 10, effective August 7, 2009.

§ 90A-61: Repealed by Session Laws 2009-443, s. 10, effective August 7, 2009.

§ 90A-62. Certification and registration of environmental health specialists registered in other states.

The Board may, without examination, grant a certificate as a registered environmental health specialist to any person who at the time of application, is registered as a registered environmental health specialist by a similar board of another state, district or territory whose standards are determined to be acceptable to the Board and comply with rules adopted by the Board. A fee to be determined by the Board and not to exceed one hundred dollars ($100.00) shall be paid by the applicant to the Board for the issuance of a certificate under the provisions of this section. (1959, c. 1271, s. 9; 1981 (Reg. Sess., 1982), c. 1274, s. 2; 2009-443, s. 11.)

§ 90A-63. Renewal of certificates.

(a) A certificate as a registered environmental health specialist or registered environmental health specialist intern issued pursuant to the provisions of this Article will expire on the thirty-first day of December of the current year and must be renewed annually on or before the first day of January. Each application for renewal must be accompanied by a renewal fee to be determined by the Board, but not to exceed one hundred twenty-five dollars ($125.00). However, for renewals postmarked before January 1 of each year, the renewal fee shall not exceed one hundred dollars ($100.00).

(b) Registrations expired for failure to pay renewal fees may be reinstated under the rules and regulations adopted by the Board.

(c) A registered environmental health specialist shall complete any continuing education requirements specified by the Board for renewal of a certificate. (1959, c. 1271, s. 10; 1981 (Reg. Sess., 1982), c. 1274, s. 2; 1989, c. 545, s. 3; 2009-443, s. 12.)

§ 90A-64. Suspensions and revocations of certificates.

(a) The Board shall have the power to refuse to grant, or may suspend or revoke, any certificate issued under provisions of this Article for any of the causes hereafter enumerated, as determined by the Board:

(1) Fraud, deceit, or perjury in obtaining registration under the provisions of this Article;

(2) Inability to practice with reasonable skill and safety due to drunkenness or excessive use of alcohol, drugs, or chemicals;

(3) Unprofessional conduct, including a material departure from or failure to conform to the standards of acceptable and prevailing practice or the ethics of the profession;

(4) Defrauding the public or attempting to do so;

(5) Failing to renew certificate as required;

(6) Dishonesty;

(7) Incompetency;

(8) Inexcusable neglect of duty;

(9) Conviction in any court of a crime involving moral turpitude or conviction of a felony;

(10) Failing to adhere to the Code of Ethics; or

(11) Failing to meet qualifications for renewal.

(a1) A registered environmental health specialist or registered environmental health specialist intern who is convicted of a felony or a crime of moral turpitude shall report the conviction to the Board within 30 days from the date of the conviction. A felony conviction shall result in the automatic suspension of a certificate issued by the Board for 60 days until further action is taken by the Board. The Board shall immediately begin the hearing process in accordance with Article 3A of Chapter 150B of the General Statutes. Nothing in this section shall preclude the Board from taking further action.

(b) The procedure to be followed by the Board when refusing to allow an applicant to take an examination, or revoking or suspending a certificate issued under the provisions of this Article, shall be in accordance with the provisions of Chapter 150B of the General Statutes of North Carolina.

(c) The Board may conduct investigations for any complaints alleged or upon its own motion for any allegations or causes for disciplinary action under subsection (a) of this section. The Board may subpoena individuals and records to determine if action is necessary to enforce this Article.

(d) The Board and its members, individually, or its staff shall not be held liable for any civil or criminal proceeding when exercising in good faith its powers and duties authorized under the provisions of this Article. (1959, c. 1271, s. 11; 1973, c. 1331, s. 3; 1981 (Reg. Sess., 1982), c. 1274, s. 2; 1987, c. 827, s. 1; 2009-443, s. 13.)

§ 90A-65. Representing oneself as a registered environmental health specialist or registered environmental health specialist intern.

A holder of a current certificate of registration may append to his or her name the letters, "R.E.H.S." or "R.E.H.S.I." (1959, c. 1271, s. 12; 1981 (Reg. Sess., 1982), c. 1274, s. 2; 2009-443, s. 14.)

§ 90A-66. Violations; penalty; injunction.

Any person violating any of the provisions of this Article or of the rules and regulations adopted by the Board shall be guilty of a Class 1 misdemeanor. The Board may appear in its own name in the superior courts in an action for injunctive relief to prevent violation of this Article and the superior courts shall have power to grant such injunctions regardless of whether criminal prosecution has been or may be instituted as a result of such violations. Actions under this section shall be commenced in the superior court district or set of districts as defined in G.S. 7A-41.1 in which the respondent resides or has his principal place of business or in which the alleged acts occurred. (1959, c. 1271, s. 13; 1981 (Reg. Sess., 1982), c. 1274, s. 2; 1987 (Reg. Sess., 1988), c. 1037, s. 104; 1993, c. 539, s. 653; 1994, Ex. Sess., c. 24, s. 14(c).)

§ 90A-67. Code of Ethics.

The Board shall prepare and adopt, by rule, a Code of Ethics to be made available in writing to all registered environmental health specialists and registered environmental health specialist interns and each applicant for registration under this Article. All registered environmental health specialists and registered environmental health specialist interns shall adhere to the Code of Ethics adopted by the Board. Publication of the Code of Ethics shall serve as due notice to all certificate holders of its contents. (2009-443, s. 15.)

§ 90A-68. Reserved for future codification purposes.

§ 90A-69. Reserved for future codification purposes.

Article 5.

Certification of On-Site Wastewater Contractors and Inspectors.

§ 90A-70. Purpose.

It is the purpose of this Article to protect the environment and public health, safety, and welfare by ensuring the integrity and competence of on-site wastewater contractors and inspectors; to require the examination of on-site wastewater contractors and inspectors and the certification of their competency to supervise or conduct the construction, installation, repair, or inspection of on-site wastewater systems; to establish minimum standards for ethical conduct, responsibility, training, experience, and continuing education for on-site wastewater system contractors and inspectors; and to provide appropriate enforcement procedures for rules adopted by the North Carolina On-Site Wastewater Contractors and Inspectors Certification Board. (2006-82, s. 1.)

§ 90A-71. Definitions.

The following definitions apply in this Article:

(1) "Board" means the North Carolina On-Site Wastewater Contractors and Inspectors Certification Board.

(2) "Contractor" means a person who constructs, installs, or repairs, or offers to construct, install, or repair an on-site wastewater system in the State.

(3) "Conventional wastewater system" has the same meaning as in G.S. 130A-343(a)(3).

(4) "Department" means the Department of Health and Human Services.

(4a) "Inspection" means an examination of an on-site wastewater system permitted under the provisions of Article 11 of Chapter 130A of the General Statutes that satisfies all of the following criteria:

a. Is requested by a lending institution, realtor, prospective homebuyer, or other impacted party as a condition of sale, refinancing, or transfer of title.

b. Meets the minimum requirements established by the Board.

(5) "Inspector" means a person who conducts an inspection in accordance with rules adopted by the Board.

(6) "On-site wastewater system" means any wastewater system permitted under the provisions of Article 11 of Chapter 130A of the General Statutes that does not discharge to a treatment facility or the surface waters of the State.

(7) "Person" means all persons, including individuals, firms, partnerships, associations, public or private institutions, municipalities, or political subdivisions, governmental agencies, or private or public corporations organized and existing under the laws of this State or any other state or country.

(8) "Wastewater treatment facility" means a mechanical or chemical treatment facility serving a site with multiple wastewater sources. (2006-82, s. 1; 2010-31, s. 13.2(e); 2011-145, s. 13.3(ll).)

§ 90A-72. Certification required; applicability.

(a) Certification Required. - No person shall construct, install, or repair or offer to construct, install, or repair an on-site wastewater system permitted under Article 11 of Chapter 130A of the General Statutes without being certified as a contractor at the required level of certification for the specified system. No person shall conduct an inspection or offer to conduct an inspection of an on-site wastewater system as permitted under Article 11 of Chapter 130A of the General Statutes without being certified in accordance with the provisions of this Article.

(b) Applicability. - This Article does not apply to the following:

(1) A person who is employed by a certified contractor or inspector in connection with the construction, installation, repair, or inspection of an on-site wastewater system performed under the direct and personal supervision of the certified contractor or inspector in charge.

(2) A person who constructs, installs, or repairs an on-site wastewater system described as a single septic tank with a gravity-fed gravel trench dispersal media when located on land owned by that person and that is intended solely for use by that person and members of that person's immediate family who reside in the same dwelling.

(3) A person licensed under Article 1 of Chapter 87 of the General Statutes who constructs or installs an on-site wastewater system ancillary to the building being constructed or who provides corrective services and labor for an on-site wastewater system ancillary to the building being constructed.

(4) A person who is certified by the Water Pollution Control System Operators Certification Commission and contracted to provide necessary operation and maintenance on the permitted on-site wastewater system.

(5) A person permitted under Article 21 of Chapter 143 of the General Statutes who is constructing a water pollution control facility necessary to comply with the terms and conditions of a National Pollutant Discharge Elimination System (NPDES) permit.

(6) A person licensed under Article 1 of Chapter 87 of the General Statutes as a licensed public utilities contractor who is installing or expanding a wastewater treatment facility, including a collection system, designed by a registered professional engineer.

(7) A plumbing contractor licensed under Article 2 of Chapter 87 of the General Statutes, so long as the plumber is not performing plumbing work that includes the installation or repair of a septic tank or similar depository, or lines or appurtenances downstream from the point where the house or building sewer lines from the plumbing system meet the septic tank or similar depository.

(8) A person employed by the Department, a local health department, or a local health district, when conducting a regulatory inspection of an on-site wastewater system for purposes of determining compliance. (2006-82, s. 1; 2010-31, s. 13.2(f).)

§ 90A-73. Creation and membership of the Board.

(a) Creation and Appointments. - There is created the North Carolina On-Site Wastewater Contractors and Inspectors Certification Board. The Board shall consist of nine members appointed to three-year terms as follows:

(1) One member appointed by the Governor who, at the time of appointment, is engaged in the construction, installation, repair, or inspection of

on-site wastewater systems, to a term that expires on 1 July of years that precede by one year those years that are evenly divisible by three.

(2) One member appointed by the Governor who, at the time of appointment, is a certified water pollution control system operator pursuant to Article 3 of this Chapter, to a term that expires on 1 July of years evenly divisible by three.

(3) One member appointed by the Governor who is a registered professional engineer licensed under Chapter 89C of the General Statutes and whose work experience includes the design of on-site wastewater systems to a term that expires on 1 July of years that follow by one year those years that are evenly divisible by three.

(4) One member appointed by the General Assembly upon recommendation of the President Pro Tempore of the Senate who, at the time of appointment, is engaged in the construction, installation, repair, or inspection of on-site wastewater systems, to a term that expires on 1 July of years that follow by one year those years that are evenly divisible by three.

(5) One member appointed by the General Assembly upon recommendation of the President Pro Tempore of the Senate who, at the time of appointment, is engaged in the business of inspecting on-site wastewater systems, to a term that expires on 1 July of years that precede by one year those years that are evenly divisible by three.

(6) One member appointed by the General Assembly upon recommendation of the President Pro Tempore of the Senate upon the recommendation of the North Carolina Home Builders Association, to a term that expires on 1 July of years evenly divisible by three.

(7) One member appointed by the General Assembly upon recommendation of the Speaker of the House of Representatives who, at the time of appointment, is engaged in the construction, installation, repair, or inspection of on-site wastewater systems, to a term that expires on 1 July of years evenly divisible by three.

(8) One member appointed by the General Assembly upon recommendation of the Speaker of the House of Representatives who, at the time of appointment, is (i) employed as an environmental health specialist, and (ii) engaged primarily in the inspection and permitting of on-site wastewater

systems, to a term that expires on 1 July of years that follow by one year those years that are evenly divisible by three.

(9) One member appointed by the General Assembly upon recommendation of the Speaker of the House of Representatives who, at the time of appointment, is (i) employed by the North Carolina Cooperative Extension Service, and (ii) is knowledgeable in the area of on-site wastewater systems, to a term that expires on 1 July of years that precede by one year those years that are evenly divisible by three.

(b) Vacancies. - An appointment to fill a vacancy on the Commission created by the resignation, dismissal, disability, or death of a member shall be for the balance of the unexpired term. Vacancies in appointments made by the General Assembly shall be filled as provided in G.S. 120-122.

(c), (d) Repealed by Session Laws 2010-31, s. 13.2(h), effective July 1, 2010.

(e) Officers. - The Board shall elect a Chair from among its members. The Chair shall serve from the time of election until 30 June of the following year, or until a successor is elected.

(f) Compensation. - Board members who are State employees shall receive no per diem compensation for serving on the Board but shall be reimbursed for their expenses in accordance with G.S. 138-6. All other Board members shall receive per diem compensation and reimbursement in accordance with the compensation rate established in G.S. 93B-5.

(g) Quorum. - A majority of the members of the Board constitutes a quorum for the transaction of business.

(h) Meetings. - The Board shall meet at least twice each year and may hold special meetings at the call of the Chair or a majority of the members of the Board.

(i) Repealed by Session Laws 2010-31, s. 13.2(h), effective July 1, 2010. (2006-82, s. 1; 2010-31, ss. 13.2(g), (h); 2011-145, s. 13.3(mm).)

§ 90A-74. Powers and duties of the Board.

The Board shall have the following general powers and duties:

(1) To adopt rules in the manner prescribed by Chapter 150B of the General Statutes to govern its actions and to implement the provisions of this Article.

(2) To determine the eligibility requirements for persons seeking certification pursuant to this Article.

(3) To establish grade levels of certifications based on design capacity, complexity, projected costs, and other features of approved on-site wastewater systems.

(4) To develop and administer examinations for specific grade levels of certification as approved by the Board. The Board may approve applications by recognized associations for certification of its members after a review of the requirements of the association to ensure that they are equivalent to the requirements of the Board.

(5) To issue, renew, deny, restrict, suspend, or revoke certifications and to carry out any of the other actions authorized by this Article.

(6) To establish, publish, and enforce rules of professional conduct of persons who are certified pursuant to this Article.

(7) To maintain a record of all proceedings and make available to persons certified under this Article, and to other concerned parties, an annual report of all Board action.

(8) To establish reasonable fees for application, certification, and renewal, and other services provided by the Board.

(9) To conduct investigations to determine whether violations of this Article or grounds for disciplining persons certified under this Article exist.

(10) To adopt a common seal containing the name of the Board for use on all certificates and official reports issued by the Board.

(10a) To employ staff necessary to carry out the provisions of this Article and to determine the compensation, duties, and other terms and conditions of employment of its staff.

(10b) To employ professional, clerical, investigative, or special personnel necessary to carry out the provisions of this Article.

(11) To conduct other services necessary to carry out the purposes of this Article. (2006-82, s. 1; 2010-31, s. 13.2(i).)

§ 90A-75. Expenses and fees.

(a) Expenses. - All salaries, compensation, and expenses incurred or allowed for the purposes of carrying out this Article shall be paid by the Board exclusively out of the funds received by the Board as authorized by this Article. No salary, expense, or other obligations of the Board may be charged against the General Fund of the State. Neither the Board nor any of its members or employees may incur any expense, debt, or financial obligation binding upon the State.

(b) Contributions. - The Board may accept grants, contributions, devises, and gifts that shall be kept in the same account as the funds deposited in accordance with this Article and other provisions of the law.

(c) Fees. - All fees shall be established in rules adopted by the Board. The Board shall establish fees sufficient to pay the costs of administering this Article, but in no event shall the Board charge a fee at an annual rate in excess of the following:

(1)	Application for basic certification	$150.00
(2)	Application for each grade level	$50.00
(3)	Certification renewal	$100.00
(4)	Reinstatement of revoked or suspended Certification	$500.00
(5)	Application for on-site wastewater system inspector	$200.00.

(c1) Use of Fees. - All fees collected pursuant to this Article shall be held by the Board and used by the Board for the sole purpose of administering this Article.

(d) Audit. - The Board is subject to the oversight of the State Auditor under Article 5A of Chapter 147 of the General Statutes. (2006-82, s. 1; 2010-31, s. 13.2(j); 2011-284, s. 66.)

§ 90A-76: Repealed by Session Laws 2010-31, s. 13.2(k), effective July 1, 2010.

§ 90A-77. Certification requirements.

(a) Certification. - The Board shall issue a certificate of the appropriate grade level to an applicant who satisfies all of the following conditions:

(1) Is at least 18 years of age.

(2) Submits a properly completed application to the Board.

(3) Completes the basic on-site wastewater education program approved by the Board for the specific grade level.

(4) Repealed by Session Laws 2010-31, s. 13.2(l), effective July 1, 2010.

(5) Completes any additional training program designed by the Board specific to the grade level for which the applicant is applying.

(6) Pays the applicable fees set by the Board for the particular application and grade level.

(7) For the specific grade level, as determined by the Board, passes a written or oral examination that tests the applicant's proficiency in all of the following areas:

a. Principles of public and environmental health associated with on-site wastewater systems.

b. Principles of construction and safety.

c. Technical and practical knowledge of on-site wastewater systems typical to the specified grade level.

d. Laws and rules related to the installation, construction, repair, or inspection of the specified on-site wastewater system.

(b) Location of Examinations. - The Board shall provide a minimum of three examinations each year; one each in the eastern, central, and western regions of the State.

(c) Approval of Certification Programs. - The Board may issue a certificate at the appropriate grade level to an applicant who has completed an approved training or continuing education program.

(d) No Degree Required. - An applicant shall not be required to hold or obtain an educational diploma or degree to obtain a certificate. An applicant that meets all the conditions for certification except for passage of the Board examination may take the examination on three successive occasions without having to file for a new application, pay an additional application fee, or repeat any applicable training program. If the applicant fails to pass the Board examination on three successive occasions, the applicant must reapply to the Board, pay an additional application fee, and repeat the training program.

(e) Certificate. - The certification shall show the full name of the certificate holder. The certificate shall provide a unique identification number and shall be signed by the Chair. Issuance of the certificate by the Board shall be prima facie evidence that the person named therein is entitled to all the rights and privileges of a certified contractor or inspector, at the grade level specified on the certificate, while the certificate remains in effect.

(f) Replacement Certificate. - A new certificate to replace one lost, destroyed, or mutilated shall be issued subject to rules adopted by the Board and with the payment of a fee set by the Board. The fee for a duplicate or replacement certificate shall not exceed twenty-five dollars ($25.00). (2006-82, s. 1; 2010-31, s. 13.2(l).)

§ 90A-78. Certification renewal.

(a) Renewal. - All certifications shall expire at intervals determined by the Board unless they are renewed. In no event may the interval determined by the Board be less than one year. To renew a certification, a contractor or inspector must meet all of the following conditions:

(1) Submit an application for renewal on the form prescribed by the Board.

(2) Meet the continuing education requirements prescribed by the Board.

(3) Pay the certification renewal fee.

(b) Late Fee. - A contractor or inspector with an expired certificate may renew the certification within 90 days of its expiration upon payment of a late fee set by the Board. The late fee shall not exceed twenty-five dollars ($25.00). If a certification is not renewed within 90 days of its expiration, the certification shall not be renewed, and the holder must apply for a new certificate. (2006-82, s. 1.)

§ 90A-79. Continuing education.

(a) Requirements. - The Board shall require continuing education as a condition of certification and renewal. The Board shall determine the number of hours, based on grade levels applied for, up to a maximum of 12 hours per year, and the subject material for the specified grade level. The Board shall maintain records of continuing education coursework successfully completed by each certified contractor or inspector.

(b) Approval of Continuing Education Programs. - The Board may approve a continuing education program or course if the Board finds that the program or course provides useful educational information or experience that will enhance the construction, installation, repair, or inspection of on-site wastewater systems. The Board may develop and offer continuing education programs. (2006-82, s. 1.)

§ 90A-80. Investigation of complaints.

(a) Misconduct. - A person may refer to the Board charges of fraud, deceit, negligence, incompetence, or misconduct against any certified contractor or inspector. The charges shall be in writing and sworn to by the complainant and submitted to the Board. These charges, unless dismissed without a hearing by the Board as unfounded or trivial, shall be heard and determined by the Board in accordance with the provisions of Chapter 150B of the General Statutes. An association that receives professional recognition of its own certification process by the Board shall be responsible for the conduct and competency of its members.

(b) Records. - The Board shall establish and maintain detailed records regarding complaints concerning each certified contractor or inspector. The records shall include those certified by recognized associations. The records shall also detail the levels of certification held by each contractor or inspector.

(c) Notification. - The Board shall provide local health departments with notification of changes in certifications, complaints, suspensions, or reinstatements under this Article. (2006-82, s. 1.)

§ 90A-81. Remedies.

(a) Denial, Suspension, and Revocation of Certification. - The Board may deny, suspend, or revoke a certificate under this Article for:

(1) A violation of this Article or a rule of the Board.

(2) The use of fraud or deceit in obtaining or renewing a certificate.

(3) Any act of gross negligence, incompetence, or misconduct in the construction, installation, repair, or inspection of an on-site wastewater system.

(4) Failure to satisfactorily complete continuing education requirements prescribed by the Board.

(b) Arbitration. - The Board may establish a voluntary arbitration procedure to resolve complaints concerning a certified contractor or inspector or any work performed by a certified contractor or inspector, or conflicts involving any certified contractor or inspector and the Division of Public Health of the Department or a local health department.

(c) Injunction. - The Board may in its own name seek an injunction to restrain any person, firm, partnership, or corporation from violating the provisions of this Article or rules adopted by the Board. The Board may bring an action for an injunction in the superior court of any county in which the violator resides or the violator's principal place of business is located. In any proceedings for an injunction, it shall not be necessary to allege or prove either that an adequate remedy at law does not exist, or that substantial or irreparable damage would result from the continued violation. Members of the Board shall not be personally or professionally liable for any act or omission pursuant to this subsection. The Board shall not be required to post a bond in connection with any action to obtain an injunction.

(d) Offenses. - A person who commits any one or more of the following offenses is guilty of a Class 2 misdemeanor:

(1) Engages in or offers to engage in the construction, installation, repair, or inspection of an on-site wastewater system without the appropriate certificate for the grade level of on-site wastewater system.

(2) Gives false or forged evidence of any kind in obtaining a certificate.

(3) Falsely impersonates a certified contractor or inspector. (2006-82, s. 1; 2010-31, s. 13.2(m); 2011-145, s. 13.3(nn).)

Chapter 90B.

Social Worker Certification and Licensure Act.

§ 90B-1. Short title.

This Chapter shall be known as the "Social Worker Certification and Licensure Act." (1983, c. 495, s. 1; 1999-313, s. 1.)

§ 90B-2. Purpose.

Since the profession of social work significantly affects the lives of the people of this State, it is the purpose of this Chapter to protect the public by setting standards for qualification, training, and experience for those who seek to represent themselves to the public as certified social workers or licensed clinical social workers and by promoting high standards of professional performance for those engaged in the practice of social work. (1983, c. 495, s. 1; 1999-313, s. 1.)

§ 90B-3. Definitions.

The following definitions apply in this Chapter:

(1) Board. - The North Carolina Social Work Certification and Licensure Board.

(2) Repealed by Session Laws 2013-410, s. 8, effective August 23, 2013.

(3) Certified Master Social Worker. - A person who is certified under this Chapter to practice social work as a master social worker and is engaged in the practice of social work.

(4) Certified Social Work Manager. - A person who is certified under this Chapter to practice social work as a social work manager and is engaged in the practice of social work.

(5) Certified Social Worker. - A person who is certified under this Chapter to practice social work as a social worker and is engaged in the practice of social work.

(6) Clinical Social Work Practice. - The professional application of social work theory and methods to the biopsychosocial diagnosis, treatment, or prevention, of emotional and mental disorders. Practice includes, by whatever means of communications, the treatment of individuals, couples, families, and groups, including the use of psychotherapy and referrals to and collaboration with other health professionals when appropriate. Clinical social work practice shall not include the provision of supportive daily living services to persons with severe and persistent mental illness as defined in G.S. 122C-3(33a).

(6a) Licensed Clinical Social Worker. - A person who is competent to function independently, who holds himself or herself out to the public as a social worker, and who offers or provides clinical social work services or supervises others engaging in clinical social work practice.

(6b) Licensed Clinical Social Worker Associate. - A person issued an associate license to provide clinical social work services pursuant to G.S. 90B-7(f).

(7) Practice of Social Work. - To perform or offer to perform services, by whatever means of communications, for other people that involve the application of social work values, principles, and techniques in areas such as social work services, consultation and administration, and social work planning and research.

(8) Social Worker. - A person certified, licensed, or associate licensed by this Chapter or otherwise exempt under G.S. 90B-10. (1983, c. 495, s. 1; 1991, c. 732, s. 1; 1999-313, s. 1; 2007-379, s. 1; 2009-88, s. 1; 2012-72, s. 2; 2013-410, s. 8.)

§ 90B-4. Prohibitions.

(a) Except as otherwise provided in this Chapter, it is unlawful for any person who is not certified as a social worker, master social worker, or social work manager under this Chapter to represent himself or herself to be certified under this Chapter or hold himself or herself out to the public by any title or description denoting that he or she is certified under this Chapter.

(b) After January 1, 1992, except as otherwise provided in this Chapter, it is unlawful to engage in or offer to engage in the practice of clinical social work without first being licensed under this Chapter as a clinical social worker.

(c) Nothing herein shall prohibit school social workers who are certified by the State Board of Education from practicing school social work under the title "Certified School Social Worker." Except as provided for licensed clinical social workers, nothing herein shall be construed as prohibiting social workers who are not certified by the Board from practicing social work. Except as provided herein for licensed clinical social workers, no agency, institution, board, commission, bureau, department, division, council, member of the Council of State, or officer of the legislative, executive or judicial branches of State government or counties, cities, towns, villages, other municipal corporations, political subdivisions of the State, public authorities, private corporations created by act of the General Assembly or any firm or corporation receiving State funds shall require the obtaining or holding of any certificate issued under this Chapter or the taking of an examination held pursuant to this Chapter as a requirement for obtaining or continuing in employment.

(d)   Nothing herein shall authorize the practice of medicine as defined in Article 1 of this Chapter or the practice of psychology as defined in Article 18A of this Chapter. (1983, c. 495, s. 1; 1991, c. 732, s. 2; 1999-313, s. 1.)

§ 90B-5. North Carolina Social Work Certification and Licensure Board; appointments; terms; composition.

(a)   For the purpose of carrying out the provisions of this Chapter, there is hereby created the North Carolina Social Work Certification and Licensure Board which shall consist of seven members appointed by the Governor as follows:

(1)   At least two members of the Board shall be Certified Social Workers or Certified Master Social Workers, three members shall be Licensed Clinical Social Workers, and two members shall be appointed from the public at large. Composition of the Board as to the race and sex of its members shall reflect the composition of the population of the State of North Carolina.

(2)   At all times the Board shall include at least one member primarily engaged in social work education, at least one member primarily engaged in social work in the public sector, and at least one member primarily engaged in social work in the private sector.

(3)   All members of the Board shall be residents of the State of North Carolina, and with the exception of the public members, shall be certified or licensed by the Board under the provisions of this Chapter. Professional members of the Board must be actively engaged in the practice of social work or in the education and training of students in social work, and have been for at least three years prior to their appointment to the Board. Such activity during the two years preceding the appointment shall have occurred primarily in this State.

(b)   The Governor may only remove a member of the Board for neglect of duty, malfeasance, or conviction of a felony or other crime of moral turpitude.

(c) The term of office of each member of the Board shall be three years. No member shall serve more than two consecutive three-year terms. Each term of service on the Board shall expire on the 30th day of June of the year in which the term expires. As the term of a member expires, the Governor shall make the appointment for a full term, or, if a vacancy occurs for any other reason, for the remainder of the unexpired term.

(d) Members of the Board shall receive compensation for their services and reimbursement for expenses incurred in the performance of duties required by this Chapter, at the rates prescribed in G.S. 93B-5.

(e) The Board may employ, subject to the provisions of Chapter 126 of the General Statutes, the necessary personnel for the performance of its functions, and fix their compensation within the limits of funds available to the Board. (1983, c. 495, s. 1; 1991, c. 732, s. 3; 1999-313, s. 1.)

§ 90B-6. Functions and duties of the Board.

(a) The Board shall administer and enforce the provisions of this Chapter.

(b) The Board shall elect from its membership, a chairperson, a vice-chairperson, and secretary-treasurer, and adopt rules to govern its proceedings. A majority of the membership shall constitute a quorum for all Board meetings.

(c) The Board shall examine and pass on the qualifications of all applicants for certificates and licenses under this Chapter, and shall issue a certificate or license to each successful applicant therefor.

(d) The Board may adopt a seal which may be affixed to all certificates and licenses issued by the Board.

(e) The Board may authorize expenditures deemed necessary to carry out the provisions of this Chapter from the fees which it collects, but in no event shall expenditures exceed the revenues of the Board during any fiscal year. No State appropriations shall be subject to the administration of the Board.

(f) Repealed by Session Laws 1999-313, s. 1, effective July 1, 1999.

(g) The Board shall have the power to establish or approve study or training courses and to establish reasonable standards for certification, licensure, and renewal of certification and licensure, including the power to adopt or use examination materials and accreditation standards of the Council on Social Work Education or other recognized accrediting agency and the power to establish reasonable standards for continuing social work education; provided that for certificate and license renewal no examination shall be required; provided further, that the Board shall not have the power to withhold approval of study or training courses offered by a college or university having a social work program approved by the Council on Social Work Education.

(h) Subject to the provisions of Chapter 150B of the General Statutes, the Board shall have the power to adopt rules to carry out the purposes of this Chapter, including but not limited to the power to adopt ethical and disciplinary standards.

(i) The Board may order that any records concerning the practice of social work and relevant to a complaint received by the Board or an inquiry or investigation conducted by or on behalf of the Board shall be produced by the custodian of the records to the Board or for inspection and copying by representatives of or counsel to the Board. A social worker licensed by the Board or an agency employing a social worker licensed by the Board shall maintain records for a minimum of three years from the date the social worker terminates services to the client and the client services record is closed. A social worker certified or licensed by the Board shall cooperate fully and in a timely manner with the Board and its designated representatives in an inquiry or investigation of the records conducted by or on behalf of the Board.

(j) The Board shall have the power to employ or retain professional personnel, including legal counsel, subject to G.S. 114-2.3, or clerical or other special personnel deemed necessary to carry out the provisions of this Chapter. (1983, c. 495, s. 1; 1987, c. 827, s. 1; 1995, c. 344, s. 1; 1999-313, s. 1; 2005-129, s. 1; 2007-379, s. 2.)

§ 90B-6.1. Board general provisions.

The Board shall be subject to the administrative provisions of Chapter 93B of the General Statutes. (1983, c. 495, s. 1.)

§ 90B-6.2. Fees.
(a) The Board shall establish fees not exceeding the following amounts:

(1) All initial applications $200.00

(2) Examination   Cost plus an

    amount not to

    exceed $40.00

(3) Repeated examination or any

    additional examination   Cost plus an

    amount not to

    exceed $40.00

(4) Renewal applications 200.00

(5) Late fees for renewal 50.00

(6) Reinstatement   200.00

(7) Duplicate license   25.00

(8) Temporary certificate or license   25.00.

(b) Notwithstanding subdivision (a)(4) of this section, the Board may establish a graduated fee schedule for renewals that is based upon the applicant's level of certification or licensure. The Board may establish fees for the actual cost of duplication services, materials, and returned bank items. All fees derived from services provided by the Board under the provisions of this Chapter shall be nonrefundable. The Board shall maintain accounts of all receipts to the Board. (1999-313, s. 1.)

§ 90B-7. Titles and qualifications for certificates and licenses.

(a) Each person desiring to obtain a certificate or license from the Board shall make application to the Board upon such forms and in such manner as the Board shall prescribe, together with the required application fee established by the Board.

(b) The Board shall issue a certificate as "Certified Social Worker" to an applicant who meets the following qualifications:

(1) Has a bachelors degree in a social work program from a college or university having a social work program accredited or admitted to candidacy for accreditation by the Council on Social Work Education for undergraduate curricula.

(2) Has passed the Board examination for the certification of persons in this classification.

(c) The Board shall issue a certificate as "Certified Master Social Worker" to an applicant who meets the following qualifications:

(1) Has a masters or doctoral degree in a social work program from a college or university having a social work program approved by the Council on Social Work Education.

(2) Has passed the Board examination for the certification of persons in this classification.

(d) The Board shall issue a license as a "Licensed Clinical Social Worker" to an applicant who meets the following qualifications:

(1) Holds or qualifies for a current certificate as a Certified Master Social Worker.

(2) Shows to the satisfaction of the Board that he or she has had two years of clinical social work experience with appropriate supervision in the field of specialization in which the applicant will practice.

(3) Has passed the Board examination for the certification of persons in this licensure.

(e) The Board shall issue a certificate as a "Certified Social Work Manager" to an applicant who meets the following qualifications:

(1) Holds or qualifies for a current certificate as a Certified Social Worker.

(2) Shows to the satisfaction of the Board that he or she has had two years of experience in an administrative setting with appropriate supervision and training.

(3) Has passed the Board examination for the certification of persons in this classification.

(f) The Board may issue an associate license in clinical social work to a person who has a masters or doctoral degree in a social work program from a college or university having a social work program approved by the Council on Social Work Education and desires to be licensed as a clinical social worker. The associate license may not be issued for a period exceeding two years and the person issued the associate license must practice under the supervision of a licensed clinical social worker or a Board-approved alternate. Notwithstanding G.S. 90B-6(g), an associate licensee shall pass the qualifying clinical examination prescribed by the Board within two years to be eligible for renewal of the associate license. The associate licensee shall complete all requirements for licensure within three renewal cycles, or a total of six years, unless otherwise directed by the Board. (1983, c. 495, s. 1; 1991, c. 732, s. 4; 1999-313, s. 1; 2007-379, s. 3; 2012-72, s. 3.)

§ 90B-8. Persons from other jurisdictions.

(a) The Board may grant a certificate or license without examination or by special examination to any person who, at the time of application, is certified, registered or licensed as a social worker by a similar board of another country, state, or territory whose certification, registration or licensing standards are substantially equivalent to those required by this Chapter. The applicant shall have passed an examination in the country, state, or territory in which he or she is certified, registered, or licensed that is equivalent to the examination required for the level of certification or licensure sought in this State.

(b) The Board may issue a temporary license to a nonresident clinical social worker who is either certified, registered, or licensed in another jurisdiction whose standards, in the opinion of the Board, at the time of the person's certification, registration, or licensure were substantially equivalent to or higher than the requirements of this Chapter. Nothing in this Chapter shall be construed as prohibiting a nonresident clinical social worker certified, registered, or licensed in another state from rendering professional clinical social work services in this State for a period of not more than five days in any calendar year. All persons granted a temporary clinical social worker license shall comply with the supervision requirements established by the Board. (1983, c. 495, s. 1; 1999-313, s. 1.)

§ 90B-9. Renewal of certificates and licenses.

(a) All certificates and licenses shall be effective upon date of issuance by the Board, and shall be renewed on or before the second June 30 thereafter.

(b) All certificates and licenses issued hereunder shall be renewed at the times and in the manner provided by this section. At least 45 days prior to expiration of each certificate or license, the Board shall mail a notice and application for renewal to the certificate holder or licensee. Prior to the expiration date, the application shall be returned properly completed, together with a renewal fee established by the Board pursuant to G.S. 90B-6.2(a)(4) and evidence of completion of the continuing education requirements established by the Board pursuant to G.S. 90B-6(g), upon receipt of which the Board shall renew the certificate or license. If a certificate or license is not renewed on or before the expiration date, an additional fee shall be charged for late renewal as provided in G.S. 90B-6.2(a)(5).

(c) A certificate or license issued under this Chapter shall be automatically suspended for failure to renew for a period of more than 60 days after the renewal date. The Board may reinstate a certificate or license suspended under this subsection upon payment of a reinstatement fee as provided in G.S. 90B-6.2(a)(6) and may require that the applicant file a new application, furnish new supervisory reports or references or otherwise update his or her credentials, or submit to examination for reinstatement. The Board shall have exclusive jurisdiction to investigate alleged violations of this Chapter by any person whose certificate or license has been suspended under this subsection and, upon proof of any violation of this Chapter, the Board may take disciplinary action as provided in G.S. 90B-11.

(d) Any person certified or licensed and desiring to retire temporarily from the practice of social work shall send written notice thereof to the Board. Upon receipt of such notice, his or her name shall be placed upon the nonpracticing list and he or she shall not be subject to payment of renewal fees while temporarily retired. In order to reinstate certification or licensure, the person shall apply to the Board by making a request for reinstatement and paying the appropriate fee as provided in G.S. 90B-6.2. (1983, c. 495, s. 1; 1999-313, s. 1; 2006-226, s. 19.)

§ 90B-10. Exemption from certain requirements.

(a) Applicants who were engaged in the practice of social work before January 1, 1984, shall be exempt from the academic qualifications required by this act for Certified Social Workers and Certified Social Work Managers and shall be certified upon passing the Board examination and meeting the experience requirements, if any, for certification of persons in that classification.

(b) The following may engage in clinical social work practice without meeting the requirements of G.S. 90B-7(d):

(1) Repealed by Session Laws 2007-379, s. 4, effective August 19, 2007.

(2) A student completing a clinical requirement for graduation while pursuing a course of study in social work in an institution accredited by or in candidacy status with the Council on Social Work Education.

(3) Repealed by Session Laws 2007-379, s. 4, effective August 19, 2007.

(c) Notwithstanding the requirements of G.S. 90B-16, any individual who is employed by an agency of a local or State governmental entity, and who is in a position holding the title of "Social Worker" or any variation of the name, and whose position title is derived from the Office of State Human Resources Social Work Series may use the title "Social Worker" or any variation of the title. This includes persons in such positions in counties whose classification and compensation systems have been certified as substantially equivalent by the State Human Resources Commission and persons serving in such positions in Human Services agencies created by counties pursuant to G.S. 153A-77. (1983, c. 495, s. 1; 1991, c. 732, s. 5; 1993 (Reg. Sess., 1994), c. 745, s. 38.1; 1996, 2nd Ex. Sess., c. 18, s. 24.11; 1997-443, s. 11.31; 2007-379, s. 4; 2009-88, s. 2; 2013-382, s. 9.1(c).)

§ 90B-11. Disciplinary procedures.

(a) The Board may, in accordance with the provisions of Chapter 150B of the General Statutes, deny, suspend, or revoke an application, certificate, or license on any of the following grounds:

(1) Conviction of a misdemeanor or the entering of a plea of guilty or nolo contendere to a misdemeanor under this Chapter.

(2) Conviction of a felony or the entering of a plea of guilty or nolo contendere to a felony under the laws of the United States or of any state of the United States.

(3) Gross unprofessional conduct, dishonest practice or incompetence in the practice of social work.

(4) Procuring or attempting to procure a certificate or license by fraud, deceit, or misrepresentation.

(5) Any fraudulent or dishonest conduct in social work.

(6) Inability of the person to perform the functions for which he or she is certified or licensed, or substantial impairment of abilities by reason of physical or mental disability.

(7) Violations of any of the provisions of this Chapter or of rules of the Board.

(b) Upon proof that an applicant, certificate holder, or licensee under this Chapter has engaged in any of the prohibited actions specified in subsection (a) of this section, the Board may, in lieu of denial, suspension, or revocation, take one or more of the following actions:

(1) Issue a reprimand or censure.

(2) Order probation with conditions deemed appropriate by the Board.

(3) Require examination, remediation, or rehabilitation, including care, counseling, or treatment by a professional designated or approved by the Board, the cost of which shall be borne by the applicant, certificate holder, or licensee.

(4) Require supervision for the services provided by the applicant, certificate holder, or licensee by a certified or licensed social worker designated and approved by the Board, the cost of which shall be borne by the applicant, certificate holder, or licensee.

(5) Limit or circumscribe the practice of social work provided by the applicant, certificate holder, or licensee with respect to the extent, nature, or location of the services provided.

(c) The Board may impose conditions of probation or restrictions upon continued practice at the conclusion of a period of suspension or as a requirement for the restoration of a revoked or suspended certificate or license. Instead of or in connection with any disciplinary proceeding or investigation, the Board may enter into a consent order with an applicant, certificate holder, or licensee relative to a discipline, supervision, probation, remediation, rehabilitation, or practice limitation.

(d) In considering whether an applicant, certificate holder, or licensee is mentally or physically capable of practicing social work with reasonable skill and safety, the Board may require an applicant, certificate holder, or licensee to submit to a mental examination by a licensed clinical social worker or other licensed mental health professional designated by the Board and to a physical examination by a physician or other licensed health professional designated by the Board. The examination may be ordered by the Board before or after charges are presented against the applicant, certificate holder, or licensee and the results of the examination shall be reported directly to the Board and shall be admissible in evidence in a hearing before the Board.

(e) The Board shall provide the opportunity for a hearing under Article 3A of Chapter 150B of the General Statutes to: (i) any person whose certification or licensure was denied or granted subject to restrictions, probation, disciplinary action, remediation, or other conditions or limitations; and (ii) any certificate holder or licensee before revoking or suspending his or her certificate or license or restricting his or her practice or imposing any other disciplinary action or remediation. If the applicant, certificate holder, or licensee waives the opportunity for a hearing, the Board's denial, revocation, suspension, or other action shall be final. No applicant, certificate holder, or licensee shall be entitled to a hearing for failure to pass a qualifying examination.

(f) In any proceeding before the Board, complaint or notice of charges against any applicant, certificate holder, or licensee, and any decision rendered by the Board, the Board may withhold from public disclosure the identity of any client who has not consented to the public disclosure of social work services provided to him or her by the applicant, certificate holder, or licensee. If necessary for the protection and rights of a client and the full presentation of relevant evidence, the Board may close a hearing to the public and receive evidence involving or concerning the delivery of social work services.

(g) Records, papers, and other documents containing information collected and compiled by or on behalf of the Board as a result of an investigation, inquiry, or interview conducted in connection with certification, licensure, or a disciplinary matter shall not be considered public records within the meaning of Chapter 132 of the General Statutes. Any notice or statement of charges, notice of hearing, or decision rendered in connection with a hearing, shall be a public record. Information that identifies a client who has not consented to the public disclosure of services rendered to him or her by a person certified or licensed under this Chapter shall be deleted from the public record. All other records, papers, and documents containing information collected and compiled by or on behalf of the Board shall be public records, but any information that identifies a client who has not consented to the public disclosure of services rendered to him or her shall be deleted. (1983, c. 495, s. 1; 1987, c. 827, s. 1; 1999-313, s. 1.)

§ 90B-12. Violation a misdemeanor.

Any person violating any provision of this Chapter is guilty of a Class 2 misdemeanor. (1983, c. 495, s. 1; 1993, c. 539, s. 654; 1994, Ex. Sess., c. 24, s. 14(c).)

§ 90B-13. Injunction.

As an additional remedy, the Board may proceed in a superior court to enjoin and restrain any person from violating the prohibitions of this Chapter. The Board shall not be required to post bond in connection with such proceeding. (1983, c. 495, s. 1.)

§ 90B-14. Third-party reimbursements.

Nothing in this Chapter shall be construed to authorize or require direct third-party reimbursement to persons certified under this Chapter. (1991, c. 732, s. 6.)

§ 90B-15. License or certificate to be displayed.

A person licensed or certified under this Chapter shall conspicuously display the license or certificate issued by the Board at the licensee's or certificate holder's primary place of practice. (2007-379, s. 5.)

§ 90B-16. Title protection.

(a) Except as provided in G.S. 90B-10, an individual who (i) is not certified, licensed, or associate licensed by this Chapter as a social worker, (ii) does not hold a bachelor's or master's degree in social work from a college or university having a social work program accredited or admitted to candidacy for accreditation by the Council of Social Work Education, or (iii) has not received a doctorate in social work shall not use the title "Social Worker" or any variation of the title.

(b) The Board is authorized to enforce title protection pursuant to this section in accordance with G.S. 90B-13.

(c) The Board shall adopt rules to implement this section. (2009-88, s. 3; 2012-72, s. 4.)

Chapter 90C.

North Carolina Recreational Therapy Licensure Act.

§§ 90C-1 through 90C-19: Repealed by Session Laws 2005-378, s. 1, effective October 5, 2005.

Chapter 90C.

North Carolina Recreational Therapy Licensure Act.

§ 90C-20. Short title.

This Chapter shall be known as the "North Carolina Recreational Therapy Licensure Act". (2005-378, s. 2.)

§ 90C-21. Purpose.

It is the purpose and intent of the Recreational Therapy Licensure Act to safeguard the health and safety of the public and to protect the public from harm by unqualified persons by establishing a minimum level of education, experience, and competence to assure the highest degree of professional care and conduct on the part of licensed recreational therapists and licensed recreational therapy assistants. (2005-378, s. 2.)

§ 90C-22. Definitions.

In this Chapter, unless the context otherwise requires, the following definitions shall apply:

(1) Board. - The North Carolina Board of Recreational Therapy Licensure.

(2) Licensed recreational therapist. - A person who holds a license pursuant to this Chapter as a recreational therapist. A person licensed as a "Recreational Therapist" under this Chapter may practice in clinical, residential, educational, and community settings and may:

a. Conduct an individualized patient or client assessment for the purpose of collecting systematic, comprehensive, and accurate data necessary to determine a course of action and subsequent individualized treatment plan.

b. Plan and develop the individualized treatment plan that identifies a patient or client's goals, objectives, and treatment intervention strategies.

c. Implement the individualized treatment plan that is consistent with the overall patient or client treatment program.

d. Systematically evaluate and compare the patient or client's response to the individualized treatment plan and suggest modifications as appropriate.

e. Develop a discharge plan in collaboration with the patient or client, his or her family, and other treatment team members.

f. Serve as a resource for patient or client recreation opportunities to promote or improve his or her general health and well-being.

g. Deliver services in accordance with the professional standards of practice and codes of ethics promulgated by national or State professional organizations.

h. Manage delivery of services in accordance with a written plan of operation based upon standards advanced by appropriate membership, regulatory, and credentialing agencies.

i. Provide professional and preprofessional education and training of recreational therapists or recreational therapy assistants.

j. Conduct research in the field of recreational therapy or therapeutic recreation.

(3) Licensed recreational therapy assistant. - A person who holds a license pursuant to this Chapter as a recreational therapy assistant to act under the supervision of a licensed recreational therapist as defined by rule. A person licensed as a "Recreational Therapy Assistant" under this Chapter may assist in the practice of recreational therapy in clinical, residential, and community settings under the supervision of a licensed recreational therapist and in accordance with a recreational therapy assistant's training, education, and scope of practice, as defined by rule.

(4) Person. - Any individual, corporation, partnership, association, unit of government, or other legal entity.

(5) Recreational therapy. - A treatment service designed to restore, remediate, or rehabilitate a patient or client's level of functioning and independence in life activities, as well as reduce or eliminate the activity

limitations and restrictions to participation in life situations caused by an illness or disabling condition.

(6)   Recreational therapy aide. - Any nonlicensed person who aids in the provision of recreational therapy services under the provisions of this Chapter, and who acts under the direction and on-site supervision of a licensed recreational therapist or licensed recreational therapy assistant. A recreational therapy aide may perform recreational therapy related duties and functions which are assigned and are commensurate with an aide's training and competency. An aide's work shall not include responding to a physician's orders; designing, conducting, or interpreting individualized recreational therapy patient assessment; determining or modifying recreational therapy treatment plans or interventions; or any independent practice or performance of recreational therapy services.

(7)   Scope of recreational therapy. - The practice of recreational therapy includes all direct patient or client services of assessment, planning, design, implementation, evaluation, and documentation of specific interventions, management, consultation, research, and education for either individuals or groups that require specific therapeutic recreation or recreational therapy intervention representing the process and knowledge base delineated in the most recent National Council for Therapeutic Recreation Certification (NCTRC) Job Analysis Study and professional standards of practice. Scope is inclusive of professional and preprofessional education and training in recreational therapy, therapeutic recreation, and related research.

(8)   Therapeutic recreation. - The provision of treatment services and the provision of recreation services to persons with illnesses or disabling conditions. The primary purposes of treatment services, which are often referred to as recreational therapy, are to restore, remediate, or rehabilitate in order to improve functioning and independence as well as reduce or eliminate the effects of illness or disability. The primary purposes of recreation services are to provide recreation resources and opportunities in order to improve health and well-being. Therapeutic recreation is provided by professionals who are trained and certified, registered, or licensed to provided therapeutic recreation. (2005-378, s. 2.)

§ 90C-23. North Carolina Recreational Therapy Licensure Board is created.

(a)   The North Carolina Recreational Therapy Licensure Board is created.

(b)   Composition. - The Board shall consist of eight members appointed as follows:

(1)   Three practicing recreational therapists, one of whom shall be appointed by the Governor, one of whom shall be appointed by the General Assembly upon the recommendation of the President Pro Tempore of the Senate, and one of whom shall be appointed by the General Assembly upon the recommendation of the Speaker of the House of Representatives.

(2)   One licensed practicing recreational therapy assistant appointed by the Governor.

(3)   One licensed practicing recreational therapist who is engaged primarily in providing education or training for recreational therapists or recreational therapy assistants appointed by the Governor.

(4)   One physician licensed pursuant to Article 1 of Chapter 90 of the General Statutes appointed by the Governor.

(5)   Two public members, one of whom shall be appointed by the General Assembly upon the recommendation of the President Pro Tempore of the Senate and one of whom shall be appointed by the General Assembly upon the recommendation of the Speaker of the House of Representatives.

The Governor shall make appointments after consultation with the North Carolina Recreational Therapy Licensure Board and other interested persons.

(c)   Qualifications. - The nonpublic recreational therapist or recreational therapy assistant members of the Board shall hold a current license. Each nonpublic recreational therapist or recreational therapy assistant member of the Board, at the time of his or her appointment and for at least two years before, shall have been actively engaged in North Carolina in the practice of recreational therapy or therapeutic recreation, in the education and training of graduate or undergraduate students of recreational therapy or therapeutic recreation, or in recreational therapy or therapeutic recreation research.

One public member shall not be a licensed health care professional or an agent or employee of any health care institution, health care insurer, health care professional school, or a member of any allied health profession. One public member shall have received recreational therapy or therapeutic recreation services. For purposes of this subsection, a person enrolled in a program to prepare him or her to be a licensed health care professional or an allied health professional shall not be eligible to serve as a public member of the Board. The spouse of any person who would be prohibited by this subsection from serving on the Board as a public member shall not serve as a public member of the Board. Public members shall reasonably reflect the population of this State.

(d)   Term. - Members of the Board shall serve three-year staggered terms and shall serve until a successor is appointed and qualified. No member shall serve more than two consecutive full terms.

(e)   Vacancies. - The Governor shall fill vacancies to the Board positions for which the Governor is the appointing authority within 30 days after a position is vacated. The General Assembly shall fill vacancies for which it is the appointing authority in accordance with G.S. 120-122. Appointees shall serve the remainder of the unexpired term and until their successors have been appointed and qualified.

(f)   Removal. - The Board may remove any of its members for gross neglect of duty, incompetence, or unprofessional conduct. A member subject to disciplinary proceedings shall be disqualified from Board business until the charges are resolved. The Governor may also remove any member for gross neglect of duty, incompetence, or unprofessional conduct.

(g)   Compensation. - Each member of the Board shall receive such per diem compensation and reimbursement for travel and subsistence as shall be set for licensing Board members generally, as provided in G.S. 93B-5.

(h)   Officers. - The officers of the Board shall be a chairman, a vice-chairman, and other officers deemed necessary by the Board to carry out the purposes of this Chapter. All officers shall be elected annually by the Board for one-year terms and shall serve until their successors are elected and qualified.

(i)   Meetings. - The Board shall hold at least two meetings each year to conduct business and shall adopt rules governing the calling, holding, and conducting of regular and special meetings. A majority of the Board members shall constitute a quorum.

(j)   Employees. - The Board may employ necessary personnel for the performance of its functions and fix their compensation within the limits of the funds available to the Board.

(k)   The total expense of the administration of this Chapter shall not exceed the total income from fees collected pursuant to this Chapter. None of the expenses of the Board, or the compensation or expenses of any officer or any employee of the Board, shall be paid or payable out of the General Fund. Neither the Board nor any of its officers or employees may incur any expense, debt, or other financial obligation binding upon the State. (2005-378, s. 2.)

§ 90C-24. Powers of the Board.

(a)   The Board shall have the following general powers and duties:

(1)   To administer this Chapter.

(2)   To issue interpretations of this Chapter.

(3)   To adopt, amend, or repeal rules and regulations in the manner prescribed by Chapter 150B of the General Statutes, as may be necessary to carry out the provisions of this Chapter.

(4)   To establish qualifications of, employ, and set the compensation of the Executive Director who shall not be a member of the Board.

(5)   To employ and fix the compensation of the personnel that the Board determines are necessary to carry out the provisions of this Chapter and to incur other expenses necessary to effectuate this Chapter.

(6)   To determine the qualifications of persons who are licensed pursuant to this Chapter.

(7)   To issue, renew, deny, suspend, or revoke licenses and carry out any of the other actions authorized by this Chapter.

(8)   To conduct investigations for the purpose of determining whether violations of this Chapter are grounds for revoking, denying, suspending, or refusing to renew the licenses of persons licensed pursuant to this Chapter.

(9) To maintain a record of all proceedings and make available to persons who hold a license and other concerned parties an annual report of all Board action.

(10) To set fees for licensure, license renewal, and other services deemed necessary to carry out the purpose of this Chapter.

(11) To adopt a seal containing the name of the Board to be used on licenses and official reports it issues.

(12) To issue annually a list stating the names of persons currently licensed under the privilege of this Chapter.

(13) To establish or approve, as defined by rule, reasonable competency requirements for licensure, including the power to adopt or use examination materials, study or training courses, and standards of recognized accrediting and credentialing agencies and professional associations and the power to establish or approve, as defined by rule, reasonable standards for renewal of licensure, including requirements for continuing recreational therapy or therapeutic recreation education.

(b) The powers and duties enumerated above are granted for the purpose of enabling the Board to protect the public from misrepresentation of licensure status as provided in this Chapter and shall be liberally construed to accomplish this objective. (2005-378, s. 2.)

§ 90C-25. Executive Director.

The Executive Director shall deposit all fees payable to the Board in financial institutions designated by the Board as official depositories. The funds shall be deposited in the name of the Board and shall be used to pay all expenses incurred by the Board in carrying out the purposes of this Chapter. The State Auditor shall audit the Board annually. (2005-378, s. 2.)

§ 90C-26. The Board may accept contributions, etc.

The Board may accept grants, contributions, devises, and gifts that shall be kept in a separate fund and shall be used by it to publicize the licensure program and its protective benefits to the public. (2005-378, s. 2; 2011-284, s. 67.)

§ 90C-27. Requirements for licensure.

(a) The Board shall license any person as a "Licensed Recreational Therapist" who meets the following education, credential, and experience requirements:

(1) Passage of an appropriate examination as a therapeutic recreation specialist or a recreational therapist by the North Carolina Recreational Therapy Licensure Board or current certification as a "Certified Therapeutic Recreation Specialist" by the National Council for Therapeutic Recreation Certification.

(2) A minimum level of education or experience, as defined by rules of the Board, inclusive of practice competency standards or guidelines promulgated by professional associations and credentialing and accrediting organizations.

(3) For purposes of this subsection, an academic major or specialization shall be defined by rules of the Board and shall be inclusive of information gathered through surveys of educational institutions in the State having a bachelors or masters degree with a specialization in recreational therapy or therapeutic recreation.

(b) The Board shall license any person as a "Licensed Recreational Therapy Assistant" who meets the following education and experience requirements:

(1) A minimum level of education or experience, as defined by rules of the Board, inclusive of practice competency standards or guidelines promulgated by professional associations and credentialing and accrediting organizations as deemed appropriate by the Board.

(2) For purposes of this section, an academic major or specialization shall be defined by rules of the Board and shall be inclusive of information gathered through surveys of educational institutions in the State having associate degree curricula in recreational therapy or therapeutic recreation. (2005-378, s. 2.)

§ 90C-28. Licensure fees.

Applications for licensure shall be made on forms prescribed and furnished by the Board. The Board may establish fees for the actual cost of duplication services, materials, and returned bank items. All fees derived from services provided by the Board under the provisions of this Chapter shall be nonrefundable. The Board shall establish the amount of fees as defined by rule not to exceed the following amounts:

(1)	Initial application for licensure fee	$200.00
(2)	Licensure renewal fee	$200.00
(3)	Record maintenance fee	$100.00
(4)	Inactive fee	$ 50.00

(2005-378, s. 2.)

§ 90C-29. License renewal.

Every license issued pursuant to this Chapter shall be renewable every two years. Within 30 days before the expiration date, a person who desires to continue to be licensed in the field of therapeutic recreation or recreational therapy shall apply for license renewal on forms furnished by the Board. The applicant shall meet criteria for renewal, including continuing education, established by the Board as defined by rule and shall pay the required fee established by the Board pursuant to this Chapter. Failure to renew the license before the expiration date shall result in automatic forfeiture of any license issued pursuant to this Chapter.

The Executive Director shall notify, in writing, every person at his or her last known address of the expiration of his or her license and the amount that is required for its two-year renewal. (2005-378, s. 2.)

§ 90C-30. Reinstatement.

A person who has allowed his or her license to lapse by failure to renew it pursuant to this Chapter must apply for licensure on a reinstatement form provided by the Board. The Board shall require the applicant to return the completed reinstatement licensure form including renewal requirements established by the Board as defined by rule. If the license has lapsed for more than two years, the Board shall require the applicant to successfully demonstrate competency as defined by rules established by the Board. If the Board determines that the license should be reinstated, it shall issue a license renewal to the applicant. (2005-378, s. 2.)

§ 90C-31. Inactive list.

When a person licensed by the Board submits a request for inactive status and pays the inactive fee, the Board shall issue to the person a statement of inactive status and shall place the person's name on the "Inactive Status' list. While on that list, the person shall not hold himself or herself out as licensed pursuant to this Chapter. When that person desires to be removed from the inactive list and returned to an active list, an application shall be submitted to the Board on a form furnished by the Board, and the fee shall be paid for license renewal. The Board shall require evidence of competency as defined by rule to resume practice before returning the applicant to the active status. (2005-378, s. 2.)

§ 90C-32. Revocation, suspension, or denial of licensure.

The Board may require remedial education, issue of a letter of reprimand, restrict, revoke, or suspend any license issued pursuant to this Chapter or deny any application for licensure if the Board determines that the licensee or applicant has done any of the following:

(1)   Given false information or withheld material information from the Board in procuring or attempting to procure a license pursuant to this Chapter.

(2)   Been convicted of, or pleaded guilty or nolo contendere to, any crime that indicates that the person is unfit or incompetent to be licensed pursuant to this Chapter.

(3) Is unable to perform the functions for which a license has been issued due to impairment of mental or physical faculties.

(4) Engaged in conduct that endangers the public health.

(5) Is unfit or incompetent to be licensed pursuant to this Chapter by reason of deliberate or negligent acts or omissions regardless of whether active injury to the patient or client is established.

(6) Engages in conduct that deceives, defrauds, or harms the public in the course of claiming licensed status or practicing recreational therapy.

(7) Willfully violated any provision of this Chapter, rules, or code of ethics enacted by the Board.

(8) Aided, abetted, or assisted any person in violating the provisions of this Chapter.

The Board may reinstate a revoked license or remove licensure restrictions when it finds that the reasons for revocation or restriction no longer exist and that the person can reasonably be expected to safely and properly practice recreational therapy. (2005-378, s. 2.)

§ 90C-33. Reciprocity.

The Board may grant a license, without examination or by special examination, to any person who, at the time of application, is licensed as a recreational therapist or therapeutic recreation specialist by a similar Board of another country, state, or territory whose licensing standards are substantially equivalent to or higher than those required by this Chapter. The Board shall determine the substantial equivalence upon which reciprocity is based. (2005-378, s. 2.)

§ 90C-34. Persons and practices not affected.

Nothing in this Chapter shall be construed to prevent or restrict:

(1) Any person qualified, registered, certified, or licensed to engage in another profession or occupation or any person working under the supervision of a person registered, certified, or licensed to engage in another profession or occupation in this State from performing work incidental to the practice of that profession or occupation as long as that person does not represent himself or herself as a recreational therapy assistant or recreational therapist or the work to be recreational therapy or therapeutic recreation as defined by this Chapter.

(2) Any person employed as a therapeutic recreation specialist, therapeutic recreation assistant, or recreational therapist or a recreational therapy assistant by the government of the United States, if he or she provides therapeutic recreation or recreational therapy solely under the direction and control of the organization by which he or she is employed.

(3) Any person pursuing a course of study leading to a degree in recreational therapy or therapeutic recreation at an accredited college or university that meets the minimum academic requirements for a major or specialization in recreational therapy as defined by the rules and regulations of the Board.

(4) Any person fulfilling the supervised fieldwork experience required for a degree and for licensure, as defined by the rules of the Board, if the person is designated by a title that clearly indicates his or her status as a student.

(5) Expired. (2005-378, s. 2; 2007-389, s. 1.)

§ 90C-35. Reports; immunity from suit.

Any person who has reasonable cause to suspect malpractice, misconduct, or incapacity of a person who is licensed pursuant to this Chapter or who has reasonable cause to suspect that any person is in violation of this Chapter should report the relevant facts to the Board. Upon receipt of a charge or upon its own initiative, the Board may give notice of an administrative hearing pursuant to Chapter 150B of the General Statutes or may, after diligent investigation, dismiss unfounded charges. Any person making a report pursuant to this section shall be immune from criminal prosecution or civil liability based on that report unless the person knew the report was false or acted in reckless disregard of whether or not the report was false. (2005-378, s. 2.)

§ 90C-36. Violations and penalties.

Any person not licensed under this Chapter who holds himself or herself out to be licensed under this Chapter or who practices recreational therapy or therapeutic recreation shall be guilty of a Class 1 misdemeanor. Any fine imposed as a result of conviction shall not exceed five hundred dollars ($500.00). (2005-378, s. 2.)

§ 90C-37. Enjoining illegal practices.

(a)   If the Board finds that a person is violating any of the provisions of this Chapter, it may apply in its own name to the superior court for a temporary or permanent restraining order or an injunction to prevent that person from continuing the illegal practices. The court is empowered to grant an injunction regardless of whether criminal prosecution or other action has been or may be instituted as a result of the violation. All actions by the Board shall be governed by the Rules of Civil Procedure.

(b)   The venue for actions brought under this Chapter shall be in the county where the defendant resides or the county where the violation occurs. (2005-378, s. 2.)

Chapter 90D.

Interpreters and Transliterators.

§ 90D-1. Title.

This Chapter may be cited as the "Interpreter and Transliterator Licensure Act". (2002-182, s. 1; 2003-56, s. 3.)

§ 90D-2. Declaration of purpose.

The practice of manual or oral interpreting and transliterating services affects the public health, safety, and welfare, and therefore the licensure of these practices is necessary to ensure minimum standards of competency and to provide the public with safe and accurate manual or oral interpreting or transliterating services. It is the purpose of this Chapter to provide for the regulation of persons offering manual or oral interpreting or transliterating services to individuals who are deaf, hard-of-hearing, or dependent on the use of manual modes of communication in this State. (2002-182, s. 1; 2003-56, s. 3.)

§ 90D-3. Definitions.

The following definitions apply in this Chapter:

(1)   Board. - The North Carolina Interpreter and Transliterator Licensing Board.

(2)   Cued speech. - A tool that utilizes a phonetically based system to enable spoken language to appear visibly through the use of eight handshapes in four locations in combination with natural mouth movements to allow sounds of spoken language to appear differently.

(3)   Educational interpreter or transliterator. - A person who provides accessible communication, using the most understandable language model, to individuals in prekindergarten through grade 12 or in any institution of higher education.

(4)   Interpreter. - A person who practices the act of interpreting as defined in this section.

(5)   Interpreting. - The process of providing accessible communication, between and among persons who are deaf or hard-of-hearing and those who are hearing. This process includes, but is not limited to, communication between American Sign Language and English. It may also involve various other modalities that involve visual, gestural, and tactile methods.

(6)   License. - A certificate that evidences approval by the Board that a person has successfully completed the requirements set forth in G.S. 90D-7 entitling the person to perform the functions and duties of an interpreter or transliterator.

(7) Provisional license. - A certificate issued by the Board under G.S. 90D-8 enabling a person to perform the functions and duties of an interpreter or transliterator until the person has successfully completed all of the requirements set forth in G.S. 90D-7.

(8) Transliterating. - The process of providing accessible communication between one or more hearing persons and one or more deaf or hard-of-hearing persons using a form of manually coded English.

(9) Transliterator. - A person who practices the act of transliterating as defined in this section. (2002-182, s. 1; 2003-56, s. 3.)

§ 90D-4. License required; exemptions.

(a) Except as provided in Chapter 8B of the General Statutes, no person shall practice or offer to practice as an interpreter or transliterator for a fee or other consideration, represent himself or herself as a licensed interpreter or transliterator, or use the title "Licensed Interpreter for the Deaf", "Licensed Transliterator for the Deaf", or any other title or abbreviation to indicate that the person is a licensed interpreter or transliterator unless that person is currently licensed under this Chapter.

(b) The provisions of this Chapter do not apply to:

(1) Persons providing interpreting or transliterating services in religious proceedings.

(2) Persons providing interpreting or transliterating services in mentoring or training programs approved by the Board.

(3) An intern under the supervision of a person licensed under this Chapter to provide interpreting or transliterating services.

(4) Persons providing interpreting or transliterating services in an emergency situation until a licensed interpreter or transliterator can be obtained. An emergency situation is one where the deaf or hard-of-hearing person is in substantial danger of death or irreparable harm if interpreting or transliterating services are not provided immediately.

(5) Educational interpreters or transliterators.

(6) Nonresident persons who are nationally certified providing interpreting or transliterating services in this State no more than 20 days per year in accordance with rules adopted by the Board. (2002-182, s. 1; 2003-56, s. 3; 2005-299, s. 1.)

§ 90D-5. Creation of the Board.

(a) The North Carolina Interpreter and Transliterator Licensing Board is created.

(b) Composition and Terms. - The Board shall consist of nine members who shall serve staggered terms. The initial Board members shall be selected on or before July 1, 2003, as follows:

(1) A member of the North Carolina Association of the Deaf (NCAD) who is deaf and familiar with the interpreting process. This member shall be appointed by the Governor and serve for a term of two years.

(2) An interpreter who is a member of the North Carolina Registry of Interpreters for the Deaf, Inc., (NCRID) with five years experience in a community setting and who is licensed to practice as an interpreter or transliterator under this Chapter. This member shall be appointed by the Governor and serve for a term of three years.

(3) An employee of the North Carolina Department of Health and Human Services. This member shall be appointed by the Governor, upon recommendation of the Secretary of the Department, and serve a term of three years.

(4) An interpreter or transliterator for deaf-blind individuals who is licensed to practice as an interpreter or transliterator under this Chapter or a deaf-blind individual who is a member of the North Carolina Deaf-Blind Association and who has knowledge of the interpreting process. This member shall be appointed by the General Assembly, upon recommendation of the President Pro Tempore of the Senate, and serve for a term of three years.

(5)   A cued speech or oral transliterator licensed to practice as an interpreter or transliterator under this Chapter. This member shall be appointed by the General Assembly, upon recommendation of the President Pro Tempore of the Senate, and serve for a term of two years.

(6)   A member of Self Help for Hard of Hearing (SHHH) with knowledge of the interpreting process and deafness. This member shall be appointed by the General Assembly, upon recommendation of the President Pro Tempore of the Senate, and serve for a term of three years.

(7)   An interpreter who is a member of the North Carolina Registry of Interpreters for the Deaf, Inc., (NCRID) with five years experience in an educational setting in grades K-12 and who is licensed to practice as an interpreter or transliterator under this Chapter. This member shall be appointed by the General Assembly, upon recommendation of the Speaker of the House of Representatives, and serve for a term of two years.

(8)   A faculty member of an Interpreter Training Program (ITP), an Interpreter Preparation Program (IPP), or a qualified or professional certified instructor of the American Sign Language Teachers Association (ASLTA). This member shall be appointed by the General Assembly, upon recommendation of the Speaker of the House of Representatives, and serve for a term of two years.

(9)   A public member. This member shall be appointed by the General Assembly, upon recommendation of the Speaker of the House of Representatives, and serve a term of two years. For purposes of this section, a public member shall not be licensed under this Chapter or have an immediate family member who is deaf or hard-of-hearing.

Upon the expiration of the terms of the initial Board members, each member shall be appointed for a term of three years and shall serve until a successor is appointed and qualified. No member may serve more than two consecutive full terms.

(c)   Qualifications. - All members of the Board who are required to be licensed under this Chapter shall reside or be employed in North Carolina and shall remain in active practice and in good standing with the Board as a licensee during their terms.

(d)   Vacancies. - A vacancy shall be filled in the same manner as the original appointment. Appointees to fill vacancies shall serve the remainder of the unexpired term and until their successors have been duly appointed and qualified.

(e)   Removal. - The Board may remove any of its members for neglect of duty, incompetence, or unprofessional conduct. A member subject to disciplinary proceedings as a licensee shall be disqualified from participating in the official business of the Board until the charges have been resolved.

(f)   Compensation. - Each member of the Board shall receive per diem and reimbursement for travel and subsistence as provided in G.S. 93B-5.

(g)   Officers. - The officers of the Board shall be a chair, a vice-chair, and other officers deemed necessary by the Board to carry out the purposes of this Chapter. All officers shall be elected by the Board for two-year terms and shall serve until their successors are elected and qualified.

(h)   Meetings. - The Board shall hold at least two meetings each year to conduct business. The Board shall establish procedures governing the calling, holding, and conducting of regular and special meetings. A majority of the Board shall constitute a quorum. (2002-182, s. 1; 2003-56, s. 1.)

§ 90D-6. Powers of the Board.

The Board shall have the power and duty to:

(1)   Administer this Chapter.

(2)   Adopt, amend, or repeal rules necessary to carry out the provisions of this Chapter, subject to the provisions of Chapter 150B of the General Statutes.

(3)   Employ and fix the compensation of personnel that the Board determines is necessary to carry into effect the provisions of this Chapter and to incur other expenses necessary to effectuate this Chapter.

(4)   Examine and determine the qualifications and fitness of applicants for licensure, renewal of licensure, and reciprocal licensure.

(5)   Issue, renew, deny, suspend, or revoke licenses and carry out any disciplinary actions authorized by this Chapter.

(6) Set fees as authorized in G.S. 90D-10.
(7) Conduct investigations for the purpose of determining whether violations of this Chapter or grounds for disciplining licensees exist.

(8) Maintain a record of all proceedings and make available to licensees and other concerned parties an annual report of all Board action.

(9) Keep on file in its office at all times a complete record of the names, addresses, license numbers, and renewal license numbers of all persons entitled to practice under this Chapter.

(10) Adopt a seal containing the name of the Board for use on all licenses and official reports issued by the Board.

(11) Adopt rules for continuing education requirements.

(12) Conduct administrative hearings in accordance with Article 3A of Chapter 150B of the General Statutes. (2002-182, s. 1; 2005-299, s. 3.)

§ 90D-7. Requirements for licensure.

(a) Upon application to the Board and the payment of the required fees, an applicant may be licensed as an interpreter or transliterator if the applicant meets all of the following qualifications:

(1) Is 18 years of age or older.

(2) Is of good moral character as determined by the Board.

(3) Meets one of the following criteria:

a. Holds a valid National Association of the Deaf (NAD), level 4 or 5 certification.

b. Is nationally certified by the Registry of Interpreters for the Deaf, Inc., (RID).

c. Has a national certification recognized by the National Cued Speech Association (NCSA).

d. Holds a quality assurance North Carolina Interpreter Classification System (NCICS) level A or B classification in effect on January 1, 2000.

(b) Effective July 1, 2008, any person who applies for initial licensure as an interpreter or transliterator shall hold at least a two-year degree from a regionally accredited institution.

(c) The Department of Justice may provide a criminal record check to the Board for a person who has applied for a new, provisional, or renewal license through the Board. The Board shall provide to the Department of Justice, along with the request, the fingerprints of the applicant, any additional information required by the Department of Justice, and a form signed by the applicant consenting to the check of the criminal record and to the use of the fingerprints and other identifying information required by the State or national repositories. The applicant's fingerprints shall be forwarded to the State Bureau of Investigation for a search of the State's criminal history record file, and the State Bureau of Investigation shall forward a set of the fingerprints to the Federal Bureau of Investigation for a national criminal history check. The Board shall keep all information pursuant to this subdivision privileged, in accordance with applicable State law and federal guidelines, and the information shall be confidential and shall not be a public record under Chapter 132 of the General Statutes.

The Department of Justice may charge each applicant a fee for conducting the checks of criminal history records authorized by this subsection. (2002-182, s. 1; 2003-56, s. 3.)

§ 90D-8. Provisional license.

(a) Upon application to the Board and the payment of the required fees, an applicant may be issued a one-time provisional license as an interpreter or transliterator if the applicant meets all of the following qualifications:

(1) Is at least 18 years of age.

(2) Is of good moral character as determined by the Board.

(3) Completes two continuing education units approved by the Board. These units must be completed for each renewable year.
(4) Satisfies one of the following:

a. Holds a quality assurance North Carolina Interpreter Classification System (NCICS) level C classification.

b. Holds a valid National Association of the Deaf (NAD) level 2 or 3 certification.

c. Holds a current Educational Interpreter Performance Assessment (EIPA) level 3 or above classification.

d. Repealed by Session Laws 2005-299, s. 2, effective August 22, 2005.

e. Holds at least a two-year interpreting degree from a regionally accredited institution.

(a1) Upon application to the Board, payment of the required fees, and meeting the requirements for a provisional license under subdivisions (1) and (2) of subsection (a) of this section, the Board may also issue a provisional license to any of the following categories of persons seeking a provisional license:

(1) A certified deaf interpreter (CDI) who completes 30 hours of training, including "Role and Function", "Code of Ethics", and interpreting professional studies coursework.

(2) An oral interpreter who completes a total of 40 hours of training in interpreting coursework or workshops related to oral interpreting.

(3) A person providing cued speech interpreting or transliterating services who completes a total of 40 hours of training in interpreting coursework or workshops related to cued speech.

(4) A person providing interpreting or transliterating services who has a recognized credential from another state in the field of interpreting or transliterating.

(5) An interpreter or transliterator who has accumulated 200 hours per year in the provision of interpreting or transliterating services, in this State or another state, totaling 400 hours for the two years immediately preceding the date of application.

(b) A provisional license issued under this section shall be valid for one year. Upon expiration, a provisional license may be renewed for an additional one-year period in the discretion of the Board. However, a provisional license shall not be renewed more than three times. The Board may, in its discretion, grant an extension after the third time the provisional license has been renewed under circumstances to be established in rules adopted by the Board.

(c) Effective July 1, 2008, any person who applies for initial licensure on a provisional basis as an interpreter or transliterator shall hold at least a two-year degree from a regionally accredited institution. (2002-182, s. 1; 2003-56, s. 3; 2005-299, s. 2.)

§ 90D-9. Reciprocity; licensure of nonresident.

(a) The Board may issue a license to a qualified applicant who resides in this State and holds an interpreter or transliterator license in another state if that state has standards of competency that are substantially equivalent to those provided in this Chapter.

(b) The Board may issue a license to a nonresident if the person meets the requirements of this Chapter or the person resides in a state that recognizes licenses issued by the Board. (2002-182, s. 1; 2003-56, s. 3.)

§ 90D-10. Expenses and fees.

(a) All salaries, compensation, and expenses incurred or allowed for the purposes of this Chapter shall be paid by the Board exclusively out of the fees received by the Board as authorized by this Chapter or from funds received from other sources. In no case shall any salary, expense, or other obligations of the Board be charged against the General Fund.

(b) The Board may impose the following fees not to exceed the amounts listed below:

(1) License
$225.00

(2) Provisional license
$225.00

(3) License renewal
$150.00

(4) Provisional license renewal
$150.00

(5) Duplicate license
$10.00.

(2002-182, s. 1; 2003-56, s. 3.)

§ 90D-11. License renewal.

Each license issued under this Chapter shall be renewed on or before October 1 of each year. All applications for renewal shall be filed with the Board and shall be accompanied by the renewal fee as required by G.S. 90D-10 and written proof of satisfactory completion of continuing education requirements adopted by the Board. Licenses that are not renewed shall automatically lapse, and the licensee shall be required to reapply for licensure in accordance with rules adopted by the Board. (2002-182, s. 1; 2003-56, s. 3.)

§ 90D-12. Disciplinary action.

The Board may deny, suspend, revoke, or refuse to license an interpreter or transliterator or applicant for any of the following:

(1) Giving false information to or withholding information from the Board in procuring or attempting to procure a license.

(2) Having been convicted of or pled guilty or no contest to a crime that indicates the person is unfit or incompetent to perform interpreter or

transliterator services or that indicates the person has deceived or defrauded the public.

(3)   Having been disciplined by the Registry of Interpreters for the Deaf, Inc., (RID).

(4)   Demonstrating gross negligence, incompetency, or misconduct in performing interpreter or transliterator services.

(5)   Failing to pay child support after having been ordered to do so by a court of competent jurisdiction.

(6)   Willfully violating any provisions of this Chapter or rules adopted by the Board. (2002-182, s. 1; 2003-56, s. 3.)

§ 90D-13. Injunctive relief.

If the Board finds that a person who does not have a license issued under this Chapter claims to be a licensed interpreter or transliterator or is engaging in practice as an interpreter or transliterator in violation of this Chapter, the Board may apply in its own name to the superior court for a temporary restraining order or other injunctive relief to prevent the person from continuing illegal practices. The action may be brought in the county where the illegal or unlawful acts are alleged to have been committed, in the county where the defendant resides, or in the county where the Board maintains its offices and records. The court may grant injunctions regardless of whether criminal prosecution or other action has been or may be instituted as a result of a violation. (2002-182, s. 1; 2003-56, s. 3.)

§ 90D-14. Civil penalties.

(a)   Authority to Assess Civil Penalties. - The Board may assess a civil penalty not to exceed one thousand dollars ($1,000) for the violation of any section of this Chapter or any rules adopted by the Board. The clear proceeds of any civil penalty assessed under this section shall be remitted to the Civil Penalty and Forfeiture Fund in accordance with G.S. 115C-457.2.

(b) Consideration Factors. - Before imposing and assessing a civil penalty, the Board shall consider the following factors:

(1) The nature, gravity, and persistence of the particular violation.

(2) The appropriateness of the imposition of a civil penalty when considered alone or in combination with other punishment.

(3) Whether the violation was willful and malicious.

(4) Any other factors that would tend to mitigate or aggravate the violations found to exist.

(c) Schedule of Civil Penalties. - The Board shall establish a schedule of civil penalties for violations of this Chapter or rules adopted by the Board.

(d) Costs. - The Board may assess the costs of disciplinary actions against a person found to be in violation of this Chapter or rules adopted by the Board. (2005-299, s. 4.)

Chapter 91.

Pawnbrokers.

Chapter 91A.

Pawnbrokers and Cash Converters Modernization Act.

§ 91A-1: Recodified as Part 1 of Article 45 of Chapter 66, G.S. 66-385 through 66-399, by Session Laws 2012-46, s. 2, effective October 1, 2012.

§ 91A-2: Recodified as Part 1 of Article 45 of Chapter 66, G.S. 66-385 through 66-399, by Session Laws 2012-46, s. 2, effective October 1, 2012.

§ 91A-3: Recodified as Part 1 of Article 45 of Chapter 66, G.S. 66-385 through 66-399, by Session Laws 2012-46, s. 2, effective October 1, 2012.

§ 91A-4: Recodified as Part 1 of Article 45 of Chapter 66, G.S. 66-385 through 66-399, by Session Laws 2012-46, s. 2, effective October 1, 2012.

§ 91A-5: Recodified as Part 1 of Article 45 of Chapter 66, G.S. 66-385 through 66-399, by Session Laws 2012-46, s. 2, effective October 1, 2012.

§ 91A-6: Recodified as Part 1 of Article 45 of Chapter 66, G.S. 66-385 through 66-399, by Session Laws 2012-46, s. 2, effective October 1, 2012.

§ 91A-7: Recodified as Part 1 of Article 45 of Chapter 66, G.S. 66-385 through 66-399, by Session Laws 2012-46, s. 2, effective October 1, 2012.

§ 91A-7.1: Recodified as Part 1 of Article 45 of Chapter 66, G.S. 66-385 through 66-399, by Session Laws 2012-46, s. 2, effective October 1, 2012.

§ 91A-8: Recodified as Part 1 of Article 45 of Chapter 66, G.S. 66-385 through 66-399, by Session Laws 2012-46, s. 2, effective October 1, 2012.

§ 91A-9: Recodified as Part 1 of Article 45 of Chapter 66, G.S. 66-385 through 66-399, by Session Laws 2012-46, s. 2, effective October 1, 2012.

§ 91A-10: Recodified as Part 1 of Article 45 of Chapter 66, G.S. 66-385 through 66-399, by Session Laws 2012-46, s. 2, effective October 1, 2012.

§ 91A-11: Recodified as Part 1 of Article 45 of Chapter 66, G.S. 66-385 through 66-399, by Session Laws 2012-46, s. 2, effective October 1, 2012.

§ 91A-12: Recodified as Part 1 of Article 45 of Chapter 66, G.S. 66-385 through 66-399, by Session Laws 2012-46, s. 2, effective October 1, 2012.

§ 91A-13: Recodified as Part 1 of Article 45 of Chapter 66, G.S. 66-385 through 66-399, by Session Laws 2012-46, s. 2, effective October 1, 2012.

§ 91A-14: Recodified as Part 1 of Article 45 of Chapter 66, G.S. 66-385 through 66-399, by Session Laws 2012-46, s. 2, effective October 1, 2012.

92-1: Deleted.

§ 92-2: Deleted.

§ 92-3: Deleted.

§ 92-4: Deleted.

§ 92-5: Deleted.

§ 92-6: Deleted.

§ 92-7: Deleted.

§ 92-8: Deleted.

§ 92-9: Deleted.

§ 92-10: Deleted.

§ 92-11: Deleted.

§ 92-12: Deleted.

§ 92-13: Deleted.

§ 92-14: Deleted.

§ 92-15: Deleted.

§ 92-16: Deleted.

§ 92-17: Deleted.

§ 92-18: Deleted.

§ 92-19: Deleted.

§ 92-20: Deleted.

§ 92-21: Deleted.

§ 92-22: Deleted.

§ 92-23: Deleted.

§ 92-24: Deleted.

§ 92-25: Deleted.

§ 92-26: Deleted.

§ 92-27: Deleted.

§ 92-28: Deleted.

§ 92-29: Deleted.

Chapter 93.

Certified Public Accountants.

§ 93-1. Definitions; practice of law.

(a) Definitions. - As used in this Chapter certain terms are defined as follows:

(1) An "accountant" is a person engaged in the public practice of accountancy who is not a certified public accountant as defined in this Chapter.

(2) "Board" means the Board of Certified Public Accountant Examiners as provided in this Chapter.

(3) A "certified public accountant" is a person who holds a certificate as a certified public accountant issued under the provisions of this Chapter.

(4) Repealed by Session Laws 1993, c. 518, s. 2.

(5) A person is engaged in the "public practice of accountancy" who holds himself out to the public as a certified public accountant or an accountant and in consideration of compensation received or to be received offers to perform or

does perform, for other persons, services which involve the auditing or verification of financial transactions, books, accounts, or records, or the preparation, verification or certification of financial, accounting and related statements intended for publication or renders professional services or assistance in or about any and all matters of principle or detail relating to accounting procedure and systems, or the recording, presentation or certification and the interpretation of such service through statements and reports.

(b) Practice of Law. - Nothing in this Chapter shall be construed as authorizing certified public accountants or accountants to engage in the practice of law, and such person shall not engage in the practice of law unless duly licensed so to do. (1925, c. 261, s. 1; 1929, c. 219, s. 1; 1951, c. 844, s. 1; 1979, c. 750, s. 3; 1983, c. 185, ss. 1, 2; 1993, c. 518, s. 2; 2009-347, s. 1.)

§ 93-2. Qualifications.

Any person who is a citizen of the United States, has declared the intention of becoming a citizen, is a resident alien, or is a citizen of a foreign jurisdiction which extends to citizens of this State like or similar privileges to be examined or certified, and who is over 18 years of age and of good moral character, and who has received from the State Board of Certified Public Accountant Examiners a certificate of qualification to practice as a certified public accountant shall be licensed to practice and be styled and known as a certified public accountant. (1925, c. 261, s. 2; 1979, c. 750, s. 4; 1993, c. 518, s. 3.)

§ 93-3. Unlawful use of title "certified public accountant" by individual.

It shall be unlawful for any person who has not received a certificate of qualification or not been granted a practice privilege under G.S. 93-10 admitting the person to practice as a certified public accountant to assume or use such a title, or to use any words, letters, abbreviations, symbols or other means of identification to indicate that the person using same has been admitted to practice as a certified public accountant. (1925, c. 261, s. 3; 2009-347, s. 2.)

§ 93-4. Use of title by firm.

It shall be unlawful for any firm, copartnership, or association to assume or use the title of certified public accountant, or to use any words, letters, abbreviations, symbols or other means of identification to indicate that the members of such firm, copartnership or association have been admitted to practice as certified public accountants, unless each of the members of such firm, copartnership or association first shall have received a certificate of qualification from the State Board of Certified Public Accountant Examiners or been granted a practice privilege admitting each member of the firm, copartnership, or association to practice as a certified public accountant; provided, however, that the Board may exempt those persons who do not actually practice in or reside in the State of North Carolina from registering and receiving a certificate of qualification under this section. (1925, c. 261, s. 4; 1979, c. 750, s. 5; 2009-347, s. 3.)

§ 93-5. Use of title by corporation.

It shall be unlawful for any corporation to assume or use the title of certified public accountant, or to use any words, letters, abbreviations, symbols or other means of identification to indicate that such corporation has received a certificate of qualification from the State Board of Certified Public Accountant Examiners admitting it to practice as a certified public accountant. (1925, c. 261, s. 5.)

§ 93-6. Practice as accountants permitted; use of misleading titles prohibited.

It shall be unlawful for any person to engage in the public practice of accountancy in this State who is not a holder of a certificate as a certified public accountant issued by the Board, unless such person uses the term "accountant" and only the term "accountant" in connection with his name on all reports, letters of transmittal, or advice, and on all stationery and documents used in connection with his services as an accountant, and refrains from the use in any manner of any other title or designation in such practice. (1925, c. 261, ss. 6, 8; 1951, c. 844, s. 2; 1993, c. 518, s. 4.)

§ 93-7: Repealed by Session Laws 1993, c. 518, s. 5.

§ 93-8. Public practice of accounting by corporations prohibited.

It shall be unlawful for any certified public accountant to engage in the public practice of accountancy in this State through any corporate form, except as provided in General Statutes Chapter 55B. (1925, c. 261, s. 6; 1951, c. 844, s. 3; 1969, c. 718, s. 17; 1983, c. 185, s. 3.)

§ 93-9. Assistants need not be certified.

Nothing contained in this Chapter shall be construed to prohibit the employment by a certified public accountant or by any person, firm, copartnership, association, or corporation permitted to engage in the practice of public accounting in the State of North Carolina, of persons who have not received certificates of qualification admitting them to practice as certified public accountants, as assistant accountants or clerks: Provided, that such employees work under the control and supervision of certified public accountants and do not certify to anyone the accuracy or verification of audits or statements; and provided further, that such employees do not hold themselves out as engaged in the practice of public accounting. (1925, c. 261, s. 9; 1993, c. 518, s. 6.)

§ 93-10. Practice privileges.

(a) An individual whose principal place of business is outside this State is granted the privilege to perform or offer to perform services, whether in person or by mail, telephone, or electronic means, in this State as a certified public accountant without notice to the Board, the submission of any other documentation, or the payment of any fee if the individual meets all of the following conditions:

(1) Holds a valid and unrevoked certificate as a certified public accountant, or its equivalent, issued by another state, a territory of the United States, or the District of Columbia.

(2) Holds a valid and unrevoked license or permit to practice as a certified public accountant issued by another state, a territory of the United States, or the District of Columbia.

(3) Has passed The Uniform CPA Examination.

(4) Has not been convicted of a felony under the laws of the United States, any state, a territory of the United States, or the District of Columbia and has never been convicted of a crime, an essential element of which is dishonesty, deceit, or fraud unless the jurisdiction in which the individual is licensed has determined the felony or other crime has no effect on the individual's license.

(5),(6) Repealed by Session Laws 2009-347, s. 4, effective July 27, 2009.

(b) An individual who satisfies the requirements of subsection (a) of this section and exercises the privilege afforded under this section by performing or offering to perform services as a certified public accountant in this State simultaneously consents as a condition of the grant of this privilege to:

(1) Comply with the laws of this State, the provisions of this Chapter, and rules adopted by the Board.

(2) Have an administrative notice of hearing served on the licensing board in the individual's principal state of business, notwithstanding the individual notice requirements of G.S. 150B-38.

(3) Be subject to personal jurisdiction, subject matter jurisdiction, and disciplinary authority of the Board.

(c) A firm whose principal place of business is outside this State and has no office in this State is granted the privilege to perform or offer to perform services, whether in person or by mail, telephone, or electronic means, in this State as a firm without notice to the Board, submission of any other documentation, or payment of any fee, except as otherwise provided in subdivision (3) of this subsection. A firm that exercises the privilege afforded under this section simultaneously consents as a condition of the grant of the privilege to:

(1) Comply with the laws of this State, the provisions of this Chapter, and rules adopted by the Board.

(2) Be subject to personal jurisdiction, subject matter jurisdiction, and disciplinary authority of the Board.

(3) Provide notice without a fee to the Board if any individual with the firm who has been granted privileges in North Carolina to practice as a certified public accountant performs any of the following services for a client in this State:

a. A financial statement audit or other engagement performed in accordance with the Statements on Auditing Standards.

b. An examination of prospective financial information performed in accordance with the Statements on Standards for Attestation Engagements.

c. An engagement performed in accordance with the Public Company Accounting Oversight Board auditing standards. (1925, c. 261, s. 10; 1993, c. 518, s. 7; 2001-313, s. 1; 2009-347, s. 4.)

§ 93-11. Not applicable to officers of State, county or municipality.

Nothing herein contained shall be construed to restrict or limit the power or authority of any State, county or municipal officer or appointee engaged in or upon the examination of the accounts of any public officer, his employees or appointees. (1925, c. 261, s. 12.)

§ 93-12. Board of Certified Public Accountant Examiners.

The name of the State Board of Accountancy is hereby changed to State Board of Certified Public Accountant Examiners and said name State Board of Certified Public Accountant Examiners is hereby substituted for the name State Board of Accountancy wherever the latter name appears or is used in Chapter 93 of the General Statutes. Said Board is created as an agency of the State of North Carolina and shall consist of seven members to be appointed by the Governor, five persons to be holders of valid and unrevoked certificates as certified public accountants issued under the provisions of this Chapter and two persons who are not certified public accountants who shall represent the interest of the public at large. Members of the Board shall hold office for the term of three years and until their successors are appointed. Appointments to the Board shall be made under the provisions of this Chapter as and when the terms of the members of the present State Board of Accountancy expire; provided, that all future appointments to said Board shall be made for a term of three years expiring on the thirtieth day of June. All Board members serving on June 30, 1980, shall be eligible to complete their respective terms. No member appointed to a term on or after July 1, 1980, shall serve more than two complete consecutive terms. The powers and duties of the Board shall be as follows:

(1) To elect from its members a president, vice-president and secretary-treasurer. The members of the Board shall receive compensation and reimbursement for travel expenses in accordance with G.S. 93B-5.

(2) To employ legal counsel, clerical and technical assistance and to fix the compensation therefor, and to incur such other expenses as may be deemed necessary in the performance of its duties and the enforcement of the provisions of this Chapter. Upon request the Attorney General of North Carolina will advise the Board with respect to the performance of its duties and will assign a member of his staff, or approve the employment of counsel, to represent the Board in any hearing or litigation arising under this Chapter. The Board may, in the exercise of its discretion, cooperate with similar boards of other states, territories and the District of Columbia in activities designed to bring about uniformity in standards of admission to the public practice of accountancy by certified public accountants, and may employ a uniform system of preparation of examinations to be given to candidates for certificates as certified public accountants, including the services and facilities of the American Institute of Certified Public Accountants, or of any other persons or organizations of recognized skill in the field of accountancy, in the preparation of examinations and assistance in establishing and maintaining a uniform system of grading of examination papers, provided however, that all examinations given by said Board shall be adopted and approved by the Board and that the grade or grades given to all persons taking said examinations shall be determined and approved by the Board.

(3) To formulate rules for the government of the Board and for the examination of applicants for certificates of qualification admitting such applicants to practice as certified public accountants.

(4) To hold written, oral, and computer-based examinations of applicants for certificates of qualification at least once a year, or more often, as may be deemed necessary by the Board.

(5) To issue certificates of qualification admitting to practice as certified public accountants, each applicant who, having the qualifications herein specified, has passed an examination to the satisfaction of the Board, in "accounting," "auditing," "business law," and other related subjects.

A person is eligible to take the examination given by the Board, or to receive a certificate of qualification to practice as a certified public accountant, if the person is a citizen of the United States, has declared the intention of becoming a citizen, is a resident alien, or is a citizen of a foreign jurisdiction which extends to citizens of this State like or similar privileges to be examined or certified, is 18 years of age or over, and is of good moral character.

To be eligible to take the examination given by the Board, a person shall submit evidence satisfactory to the Board that the person holds a bachelors degree from a college or university that is accredited by one of the regional accrediting associations or from a college or university determined by the Board to have standards that are substantially equivalent to a regionally accredited institution. The degree studies shall include a concentration in accounting as prescribed by the Board or shall be supplemented with courses that are determined by the Board to be substantially equivalent to a concentration in accounting.

The Board may, in its discretion, waive the education requirement of any candidate if the Board is satisfied from the result of a special written examination given the candidate by the Board to test the candidate's educational qualifications that the candidate is as well qualified as if the candidate met the education requirements specified above. The Board may provide by regulation for the general scope of such examinations and may obtain such advice and assistance as it deems appropriate to assist it in preparing, administering and grading such special examinations.

To be eligible to receive a certificate of qualification to practice as a certified public accountant, a person shall submit evidence satisfactory to the Board that:

a. The person has completed 150 semester hours and received a bachelors degree with a concentration in accounting and other courses that the Board may require from a college or university that is accredited by a regional accrediting association or from a college or university determined by the Board to have standards that are substantially equivalent to those of a regionally accredited institution.

b. The person has the endorsement as to the person's eligibility of three certified public accountants who currently hold licenses in any state or territory of the United States or the District of Columbia.

c. The person has one of the following:

1. One year's experience in the field of accounting under the direct supervision of a certified public accountant who currently holds a valid license in any state or territory of the United States or the District of Columbia.

2. Four years of experience teaching accounting in a four-year college or university accredited by one of the regional accrediting associations or in a college or university determined by the Board to have standards substantially equivalent to a regionally accredited institution.

3. Four years of experience in the field of accounting.

4. Four years of experience teaching college transfer accounting courses at a community college or technical institute accredited by one of the regional accrediting associations.

5. Any combination of such experience determined by the Board to be substantially equivalent to the foregoing.

The Board may permit persons otherwise eligible to take its examinations and withhold certificates until the person has had the required experience.

(6) In its discretion to grant certificates of qualification admitting to practice as certified public accountants such applicants who shall be the holders of valid and unrevoked certificates as certified public accountants, or the equivalent, issued by or under the authority of any state, or territory of the United States or the District of Columbia, when in the judgment of the Board the requirements for the issuing or granting of such certificates or degrees are substantially equivalent to the requirements established by this Chapter: Provided, however, that the state or political subdivision of the United States upon whose certificate the reciprocal action is based grants the same privileges to holders of certificates as certified public accountants issued pursuant to the provisions of this Chapter. The Board, by general rule, may grant temporary permits to applicants under this subsection pending their qualification for reciprocal certificates.

(7) To charge for each examination provided for in this Chapter a fee not exceeding four hundred dollars ($400.00). In addition to the examination fee, if the Board uses a testing service for the preparation, administration, or grading of examinations, the Board may charge the applicant the actual cost of the examination services. The applicant shall pay all fees and costs associated with the examination at the time the application is filed with the Board. Examination fees and costs shall not be refunded unless the Board deems the applicant ineligible for examination.

(7a) To charge for each initial certificate of qualification provided for in this Chapter a fee not exceeding one hundred fifty dollars ($150.00).

(7b) To require an annual registration of each firm and to charge an annual registration fee not to exceed two hundred dollars ($200.00) for each firm with one office, and a fee not to exceed twenty-five dollars ($25.00) for each additional North Carolina office of the firm, to defray the administrative costs of accounting practice review programs. The Board may charge an annual fee not to exceed twenty-five dollars ($25.00) for each firm application for exemption from the accounting practice review program.

(8) To require the renewal of all certificates of qualification annually on the first day of July, and to charge an annual renewal fee not to exceed one hundred dollars ($100.00).

(8a) To require the registration of certified public accountant firms which have offices both within and outside of North Carolina, and the payment by such firms of an annual registration fee based on the total number of partners in each such firm, but not to exceed two thousand five hundred dollars ($2,500) per firm per year.

(8b) To formulate rules for the continuing professional education of all persons holding the certificate of certified public accountant, subject to the following provisions:

a. After January 1, 1983, any person desiring to obtain or renew a certificate as a certified public accountant must offer evidence satisfactory to the Board that the person has complied with the continuing professional education requirement approved by the Board. The Board may grant a conditional license for not more than 12 months for persons who are being licensed for the first time, or moving into North Carolina, or for other good cause, in order that the person may comply with the continuing professional education requirement.

b.   The Board shall adopt rules for the administration of the continuing professional education requirement with a minimum number of hours of 20 and a maximum number of hours of 40 per year, and the Board may exempt persons who are retired or inactive from the continuing professional education requirement. The Board may also permit any certified public accountant to accumulate hours of continuing professional education in any calendar year of as much as two additional years annual requirement in advance of or subsequent to the required calendar year.

c.   Any applicant who offers satisfactory evidence on forms promulgated by the Board that the applicant has participated in a continuing professional education program of the type required by the Board shall be deemed to have complied with this subdivision.

(8c)   The Board may formulate rules and regulations for report review and peer review of audits, reviews, compilations, and other reports issued on financial information in the public practice of accountancy of all firms, as herein defined, subject to the following provisions:

a.   After June 30, 1992, any firm desiring to obtain or maintain a registration as a firm must offer satisfactory evidence to the Board that such firm has complied with the peer review and report review requirements approved by the Board; provided, however, that the Board shall give to every firm subject to this section not less than 12 months advance notice of each peer review and report review required of the firm.

b.   The Board may grant a conditional registration for not more than 24 months for firms which are being registered for the first time, or moving into North Carolina, or for other good cause, in order that such firm may comply with the report review and peer review requirements, and in order that the Board may develop a system of review rotation among the various firms that must comply with this section.

c.   The peer review and report review shall be valid for a minimum of three years subject to the power of the Board to require remedial action by any firm with a deficiency in the review according to the rules established by the Board.

d.   The Board shall promulgate rules and regulations for the administration of the report review and peer review requirements and the Board shall exempt firms that show to the satisfaction of the Board that they are not engaged in the public practice of accountancy or that the scope of their practice does not come within the peer review and report review guidelines established by the Board.

e.   Any firm that offers satisfactory evidence to the Board that the firm has satisfactorily participated in and successfully completed a peer review or a report review of the type required by the Board shall be deemed to have complied with this section and the Board shall promulgate rules and regulations for the administration of this procedure.

f.   For purposes of this section, a firm means an entity, sole proprietorship, partnership, registered limited liability partnership, professional limited liability company, or professional corporation through which one or more certificate holders engage in the public practice of accountancy through an office.

(9)   Adoption of Rules of Professional Conduct; Disciplinary Action. - The Board shall have the power to adopt rules of professional ethics and conduct to be observed by certified public accountants in this State and persons exercising the practice privilege authorized by this Chapter. The Board shall have the power to revoke, either permanently or for a specified period, any certificate issued under the provisions of this Chapter to a certified public accountant or any practice privilege authorized by the provisions of this Chapter or to censure the holder of any such certificate or person exercising the practice privilege authorized by this Chapter. The Board also shall have the power to assess a civil penalty not to exceed one thousand dollars ($1,000) for any one or combination of the following causes:

a.   Conviction of a felony under the laws of the United States or of any state of the United States.

b.   Conviction of any crime, an essential element of which is dishonesty, deceit or fraud.

c.   Fraud or deceit in obtaining a certificate as a certified public accountant.

d.   Dishonesty, fraud or gross negligence in the public practice of accountancy.

e.   Violation of any rule of professional ethics and professional conduct adopted by the Board.

Any disciplinary action taken shall be in accordance with the provisions of Chapter 150B of the General Statutes. The clear proceeds of any civil penalty assessed under this section shall be remitted to the Civil Penalty and Forfeiture Fund in accordance with G.S. 115C-457.2.
(10), (11) Repealed by Session Laws 1993, c. 518, s. 8.

(12) To submit annually on or before the first day of May to the Secretary of Revenue the names of all persons who have qualified under this Chapter as certified public accountants. Privilege license issued under G.S. 105-41 shall designate whether such license is issued to a certified public accountant or an accountant.

(13) The Board shall keep a complete record of all its proceedings and shall annually submit a full report to the Governor.

(14) All fees collected on behalf of the Board and all receipts of every kind and nature, as well as the compensation paid the members of the Board and the necessary expenses incurred by them in the performance of the duties imposed upon them, shall be reported annually to the State Treasurer. All fees and other moneys received by the Board pursuant to the provisions of the General Statutes shall be kept in a separate fund by the treasurer of the Board, to be held and expended only for such purposes as are proper and necessary to the discharge of the duties of the Board and to enforce the provisions of this Chapter. No expense incurred by the Board shall be charged against the State.

(15) Any certificate of qualification issued under the provisions of this Chapter, or issued under the provisions of Chapter 157 of the Public Laws of 1913, shall be forfeited for the failure of the holder to renew same and to pay the renewal fee therefor to the State Board of Accountancy within 30 days after demand for such renewal fee shall have been made by the State Board of Accountancy.

(16) To apply to the courts, in its own name, for injunctive relief to prevent violations of this Chapter or violations of any rules adopted pursuant to this Chapter. Any court may grant injunctive relief regardless of whether criminal prosecution or any other action is instituted as a result of the violation. A single violation is sufficient to invoke the injunctive relief under this subdivision.

(17) The Board shall have the power to acquire, hold, rent, encumber, alienate, and otherwise deal with real property in the same manner as a private person or corporation, subject only to approval of the Governor and the Council

of State as to the acquisition, rental, encumbering, leasing, and sale of real property. Collateral pledged by the Board for an encumbrance is limited to the assets, income, and revenues of the Board. (1925, c. 261, s. 11; 1939, c. 218, s. 1; 1951, c. 844, ss. 4-9; 1953, c. 1041, s. 20; 1959, c. 1188; 1961, c. 1010; 1971, c. 738, ss. 1-3; 1973, c. 476, s. 193; c. 1331, s. 3; 1975, c. 107; 1975, 2nd Sess., c. 983, s. 69; 1977, c. 804, ss. 1, 2; 1979, c. 750, ss. 6-10; 1979, 2nd Sess., c. 1087, ss. 1, 2; 1981, c. 10; 1983, c. 185, ss. 4-11; 1985, c. 149; 1987, c. 353; c. 827, ss. 1, 79; 1989, c. 624; 1991, c. 214, s. 1; 1991 (Reg. Sess., 1992), c. 1011, s. 6; 1993, c. 518, s. 8; 1995, c. 137, s. 1; 1997-157, s. 1; 1997-284, s. 1; 1998-215, s. 130; 1998-216, s. 6; 1998-217, s. 51; 1999-440, s. 3; 2001-313, ss. 2, 3, 4, 5; 2009-347, s. 5.)

§ 93-12.1. Effect of new requirements.

Any person who applies to the Board of Certified Public Accountant Examiners before July 1, 1983, to take the examination, who meets the educational requirement as it existed prior to June 4, 1979, and complies with any of the experience requirements of this Chapter shall be deemed to have met the prerequisites to taking such examination. (1979, c. 750, s. 11.)

§ 93-12.2. Board records are confidential.

Records, papers, and other documents containing information collected or compiled by the Board, its members, or employees, as a result of a complaint, investigation, inquiry, or interview in connection with an application for examination, certification, or registration, or in connection with a certificate holder's professional ethics and conduct, shall not be considered public records within the meaning of Chapter 132 of the General Statutes. Any notice or statement of charges against a certificate holder or applicant, or any notice to a certificate holder or applicant of a hearing to be held by the Board is a public record, even though it may contain information collected and compiled as a result of a complaint, investigation, inquiry, or interview conducted by the Board. If any record, paper, or other document containing information collected and compiled by the Board is admitted into evidence in a hearing held by the Board, it shall then be a public record within the meaning of Chapter 132 of the General Statutes. (1997-157, s. 2.)

§ 93-13. Violation of Chapter; penalty.

A violation of G.S. 93-3, 93-4, 93-5, 93-6, or 93-8 shall be a Class 1 misdemeanor. (1925, c. 261, s. 11; 1983, c. 185, s. 12; 1993, c. 539, s. 656; 1994, Ex. Sess., c. 24, s. 14(c); 2007-83, s. 1.)

Vision Books Order Form

Fax Orders:	1-980-299-5965
Phone Orders:	1-704-898-0770
E-mail Orders:	www.visionbooks.org
Mail Orders:	Vision Books, LLC P.O. Box 42406 Charlotte, NC 28215

Shipp To:
Name_____
Address_____
City_____State_____Zip_____
Phone_____Fax_____
Email_____@_____

Bill To: We can bill a third party on your behalf.
Name_____
Address_____
City_____State_____Zip_____
Phone____(_____)_____Fax_____
Email_____@_____

Pamphlet Number ($15.00 Each)	Qty	Total Cost
_____	_____	_____
_____	_____	_____
_____	_____	_____
_____	_____	_____
_____	_____	_____
_____	_____	_____
_____	_____	_____
_____	_____	_____
Full Volume Set 1-92	92 Pamphlets	1,380.00

Free Shipping Shipping & Handling on Full Volume Orders
Add $1.00 Shipping & Handling per pamphlet $_____

Total Cost $_____

Thank you for your support. Management!

DID YOU ENJOY THIS BOOK?

Vision Books, LLC would like to hear from you! If you or someone you know has been fasely imprisoned, we would like to hear your story. If the 'North Carolina Criminal Law and Procedure' has had an effect in your life or if you have suggestions, we would like to hear from you. Send your letters to:

Vision Books, LLC
Attn: Staff Writers
P.O. Box 42406
Charlotte, NC 28215
Email: staff@visionbooks.org

Order Additional Copies:

Fax Orders:	1-980-299-5965
Phone Orders:	1-704-898-0770
E-mail Orders:	www.visionbooks.org
Mail Orders:	Vision Books, LLC P.O. Box 42406 Charlotte, NC 28215

www.ingramcontent.com/pod-product-compliance
Lightning Source LLC
Chambersburg PA
CBHW051628170526
45167CB00001B/105